Wild Scenes in the Forest and Prairie

Volume I

Charles Fenno Hoffman

LITERATURE HOUSE / GREGG PRESS
Upper Saddle River, N. J.

Republished in 1970 by
LITERATURE HOUSE
an imprint of The Gregg Press
121 Pleasant Avenue
Upper Saddle River, N. J. 07458

Standard Book Number—8398-0784-8
Library of Congress Card—76-104485

Printed in United States of America

WILD SCENES

IN THE

FOREST AND PRAIRIE.

BY C. F. HOFFMAN, Esq.

AUTHOR OF "A WINTER IN THE FAR WEST."

IN TWO VOLUMES.

VOL. I.

LONDON:

RICHARD BENTLEY, NEW BURLINGTON STREET,
Publisher in Ordinary to Her Majesty.

Price Sixteen Shillings.

1839.

WHITING, BEAUFORT HOUSE, STRAND

PREFACE.

" I reckon our folks don't want none of them fixings," said an Ohio housewife to a Connecticut pedler who produced a pair of beaded moccassins, a shooting pouch, and other hunting paraphernalia from his pack: " the boys have plenty of such trash of their own providing."

The patient pedestrian offered next some prettily woven basket-ware and carved wooden bowls to tempt a purchase from the settler's wife.

" No! nor them nother," cried the virago:

" the Miami Injuns do our basketing, and the Buck-eyes make better bowls than you can carve from your Yankee poplars. What does the fool mean by trying to sell us things we can make better nor him? Throw open your pack, manny, and let me choose for myself among your knicknacks."

The recollection of this shrewish monologue as once overheard by the author in a western cabin came vividly to his mind when about to select and remodel some of his lucubrations for a London publisher; and after cutting and carving, altering and amending, never to his own satisfaction, he finally concluded to abide by the lesson given to the worthy pedler. Instead, therefore, of attempting to cater for, or conform to tastes of which as an untravelled foreigner he knows but little, he has thrown open his pack to let the British reader choose for himself from its contents.

In a word, these American sketches, written in the first instance without any view to European publication, are here committed to the hospitality of strangers, precisely in their original shape, as they have from time to time accumulated during the rambles of the Author.

C. Fenno Hoffman.

New York, Dec. 1838.

CONTENTS OF VOL. I.

WILD SCENES

AT THE

SOURCES OF THE HUDSON.

CHAPTER I.

THE LAND OF LAKES.

"The Land of Lakes," as the region of country which now forms the state of New York is termed in one of our aboriginal dialects, could hardly be characterized by a more appropriate name; as without counting the inland seas which bound her western shores, or pausing to enumerate the willowy ponds which freshen the verdure of her lowlands, or these deep and caldron-like pools which are so singularly set here and there upon the summits of her mountains, New York may still count a thousand lakes within her borders. Upon some of these fleets might engage in battle; and their outlets, broken at first by cataracts which Switzerland alone can rival, soon swell into rivers upon which the voyager may safely glide to climes a thousand miles away: while the Ohio, the Susquehannah, the Delaware, Hudson, and St. Lawrence, whose tributaries all interlace within a circle of a dozen miles in the heart of the state, give him a choice between the frozen shores of Labrador and the tropic seas of Mexico, in selecting the point where he would emerge upon the Atlantic main.

In connecting these wonderful links of internal navigation, whose union an enlightened policy has now effected, it is singular that in the various topographical *reconnoissances* of the state the sources of so important a stream as

the Hudson should only during the last year
have been fully and satisfactorily explored.
One would think that however the subject
might be overlooked by the legislature, it could
never have escaped the Argus eyes of our inqui-
sitive, fidgety, and prying countrymen, until
the year of grace '37.

Every body was, indeed, aware that the Hud-
son rose among a group of mountains in the
northern part of the state of New York; and if
you looked upon the map some of the lakes
which formed its head waters seemed to be laid
down with sufficient particularity. Few, how-
ever, until the legislature instituted the geolo-
gical survey which is now in progress, had any
idea that the mountains upon which this noble
river rises overtopped the Catskills and the
Alleghanies, and were among the loftiest in the
United States; or that the lakes from which it
draws its birth were equally remarkable for their

prodigal numbers, their picturesque variety, and their wild and characteristic beauty.

Tourists steamed upon the estuary of the Hudson, or loitered through the populous counties between the cities of New York and Albany, and, ignorant or unmindful that in ascending to the head of tide-water they had not seen quite one-half of the lordly stream, discussed its claims to consideration with an amiable familiarity, and, comparing its scenery with that of other celebrated rivers, they settled its whole character after a most summary fashion.

The worthy Knickerbockers were therefore not a little surprised, when they learned from the first official report of the surveying corps, that their famous river was fed by mountain snows for ten months in the year ;* and that

---

* Snow remained on Mount Marcy until the 17th of July, and appeared again on the 11th of September, 1837.

there were a dozen cascades about its head-
waters, to which Glen's falls, however endeared
to association by the genius of Cooper, must
hereafter yield in romantic interest and attrac-
tion. Many were eager at once to visit the
sources of the Hudson; and, having in very early
youth been much in the then savage district
where some of the northern branches take their
rise, the writer was so eager to penetrate farther
into the same region, and behold the real head
of the river, that he found himself rambling
among the mountains of Essex county, within
a few days after the state geologist had pro-
nounced upon it as now distinctly ascertained.

The Hudson is formed by three mountain-
torrents which unite within a few miles of their
birthplace. The source of the highest fork is
proved by observation to be 4700 feet above
tide-water. It rises in an open mountain-
meadow with two adjacent mountains swelling

in easy slopes from its sides. There is a still larger fountain-head west of this, in the same vicinity, rising in a singular gorge called "The Indian Pass:" while the northernmost source is in Lake Colden, or rather in Avalanche Lake; a small mountain tarn separated from the former by heavy earth-slides from the adjacent mountain summits, whose granite rocks glitter where the soil and trees have been swept down their denuded sides. The elevation of these two lakes, which have a fall of eighty feet between them, is between 2900 and 3000 feet above the ocean; being undoubtedly the highest lakes in the United States of America.*

* Emmons's Report—Redfield, &c.

CHAPTER II.

THE EXCURSION.

It was early in September when, accompanied by a friend—the companion of more than one pleasant ramble—I started upon the brief but novel tour. The winter sets in so early in the high mountain-region for which we were bound, that deeming we had no time to lose we struck for it by the nearest route ; and instead of following the various windings of the river— which offer a delicious summer excursion for the man of leisure—we left tide-water at Lausingburgh, and passing eastward of Lake

George, went directly north by the way of Lake Champlain.

Embarking upon this lake at Whitehall, a few hours brought our steamer abreast of Port Henry, a small village which heaves in sight immediately after passing the crumbling fortifications of Crown Point. A pretty cascade tumbles from the rocks near the landing, and is the first thing that strikes you when approaching the shore. Several wooded hills rise in succession behind it, and give a picturesque appearance to a straggling hamlet along their base. Our route hence was due westward, and the evening being fine we engaged a conveyance to carry us on at once some twenty miles, through an almost unbroken forest, into the interior.

The autumnal moon was shining brightly as we commenced ascending the hills in the rear of Port Henry, rising continually until we reached the village of Moriah, situated about three miles from the lake. The rearward view, in the mean time, was exceedingly fine. Indeed, I do not hesitate to say, that Lake Champlain, as seen from those hills, presents one of the very finest lake views in the United States. Broad enough for majestic effect, yet not too broad for the picturesque character, which, I think, is worth every thing else in scenery, the placid sheet of the lake lay silvered by the moonbeams below us. The promontory of Port Henry, with a headland of rival rock and forest opposite, nearly locked it upon the north On the south, the narrow peninsula of Crown-Point, projecting longitudinally several miles into the lake, divided it into two friths, which gradually disappeared amid hill and forest, far in the distance; while immediately in front, though far beyond the broad, bright expanse of water, a dozen spurs of the Green Mountains,

and a dozen main peaks beyond them, loomed
in the dewy atmosphere of evening, like some
vast Alpine chain.

It was after midnight when we stopped at a
log cabin about twenty miles from the lake.
The hospitable settler, although his house was
already filled with neighbours, who had come in
to help him with his harvest, seemed to take
the being roused from his slumbers at that late
hour, to accommodate us, very kindly. A log-
cabin and a pair of saddlebags are never so full,
but that room can be found for something more,
and we were soon packed beneath the same
roof with the rest.

Let me here initiate the reader into a mode
of travelling which is much in fashion about the
sources of the Hudson. Did he ever see a
teamster riding upon a buckboard? a stout,
springy plank, laid upon the bare bolsters of a
waggon! Well, now just spread a buffalo-skin

upon that buckboard, and rig the iron chain from the fore and aft stakes, so as to form a stirrup for your feet, and you have the best sort of carriage that can be contrived for rough roads. Upon such a convenience our luggage was lashed about six o'clock the next morning, and the active little settler, our host of the log-cabin, taking his axe in hand to remove any fallen tree that might obstruct our road through the woods, whistled to his dog, Buck, jumped on the board beside us, cracked his whip, and off we went into the forest. Our driver was a right-merry, stout-hearted, dashing little fellow; he had been brought up in the " Schroon country," as he called it, and had cleared every acre upon his thriving farm with his own hand; and after roughing it for several years in his log-cabin, was now prepared to build a snug framehouse upon his own ground. Our road was the worst

that I ever saw, except a *turnpike* through
the bed of a mountain-torrent, which I once
travelled in Eastern Kentucky. But stony de-
clivities, stumps, quagmires, or fallen trees, had
no terrors for our little Schroon hero; and his
lean, but mettlesome horses, dashed through
every thing. Such was the road, however, that
as it slammed about among trees and logs, the
motion of our vehicle was as much lateral as
forwards, and we were several hours in making
the first eight miles.

Accomplishing this stage at last, however, we
came to an opening in the forest, where, upon
the bank of a lake, and in the midst of a clear-
ing of about a hundred acres, stood the log-
cabin of a settler, at which we stopped to dine.
The lake, or pond, as the people call it, was a
limpid pool upon the top of a mountain, or
rather an immense globular hill, flattened at top

like an old-fashioned goblet, and surrounded with mountain peaks from which it stood wholly isolated.

Upon the outlet of this lake was a saw-mill, and we here saw a model of a wooden railroad, contrived by a forester who has never seen a specimen of either, but whose ingenuity has found a field for its exercise, even in the depths of the woods.

After refreshing ourselves and our horses at this place, we started again, and by nightfall accomplished twenty-three miles more, the whole distance being through a continuous forest, with not a single house by the way.

About twilight we emerged from the forest, at the base of a lofty, cleared, and grassy hill, with a log-cabin on the summit, prettily situated in front of a grove of tall maples, called, in the language of the country, a " sugar-bush." This grassy domain, for the whole clearing of several hundred acres, produced hay only, had a most singular effect in the bosom of a dark forest, surrounded, as it was, upon every side by mountains, which lapped each other as far as the eye could reach.

This farm—if so neglected a tract could be thus characterized—presented a scene of solitude and desertion, not uncommon in this part of the State. It had been cleared some ten or fifteen years since, but the original settler, seized with the emigrating fever which carries so many from our woodland region to the prairies of the far-west, had long deserted his mountain-home: and the place had been so neglected until the present season, that it was in danger of relapsing into the half-savage and almost irreclaimable state of what in the language of the country is called " a dead clearing." That is when thickets and briers so overrun the land and spread their roots and tendrils through the soil, that they become more difficult to eradicate than the original forest-growth, which yields at once to the axe of the woodman.

The new owners of the property, however, had now sent in some labourers from a more flourishing settlement to harvest the wild hay—the native grasses of these mountains being peculiarly fine—and the overseer of the proprietors being present—a frank, intelligent yeoman, to whom we had a letter from his employers—our reception was as hearty and hospitable as he could make it with the rude appliances about him. There was no womankind about the establishment, and after eating a hearty supper of fried pork and potatoes, cooked by a young hunter, of whom I may speak hereafter, we made a bed of fresh hay in a corner, and stretching a buffalo-skin over, by way of ticking, threw ourselves down and slept with a soundness that would have been commendable in either of those celebrated disciples of Morpheus, the seven sleepers.

During the last day's drive we had crossed many of the streams which form the head waters of the Hudson; and on the morrow, we for the first time saw one of the most beautiful of the lakes which form its sources. Hereafter, therefore, I shall copy the scenes that came under my observation as taken down separately in my note-book upon the spot.

CHAPTER III.

LAKE SANDFORD.

STRIKING the outlet of Lake Sandford where it flows through a forest of dark cedars, our luggage was shifted from the buckboard and transferred with ourselves to a canoe; we embarked at the foot of a steep hill, but our course lay for some time through low swampy ground, where the canoe could sometimes with diffi culty find a deep-enough channel through the sedge and water-lilies that by turns covered the surface. This amphibious track, however, soon disappeared where the hills again coming down

to the edge of the stream confined and deep-
ened its current; and now, after a pull of a few
hundred yards through a straight narrow passage,
we launched out upon the bosom of one of
those beautiful lakes with which this region
abounds.   Not a sign of a house or a clearing,
nor any mark of the handiwork of man was to
be seen any where, save in the rude shallop
that bore us.   The morning was still and low-
ering.   There was not breeze enough to lift the
fog from the mountains round.   Every rock
and tree was reflected, with each leaf and wild
flower however minute, in the glassy surface;
the islands among which we wound our course,
floated double;   the hermit-like loon that
glanced from beneath their embowering shelter,
and sent his wild cry with a dozen echoes far
among the hills, was the only object that moved
or gave a sound of life across the waters.

We landed upon one islet, and I paused to

observe what I have never been tired of study-
ing, the manner in which nature effects her
work of clothing the barren crags with soil.

Here, on this rocky islet, some fifty feet in
diameter, the whole process may be seen—the
first covering of moss and lichens; the larger
growth of the same; the light black soil that is
formed from their decay; the taller plants that
again, in succession, are doomed to die and be
decomposed, and afford earthy nourishment to
the first hardy forest growth; still, in its turn,
to be succeeded by softer woods, may all be
traced upon Inch-Hamish.

Here, on this little spot, where you can run
a stick some three feet down, through the pri-
mitive mosses that form the first covering of
the rock; you have, also, the towering spruce,
the ragged arbor-vitæ, and several other hardy
evergreen varieties; while a single delicate

white-ash has put forth its deciduous leaves, and hung its scarlet berries over the lake. An accomplished botanist has, I am told, found upwards of a hundred varieties of plants and trees upon this islet, which is less than an acre in extent.

Cruising leisurely up the lake in this way—pausing ever and anon to admire the change of prospect as we wound round some green headland, or lying upon our oars while trying the fine echoes which the mountains gave back to our voices whenever our course lay far from the margin,—it was afternoon before we reached the point for debarking, which we attained by piercing deep within a forest that overshadows the inlet. Our canoe left the cheerful lake, and floating beneath the boughs of ancient trees that sometimes interlaced above our heads, startled the trout from the black pools which bathed their roots, and grated at last upon a

gravelly bank where it was drawn up and se-
cured.

Not far from this point a portage of a few
hundred yards enables the hunter to launch
again upon lake Henderson, and strike the first
link in a chain of lakes, which with a few more
brief portages will float his shallop all the way
to the St. Lawrence.

CHAPTER IV.

M'INTYRE.

THE portage to Lake Henderson is occasioned by rapids which extend for about half a mile between that water and Lake Sandford. They run over a bed of iron-ore which ribs the sides of two mountains that overhang the valley through which the Hudson flows from one lake into the other.

This little valley which is already cleared and under partial cultivation, is the site of a projected manufacturing town, and here we made our head-quarters at a comfortable farm-house. We were inducted into them by the overseer already mentioned, and under his cordial auspices, my friend and myself for some days enjoyed the hospitality of the pro-prietors of the M'Intyre iron-works. The situation abounding, as it does, in excellent iron-ore, and affording a dozen mill sites, is admirably adapted for a manufacturing town, and might form the site of one of the most romantic villages in the Union.

The newness of the improvements, and the large clearings, marked only by stumps, give the place, as yet, a somewhat desolate appear-ance : care and capital will, however, soon remedy this, and when the legislature does justice to this much-neglected portion of the State, and opens a good road or canal along the beautiful lakes with which it abounds, M'Intyre will become one of the most favourite places of resort near the sources of the Hudson.

Its present loneliness and seclusion, however, would render M'Intyre not less pleasing to some tastes; while though the hand of improvement may soon make the district in which it lies, more accessible than it now is, and add some features of cultivation to the adjacent scenery, it can never soften its wildness. In fact, a partial clearing of the country will, in this region, only serve to heighten the bold features of the landscape. For the trees whose foliage now softens the sharper outlines of the mountains, and curtains many a tall crag and deep fell from view—will, when swept away, reveal scenes of desolate grandeur, which no culture can rob of their sternness. In some places the hunters' fires have already bared the pinnacles of some of these granite mountains : and earth-slides, caused by frequent rains, or slight earthquakes, which still prevail in this region, strip them here and there of their verdurous vesture, leaving only parapets of naked rock frowning upon the deep forests below them.

CHAPTER V.

AN INKLING OF AN EARTHQUAKE.

Apropos to earthquakes, we had an inkling of one on the first night of our arrival at M'Intyre. The shock, if so slight a tremour may be thus characterized, took place about midnight; and though it woke me, I deemed it at the time the effect of fancy, until I compared notes in the morning with my fellow-traveller, who, having experienced the sensation while in Caraccas some years since, could readily recognise it now. We occupied two rooms communicating with each other — the outer one, where my friend had his bed, opened upon the clearing. The door of this latter chamber being badly hung, shut with great difficulty, and was generally left ajar; but on this occasion, the night being cold and frosty, I took particular pains to secure it—driving it to by planting my foot against it, and forcing the latch completely home. We retired early that night, and the fatigue of travelling made our sleep particularly sound, when suddenly, about an hour after midnight, both of us were awakened at the same moment, and, notwithstanding both were struck by the circumstance, the cause did not occur to us till the morning, though our surprise was expressed after the wonted manner of sleepy men when startled from their slumbers.

" Hallo !"

" Hallo !"

" What's that ?"

" Are you up ?"

" No ! are you ?"

" My bed shakes !"

" It's that infernal hound, he's pushed my door wide open, and I must get up and shut it."

" There's no dog here in my room."

" The rascal's cleared out, then.—Confound the door, I can't get it close again."

" How's the night ?"

" Clear and starry, and still as one in the tropics, but devilish cold."

With these words, my friend commenced jamming at the door, secured it anew, jumped into bed again, and we were soon after dreaming as before. No noise accompanied this tremour; but they tell us here that a sound like that of a heavy waggon upon a frozen road is often heard among these mountains, where there are no roads which a waggon can traverse. I need hardly add that no dog could have opened the door which it cost me so much trouble to shut; nor, in fact, would the well-trained hound have ventured upon leaving his quarters to disturb ours.

CHAPTER VI.

AN UNFINISHED COUNTRY.

ADMITTING the existence of occasional slight earthquakes in this region, I am not enough of a naturalist to surmise what may be their effect upon the geological features of the country. They seem, however, among other things, to indicate the *unfinished state of the country*, if I may so express myself.

They are among the agents of nature, still at work in completing a portion of the world hardly yet ready to pass from her hands into those of man. The separation of the water from the land, which classic cosmogonists tell us followed the birth of light, in evolving the earth from chaos, is not here completed yet. There are lakes on the tops of mountains, and swamps among wildernesses of rocks, which are yet to be drained by other means than the thick exhalations which carry them into the atmosphere, or the dripping mosses through which they ooze into the valleys, where day by day the new soil for future use accumulates.

Had our New York Indians, who now find it so difficult to hold on to their level and fertile lands in the western part of the state, but " located " their reservations among these mountains, they might have escaped the cupidity of the whites for centuries yet to come, and have hunted the deer, the moose, and the bear, or trapped for the martin, the sable, and the ermine, all of which still abound here, without molestation, save from the occasional white hunter that might intrude upon their grounds when chasing the wolf or panther from the settled regions, to the east and west of them. There are settlements upon some of these lakes, which were commenced more than thirty years since, and which can now boast of but two or three families as residents, and these are isolated from the rest of the world, with twenty miles of unbroken forest between them and more prosperous hamlets. But the immense beds of iron-ore and other minerals recently discovered, with the increased demand for timber in our Atlantic cities, and of charcoal to work the mines here, must now bring the country into general notice, and hasten its settlement. The demolition of the pine forests, and the conversion of less valuable wood into charcoal, will rapidly clear the country, and convert the lumber-men and charcoal-burners into farmers; while the old race of hunters already begin to find a new employment in acting as guides to the owners of lands, and projecting roads for them through districts where an ordinary surveyor could hardly be paid for the exercise of his profession. One of these hunters, a sturdy original, by the name of Harvey Holt, a redoubtable hunter and celebrated axe-man, has already marked out a road for some of the large landed proprietors through the very heart of the region. He is said to have run his lines with the skill and accuracy of an accomplished engineer; and, before another year elapses, the road will probably be opened.

Other foresters, again, finding their ancient haunts thus invaded by the pioneers of improvement, have fled to wilds beyond the Wisconsan; and a friend who hunted lately upon a tract a little to the north-west of this, in Hamilton county, told me that he heard a veteran hunter of seventy complaining bitterly that he was too old to move, now that the settlers had pushed within thirty miles of him. It seems strange to find so wild a district in " one of the old thirteeners," the " empire state of New York." But the great western canal, in facilitating emigration to the new states, has retarded the improvement of this region for at least one generation, in luring off the young men as fast as they become of an age to choose a home for themselves. Some, however, like the mountaineer who is the subject of the following sketch, are so attached to the woods and streams of their native hills, that no inducement could lure them to the prairies.

CHAPTER VII.

A MOUNTAINEER OF THE HUDSON.

I was lately looking over Mr. Cooper's "Pioneers," and re-reading it after the lapse of years found myself as much delighted as ever with the best character he ever drew—"The Leather-stocking." If it did not involve an anachronism, I could swear that Cooper took the character of Natty Bumpo, from my mountaineer friend, John Cheney. The same silent, simple, deep love of the woods—the same gentleness and benevolence of feeling toward all who love his craft—the same unobtrusive kindness

D 2

toward all others; and, lastly, the same shrewd-
ness as a woodman, and gamesomeness of spirit
as a hunter, are common to both; and each,
while perhaps more efficient, are wholly unlike
the dashing swash-buckler of the far west, the
reckless ranger of the prairies. In appearance,
dress, language, and manner, those two varie-
ties of the *genus venator* are totally different.
Mr. Irving in his account of Captain Bonne-
ville's expedition has given the best description
of the latter; but though the pen of Cooper
has made the former immortal, I think his
genius might gather some new touches from
John Cheney. Worthy John! if he chances
to see himself thus drawn at full-length, I hope
he will not take it amiss. I had heard of some
of his feats before coming into this region, and
expected of course, to see one of those royster-
ing, cavorting, rifle-shirted blades that I have
seen upon our western frontier, and was at first

not a little disappointed when a slight-looking man of about seven-and-thirty, dressed like a plain countryman, and of a peculiarly quiet, simple manner, was introduced to me as the doughty slayer of bears and panthers; a man that lived winter and summer three-fourths of the time in the woods, and a real *bonâ fide* hunter by profession. Nay, there struck me as being something of the ridiculous about his character when I saw that this formidable Nimrod carried with him, as his only weapons and insignia of his art, *a pistol* and *a jack-knife!* But when, at my laughing at such toys, I was told by others of the savage encounters which John, assisted by his dog, and aided by these alone, had undertaken successfully—not to mention the number of deer which he sent every winter to market—my respect for his hunting-tools was mightily increased, and a few days in the woods with him sufficed to extend that respect to himself.

We were on a fishing excursion one day on a lake near M'Intyre; and after storing our canoe with a good supply of brook and lake trout, we weighed anchor, and pulled for a romantic promontory, commanding a delicious prospect, where we lay under the trees for hours, enjoying our pic-nic, and listening to hunters' stories. The air being cool and bracing, did not make the fire by which we cooked our dinner unacceptable. Our cloaks were stretched beneath a clump of cedars, and, after taking a plunge into the lake, which I was glad to make as brief as possible, I laid by the fire, watching the blue smoke curl up among the trees, or listening to my fellow-traveller, as he discoursed curiously with John about his cooking, or plied him from time to time with questions, that elicited some anecdotes of wild-wood sports, of which my quiet friend has been no feeble practiser himself.

" Well!" said Cheney, after he had cooked the trout to a turn, and placed a plump, red, juicy fellow, upon a clean cedar chip before each of us, with an accompaniment of roast potatoes and capital wheaten bread; " now isn't this better than taking your dinner shut up in a close room ?"

" Certainly, John," said I. " A man ought never to go into a house except he is ill, and wishes to use it for a hospital."

" Well, now, I don't know whether you are in airnest in saying that, but that's jist my way of thinking. Twice I have given up hunting, and taken to a farm : but I always get sick after living long in housen. I don't sleep well in them; and sometimes when I go to see my friends, not wishing to seem particular-like, I jist

let them go quietly to bed, and then slip out of
a window with my blanket, and get a good nap
under a tree in the open air. A man wants
nothing but a tree above him to keep off the
dew, and make him feel kind of homelike, and
then he can enjoy a real sleep."

In Tanner's narrative, that singular character
makes nearly the same remark, when speaking
of the usages which annoyed him while trying
to abandon the habits of a free hunter, and
conform to the customs of civilized life.

"But are you never disturbed by any wild
animal when sleeping thus without fire or a
camp?" one of us asked.

"Well, I remember once being wakened by
a creetur. The dumb thing was standing right
over me, looking into my face. It was so dark,
that neither of us, I suppose, could see what
the other was: but he was more frightened
than I was, for when I raised myself a little he

ran off so fast that I couldn't make out what he was; and seeing it was so dark, that to follow him would be of no account, I laid down again and slept till morning, without his disturbing me again."

" Suppose it had been a bear?"

"Well, a bear isn't exactly the varmint to buckle with so off-hand; though lying on your back is about as good a way as any to receive him, if your knife be long and sharp; but afore now, I've treed a bear at nightfall, and sitting by the root of the tree until he should come down, have fallen asleep, from being too tired to keep good watch, and let the fellow escape before morning, but if I had such luck as to have a good fat bear come to me in that way I would never let him go as that man did down at Ti."

I asked the story of this unworthy follower of the chase at *Ti*, into which familiar mono-

syllable, Cheney abbreviated the celebrated
name of Ticonderoga, and give it here to the
reader as nearly as possible in worthy John's
own words.

CHAPTER VIII.

A BEAR STORY.

"I DON'T want to say any thing against any man, but some people, till they get lost in them, seem to think a knowledge of the woods a mighty small matter; but this is neither here nor there though, but it's a fact that, however big they may talk at home, folks that ain't used to the woods, sometimes get mightily flurried when they meet with these wild animals. There now's a man in the next town who went out after moose, and when he heard one trotting along the same trail he was travelling, squatted behind a stump to shoot him; but the fellow having never seen a moose, had no idea of the sort of game he was after; and when a great bull, six year old, bigger than a horse, with horns that looked for all creation as if they never could pass between the trees of these woods, came crashing the branches with his broad hoofs, the mankinder shrunk behind a log, and says he to the moose, ' If you'll only let me alone, I'll let you alone!' Now, the fellow in Ti only knew about bears as he had heard us trappers speak of them, as carrying a half-a-dozen balls in their bodies, and some-times killing our dogs for us when we go to take them out of our traps, after being held there by the paw, starving, you don't know how many days. Well, this man was on a lake watching in his boat for deer, when hearing a plunge and a splash, he pulls round an island, and finds a great she-bear swimming straight across the lake. Being a good fellow with his oars, he pulls at once to cut off the bear from the opposite shore, which made the creetur change her course and try and swim round the boat. The man, however, again turned her, and the bear once more altered her course, but still kept for the same shore to which she had been steering. Gathering spunk now, the man, in turning the third time, rowed nearer to the beast, expecting in this way to drive her back a little, so as to keep the bear out in the middle of the lake until some one could come to help him. But when the starn of the boat, in swinging round, came near the bear, she put her paws upon it, and raised herself right into the boat, and there she sat on eend, looking the man in the face jist as quiet, now, as a bear could look. Well, the man, if he'd only know'd where to hit a bear, might have brought one of his oars down on the back of her skull, just as

easy as say so; and tough ash is better than a
rifle-ball with these varmint. But he didn't
like that kind o' quiet look the creetur gave
him; and there they sat, the bear looking at
the man, and the man looking at the bear. At
last, when he got over his fright a little, he
began to move his oars slowly, in order to
creep toward the shore from which the bear
had started; but the creetur wouldn't allow
this; she moved from her seat a little toward
the man, and showed her teeth in a way he
didn't like; but as soon as the man turned the
boat, the bear took her old place again, and sat
there jist as contented as you please; so the
man pulled for the shore to which the bear had
been swimming, watching the bear's face all the
while. And would you believe it, now, that
bear made him back his boat in toward a rock,
upon which the creetur stepped from the starn,
and turning round, gave the man a growl for

his pains afore she walked off into the woods. Tormented lightening! to be treated so by a bear! Why, I would have died upon the spot before that bear should have left the boat without our trying which was the best of us."

CHAPTER IX.

LAKE HENDERSON.

Leaving the cleared fields of M'Intyre one morning under the guidance of John Cheney, we struck the arm of a lake entirely surrounded by primitive forest, and locked up in mountains wooded to the summit. The frith upon which we embarked was the outlet of Lake Henderson; and emerging from its shadowy embrace as we laid our course up the lake, we soon shot out upon the bosom of that beautiful water.

The form of the lake, for want of a better simile, I can only compare to that most re-

spectable ancient head-gear, a three-cornered
hat, a little knocked out of shape. Its several
friths, too, strike in among the mountains with
the same sort of devil-me-care air that a
fiercely - cocked beaver did whilome put on.
Yet so completely do the dense woods around
soften away all the harder lines of the land-
scape, that the general effect is that of beauty
rather than savageness in the picture. We
pulled for about two miles through this lake,
where at each boat's length some new fold of
mountain scenery was unfurled upon our left,
while the two peaks of the Indian Pass and the
Panther Gap kept their bold heights con-
tinually in view upon our right. We landed
upon the margin of a heavy swamp, near the
inlet of the lake, floating some twenty yards
within the forest, and mooring our boat at last
among ancient trees, whose long moss some-
times swept the water.

We were bound for " The Indian Pass," one
of the most savage and stupendous among the
many wild and imposing scenes at the sources
of the Hudson.   It has been visited, I believe,
by few except the hunters of these mountains,
but it must at some day become a favourite
resort with the lovers of the picturesque.   It is
a tremendous ravine, cloven through the sum-
mit of a mountain, presenting the finest piece
of rock scenery I ever beheld—a cradle worthy
of the infant Hudson.

Many of the difficulties in exploring this
scene will probably vanish in a few years ; but
as the wildness of the approach now adds not
a little to its majesty, I can best convey the
true character of the place by leading the reader
thither in the mode I reached it.

CHAPTER X.

A ROUGH TRAMP.

THE walk to the Indian Pass is difficult enough at any time, but, soon after leaving our boat at the inlet of Lake Henderson, the morning, which had hitherto been cloudy, broke into a cold rain, which, wetting our clothes through, increased the weight that we had to drag through a primitive swamp, where each step was upon some slippery log, affording a precarious foothold; some decayed tree, into whose spongy body you would sink kneedeep, or upon quaking mosses that threatened to swallow one

E 2

up entirely. Here, though, while wading through the frequent pools, or stumbling over the fallen boughs which centuries had accumulated, I would often pause to admire some gigantic pine, which, drawing vigour from the dankness and decay around it, would throw its enormous column into the air, towering a hundred feet above hemlocks and cedars near, which would themselves seem forest giants when planted beside the modern growth of our Atlantic border.

After a mile of such walking, the ground began to rise, and, instead of wading through pools, we now crossed several brisk streams, which murmured among the rocks, as their pellucid waters ran to join the main inlet of the lake. Our path lay next along the border of this inlet, which is, in truth, the main branch of the Hudson. Sometimes we would ascend for several hundred yards among mossy rocks, thickets of white cedar, and an undergrowth of juniper; then we would come to a sort of plateau of swampy land, overgrown with moose-maple, or tangled with fern and interspersed with cranberry bogs. Another slope of rocky ground, seamed with numerous rills, that gurgled beneath the roots of hoary birches, or amid thickets of young maple, succeeded; while again and again we would cross and recross the main stream, upon fallen logs, generally lying either immediately upon or below one of the numerous cascades which diversify the river. Now we would scale some rocky hill-side, and hear the torrent roaring far beneath us, and now we found a narrow passage-way between its border and the impending cliffs.

In the mean time, though winding up and down continually, we were in the main ascending gradually to a lofty elevation. The number of the swamps were diminished, the frequent rills flashed more rapidly amid the loose boulders of rock, which soon began to cover the soil entirely; while the boulders themselves became lofty hillocks of solid stone, covered with moss, and sustaining a vigorous growth of the birch, the mountain-ash, or clumps of the hardy white cedar upon their summits.

Wet, bruised, and weary, we sat down beneath one of those enormous masses of displaced rock, after scaling a difficult ascent, and purposed to encamp there for the night; but, looking up through an opening in the trees, we saw the cliffs of the Indian Pass almost immediately above us, as they were swathed in mist, and the heavy scud, impelled by the wind which drew strongly through the gap, drifted past the gray precipice, and made the wall look as if in motion to crush us when just entering the jaws of the ravine.

But there were still two hours of daylight

left, and though the mile that was yet to be traversed before we gained the centre of the pass, was the most arduous task of the whole route, we again commenced the ascent. It took the whole two hours to accomplish this mile, but as the glen narrowed, our further advance was animated by a new object of interest, in the shape of a fresh moose-track; and we followed the trail until it broke abruptly in a rocky gorge, wilder than any I had yet beheld.

CHAPTER XI.

A WILD GORGE.

It was new to me to find the footprints of so large an animal among rocks that seemed only accessible to a goat. We saw several places where the moose had slipped upon the thin and slimy soil, or dashed the moss from the crags with his hoofs as he leaped a chasm. Following on the trail with caution, our guide held himself in readiness to shoot, confident that we must soon overtake our noble quarry as no animal of the kind could possibly make his way completely through the defile; but we soon came to a passage among the rocks, where the discreet brute, perceiving that there was but one way of returning if he ascended higher, had, after making a slight attempt to force himself through, struck into a lateral ravine, and sought some other path down the mountain.

I must adopt a homely resemblance to give the reader an idea of the size of the rocks, and their confused appearance in this part of the defile: he may imagine, though, loose boulders of solid rock, the size of tall city dwelling-houses, hurled from a mountain summit into a chasm a thousand feet in depth, lying upon each other as if they had fallen but yesterday; each so detached from each, that it is only their weight which seems to prevent them from rolling further down the defile: their corners meeting in angles that defy the mathematician to describe, and forming caverns and labyrinthine passages beneath them that no draughtsman could delineate.   The position of these tremendous crags seems so recent and precarious, that were it not for other indications around them, you would almost fear that your footsteps might topple over the gigantic masses, and renew an onward motion that was but now arrested. But Time has stamped the date of ages in other language upon their brows. Their tops are thatched with lichens that must be the growth of centuries; ancient trees are perched upon their pinnacles, and enormous twisted roots, which form a network over the chasms between them, and save your limbs from destruction when stepping over the treacherous moss that hide these black abysses, prove that the repairing hand of nature has been here at work for ages in covering up the ruin she has wrought in some one moment of violence.

But we are now in the bosom of the pass, and the shadows of night are veiling the awful precipice which forms the background of the picture. We have climbed the last ascent, steeper than all the rest, and here, in a clump of birches and balsam-firs, surrounded by steeps and precipices on every side, is our place to bivouac for the night.

CHAPTER XII.

CAMPING OUT.

"It ain't so bad a place for camping out," said John Cheney, as he rose from slaking his thirst at a feeble rill which trickled from beneath the roots of a rifted cedar over which he leaned—"it ain't so bad a place to camp, if it didn't rain so like all natur. I wouldn't mind the rain much, nother, if we had a good shantee; but you see the birch bark won't run at this season, and it's pretty hard to make a waterproof thatch, unless you have hemlock boughs —hows'ever, gentlemen, I'll do the best by ye."

And so he did! Honest John Cheney, thou art at once as stanch a hunter, and as true and gentle a practiser of woodcraft as ever roamed the broad forest; and beshrew me when I forget thy services that night in the Indian Pass.

The frame of a wigwam used by some former party was still standing, and Cheney went to work industriously tying poles across it with withes of yellow birch, and thatching the roof and sides with boughs of balsam-fir. Having but one axe with us, my friend and myself were, in the mean time, unemployed, and nothing could be more disconsolate than our situation, as we stood dripping in the cold rain, and thrashing our arms, like hackney-coachmen, to keep the blood in circulation. My hardy friend, indeed, was in a much worse condition than myself. He had been indisposed when he started upon the expedition, and was now so hoarse that I could scarcely hear him speak amid the gusts of wind which swept through the ravine. We both shivered as if in an ague, but he suffered under a fever which was soon super-added. We made repeated attempts to strike a fire, but our "loco foco" matches would not ignite, and when we had recourse to flint and steel, every thing was so damp around us that our fire would not kindle. John began to look exceedingly anxious :—

"Now, if we only had a little daylight left, I would make some shackleberry-tea for you; but it will never do to get sick here, for if this storm prove a north-easter, God only knows whether all of us may ever get away from this notch again. I guess I had better leave the camp as it is, and first make a fire for you."

Saying this, Cheney shouldered his axe, and striking off a few yards, he felled a dead tree, split it open, and took some dry chips from the heart. I then spread my cloak over the spot where he laid them to keep off the rain, and stooping under it he soon kindled a blaze, which we employed ourselves in feeding until the "camp" was completed. And now came the task of laying in a supply of fuel for the night. This the woodman effected by himself with an expedition that was marvellous. Measuring three or four trees with his eye, to see that they would fall near the fire without touching our wigwam, he attacked them with his axe, felled, and chopped them into logs, and made his wood-pile in less time than could a city sawyer, who had all his timber carted to hand. Blankets were then produced from a pack which he had carried on his back; and these, when stretched over a carpeting of leaves and branches, would have made a comfortable bed, if the latter had not been saturated with rain. Matters, however, seemed to assume a comfortable aspect, as we now sat under the shade of boughs, drying our clothes by the fire; while John busied himself in broiling some bacon which we had brought with us. But our troubles had only yet begun; and I must indulge in some details of a night in the woods, for the benefit of "gentlemen who sit at home at ease."

CHAPTER XIII.

A NIGHT IN THE WOODS.

Our camp, which was nothing more than a
shed of boughs open on the side toward the fire,
promised a sufficient protection against the rain
so long as the wind should blow from the right
quarter; and an outlying deer-stalker might
have been content with our means and appli-
ances for comfort during the night. Cheney,
indeed, seemed perfectly satisfied as he watched
the savoury slices which were to form our sup-
per steaming up from the coals.

" Well," said the woodsman, " you see there's

no place but what if a man bestirs himself to do his best, he may find some comfort in it. Now, many's the time that I have been in the woods on a worse night than this, and having no axe, nor nothing to make a fire with, have crept into a hollow log, and lay shivering till morning; but here, now, with such a fire as that—"

As he spoke a sudden puff of wind drove the smoke from the green and wet timber full into our faces, and filled the shantee to a degree so stifling, that we all rushed out into the rain, that blew in blinding torrents against us.

"Tormented lightning !" cried John, aghast at this new annoyance. "This is too pesky bad; but I can manage that smoke if the wind doesn't blow from more than three quarters at a time." Seizing his axe upon the instant, he plunged into the darkness beyond the fire, and in a moment or two a large tree came crashing

with all its leafy honours, bearing down with it
two or three saplings to our feet. With the
green boughs of these he made a wall around
the fire to shut out the wind, leaving it open
only on the side toward the shantee. The sup-
per was now cooked without further interrup-
tion. My friend was too ill to eat; but, though
under some anxiety on his account, I myself
did full justice to the culinary skill of our guide,
and began to find some enjoyment amid all the
discomfort of our situation. The recollection of
similar scenes in other days gave a relish to the
wildness of the present, and inspired that
complacent feeling which a man of less active
pursuits sometimes realizes, when he finds that
the sedentary habits of two or three years have
not yet warped and destroyed the stirring tastes
of his youth.

We told stories and recounted adventures.
I could speak of these northern hills, from

having passed some time among them upon a
western branch of the Hudson, when a lad of
fourteen; while the mountain-hunter would
listen with interest to the sporting scenes that
I could describe to him upon the open plains of
the far west; though I found it impossible to
make him understand how men could find their
way in a new country where there were so few
trees! With regard to the incidents and
legends that I gathered in turn from him, I
may hereafter enlighten the reader. But our
discourse was suddenly cut short by a catas-
trophe which had nearly proved a very serious
one. This was nothing more nor less than the
piles of brush which encircled our fire, to keep
the wind away, suddenly kindling into a blaze,
and for a moment or two threatening to con-
sume our wigwam. The wind, at the same time,
poured down the gorge in shifting, angry blasts,
which whirled the flames in reeling eddies high

into the air, bringing the gray cliffs into momentary light—touching the dark evergreens with a ruddy glow—and lighting up the stems of the pale birches, that looked like sheeted ghosts amid the surrounding gloom.

A finishing touch of the elements was yet wanting to complete the agreeableness of our situation, and finally, just as the curtain of brush on the windward side of the fire was consumed, the cold rain changed into a flurry of snow; and the quickly-melted flakes were driven with the smoke into the innermost parts of our wigwam. Conversation was now out of the question. John did, indeed, struggle on with a panther story for a moment or two, and one or two attempts were made to joke upon our miserable situation, but sleet and smoke alternately damped and stifled every effort, and then all was still except the roar of the elements. My sick friend must have passed a horrible night, as he woke me once or twice with his coughing; but I wrapped myself in my cloak, and placing my mouth upon the ground to avoid choking from the smoke, I was soon dreaming as quietly as if in a curtained chamber at home. The last words I heard John utter, as he coiled himself in a blanket, were—

"Well, it's one comfort, since it's taken on to blow so, I've cut down most of the trees around us that would be likely to fall and crush us during the night."

CHAPTER XIV.

THE INDIAN PASS.

THE ringing of Cheney's axe was the first sound that met my ear in the morning, which broke excessively cold. The fire had burnt low, though frequently replenished by him during the night, and he was now engaged in renewing it to cook our breakfast, which was soon ready, and for which the frosty mountain air gave me a keen appetite. The kind fellow, too, prepared some toast and a hot draught for my enterprising companion, whom nothing could prevent from further exploring the pass.

With this view we began descending a precipice in the rear of our camp, to a place called the ice-hole. The trees on the side of this precipice have a secret for growing peculiarly their own, or they could never flourish and maintain their place in such a position. The wall, some sixty or eighty feet high, and almost perpendicular, is covered with moss, which peels off in flakes of a yard square, as you plant your heels in it in descending; yet this flimsy substitute for soil supports a straggling growth of evergreens, that will bear the weight of a man as he clings to them, to avoid being dashed to pieces in the glen below. The snow of the last night which covered the mountain-tops made the stems of these saplings so slippery and cold, that our hands became numb in grasping them before we were halfway down the descent. The river runs through the bottom of this ravine, but its passage is so cavernous, that it is only by letting yourself down into the fissures between the immense boulders, which are here wedged together in indescribable confusion, and crawling beneath the rocks, that you can obtain a sight of its current. From this chasm you view the sky as from the bottom of a well. A pair of eagles that have their nest in the cliff above, showed like swallows as they hovered along its face. The sun never penetrates into this gloomy labyrinth; and here, unless the waters are unusually high, you may find cakes of ice at Midsummer.

Emerging from this wild chaos of rocks we clambered a short distance up the sides of the glen, and penetrated a few hundred yards further into the pass to a sloping platform amidst the rocks, where the finest view of the whole scene is to be obtained. And here, within a few yards of its first well-springs, you behold one of the strongest features of the mighty

Hudson developed even in its birth. It has already cloven its way through a defile as difficult as that through which it rushes near West Point, and far more stupendous. A rocky precipice of twelve hundred feet rises immediately in front of you, and the jaws of the pass open barely wide enough to admit the egress of the stream at its highest stages of water. The cliff opposite looks raw and recent as if riven through but yesterday: and ponderous blocks of stone, that would almost make mountains themselves, wrenched from their former seat, in what is now the centre of the pass, stand edgwise leaning down the glen, as if waiting some new throe of this convulsion of nature to sweep them further on their terrific career. Many of these features of the place you have already seen while climbing to the point where we stand; but now, upon turning round as you gain the head of the pass, and look out from its bosom upon the mountain region below, a view of unequalled beauty and grandeur greets the eye. The morning sun, which will not for hours yet reach the place where you stand, is shining upon airy peaks and wooded hills which shoulder each other as far as the eye can reach, while far down the glen, where the maple and beech find a more genial soil to nourish them, the rainbow hues of autumn are glistening along the stream, which, within a few miles of its fountain-head, has already expanded into a beautiful lake.

CHAPTER XV.

MOUNT MARCY.

THE group of wild hills among which the Hudson rises stand wholly detached from any other chain in North America. The highest peak of the Aganuschion range, or the Black Mountains, as some call them, from the dark aspect which their sombre cedars and frowning cliffs give them at a distance, was measured during last summer, and found to be nearly six thousand feet in height.

Mount Marcy, as it has been christened, not improperly, after the public functionary who first suggested the survey of this interesting region, presents a perfect pyramidal top, when viewed from Lake Sandford. Its alpine climate is very different from that prevailing in the valleys below, and I observed its cone sheathed in snow one day when I found the water temperate enough to enjoy swimming in the lake. The effect was equally beautiful and sublime. The frost had here and there flecked the forest with orange and vermilion, touching a single sumach or a clump of maples at long intervals, but generally, the woods displayed as yet but few autumnal tints: and the deep verdure of the adjacent mountains set off the snowy peak in such high contrast, soaring as it did far above them, and seeming to pierce, as it were, the blue sky which curtained them, that the poetic Indian epithet of TA-HA-WUS (*he splits the sky*), was hardly too extravagant to characterize its peculiar grandeur. The ascent of Mount

Marcy, and the view from the summit will hereafter puzzle many an abler pen than mine in the attempt to describe them.

The wild falls of KAS-KONG-SHADI (*broken water*)—the bright pools of TU-NE-SAS-SAH (*a place of pebbles*)—and the tall cascade of SHE-GWI-EN-DAUKWE (*the hanging spear*) — will hereafter tempt many to strike over to the eastern branch of the Hudson, and follow it up to Lake Colden; while the echoing glen of TWEN-UN-GA-SKO (*a raised voice*), though now as savage as the Indian Pass already described, will reverberate with more musical cries than the howl of the wolf or the panther, whose voices only are now raised to awaken its echoes. The luxurious cit will cool his champagne amid the snows of Mount Marcy: and his botanizing daughter, who has read in Michaux's American Sylva, of pines some two hundred feet in height! will wonder to pluck full-grown trees of the same genus, which she can put into her reticule.

At present, however, the mountain is a desert. Wolverines, lynxes, and wild-cats, with a few ravens, who generally follow in the track of beasts of prey, are almost the only living things that have their habitations in these high solitudes: and save when their occasional cry breaks the stillness, the solemn woods are on a calm day as silent as the grave. The absence of game birds, and of the beasts of chase, which give his subsistence to the hunter, prevents him from wasting his toil in climbing to the loftiest pinnacles: and so far as I learned, it is only lately that curiosity has prompted those who have passed a great part of their lives in the neighbourhood to make the ascent. The view, however, when once realized, seems to strike them not less than it does more cultivated minds. "It makes a man feel," said a hunter, to me, "what it is to have all creation placed beneath his feet. There are woods there, over which it would take a lifetime to hunt; mountains that seem shouldering each other up and away, heaven knows where. Thousands of little lakes are let in among them. Old Champlain, though fifty miles off, glistens below you like a strip of white birch-bark; and the green mountains of Vermont beyond it, fade and fade away, till they disappear as gradually as a cold scent when the dew rises."

CHAPTER XVI.

A WOLF ENCOUNTER.

THE hunter, Holt, of whom I have before spoken, has had some strange encounters with wild animals among these lonely defiles which I have attempted to describe : and John Cheney had, sometime since, a fight with a wolf, which is almost as well worthy of commemoration as the doughty feat of old Putnam.

It was in winter ; the snows were some four or five feet deep upon a level, and the hunter, upon whom a change of seasons seems to produce but little effect, could only pursue his game upon snow-shoes; an ingenious contrivance for walking upon the surface, which, though so much used in our northern counties, is still only manufactured in perfection by the Indians; who drive quite a trade in them along the Canada border. Wandering far from the settlements, and making his bed at nightfall in a deep snowbank, Cheney rose one morning to examine his traps, near which he will sometimes lie encamped for weeks in complete solitude; when, hovering round one of them, he discovered a famished wolf, who, unappalled by the presence of the hunter, retired only a few steps, and then, turning round, stood watching his movements.

" I ought, by rights," quoth John, " to have waited for my dogs, who could not have been far off, but the creetur looked so sarcy, standing there, that though I had not a bullet to spare, I couldn't help letting into him with my rifle."

He missed his aim; the animal giving a spring
as he was in the act of firing, and then turning
instantly upon him before he could reload his
piece. So effective was the unexpected attack
of the wolf, that his forepaws were upon Che-
ney's snow-shoes before he could rally for the
fight. The forester became entangled in the
deep drift, and sank upon his back, keeping the
wolf only at bay by striking at him with his
clubbed rifle. The stock was broken to pieces
in a few moments, and it would have fared ill
with the stark woodsman, if the wolf, instead of
making at his enemy's throat when he had him
thus at disadvantage, had not, with blind fury,
seized the barrel of the gun in his jaws. Still
the fight was unequal, as John, half buried in
the snow, could make use of but one of his
hands. He shouted to his dogs; but one of
them only, a young untrained hound, made his
appearance; emerging from a thicket he caught

sight of his master lying apparently at the
mercy of the ravenous beast, uttered a yell of
fear, and fled howling to the woods again.
"Had I had one shot left," said Cheney, "I
would have given it to that dog instead of de-
spatching the wolf with it."   In the exaspera-
tion of the moment, John might have extended
his contempt to the whole canine race, if a
stancher friend had not opportunely interposed
to vindicate their character for courage and
fidelity.

All this had passed in a moment; the wolf
was still grinding the iron gun-barrel in his
teeth: he had even once wrenched it from the
hand of the hunter, when, dashing like a thun-
derbolt between the combatants, the other
hound sprang over his master's body, and
seized the wolf by the throat.   "There was no
let go about that dog when he once took hold.
If the barrel had been red hot, the wolf couldn't

have dropped it quicker; and it would have done you good, I tell ye, to see that old dog drag the creetur's head down in the snow, while I, just at my leisure, drove the iron into his skull. One good, fair blow, though, with a heavy rifle-barrel, on the back of the head finished him. The fellow gave a kind o' quiver, stretched out his hind legs, and then he was done for. I had the rifle stocked afterwards, but she would never shoot straight after that fight; so I got me this pistol, which being light and handy, enables me more conveniently to carry an axe upon my long tramps, and make myself comfortable in the woods."

Many a deer has John since killed with that pistol. It is curious to see him draw it from the left pocket of his gray shooting-jacket, and bring down a partridge. I have myself witnessed several of his successful shots with this

unpretending shooting-iron, and once saw him
knock the feathers from a wild duck at eighty
or a hundred yards !

CHAPTER XVII.

THE DOG AND THE DEER-STALKER.

The Deer-stalkers, or "Still-hunters" as they are called in this part of the country, are very inveterate against those who hound the deer. For even in these woods, where you travel through twenty miles of unbroken forest in passing from house to house, people array themselves in factions, and indulge their animosities by acting in separate bodies with true partisan spirit. In fact, the deer-drivers and the still-hunters, only want their poet, or historian, to make their interminable bickerings, as celebrated as those of the Guelphs and Ghibbelines, or any other redoutable bone-breakers whose feudal " yesterdays have lighted fools the way to dusty death."

" What business has a man got in the woods," quoth the still-hunter, " who can't take home a piece of venison to his shantee without scaring all the deer for ten miles around before he gets at it. The flesh of the poor creeturs is worth nothing neither, after their blood is heated by being driven to death with dogs."

" How can a man sleep sound in the woods," saith John Cheney, on the other side, " when he has had the heart to lure the mother of a fawn to the very muzzle of his rifle by bleating at her: or who has shot down the dumb brutes by torchlight, when they come to the waterside to cool themselves at nightfall? It ain't nateral, and such hunting—it hunting they call it—will never prosper." Honest John! whatever may be the merits of the question, he has reason to feel sore upon the subject, from the sad and ignoble death which the hound who played so gallant a part in his wolf encounter, met with at the hands of the still-hunters.

Some of the best hounds in the country having been killed by these forest-regulators, Cheney would never allow his favourite dog to wander near the streams most frequented by them : but it chanced one day that the poor fellow met with an accident which withdrew his care from the dog. The trigger of his pistol caught against the thwart of a boat while he was in the act of raising it to shoot a deer, and the piece going off in a perpendicular direction, sent the whole charge into his leg, tearing off the calf, and driving the ball out through the sole of his foot. With this terrible wound, which, however, did not prevent him from reloading and killing the deer before he could swim to the shore, Cheney dragged himself fifteen miles through the woods, to the nearest log cabin. A violent fever, and the threatened loss of the limb, confined him here for months. But his dog, to whom, while idling in the forest, he had taught a hundred amusing tricks, was still his company and solace; and though Tray looked wistfully after each hunter that strayed by the cabin, no eagerness for the chase could impel him to leave his master's side.

At last, however, upon one unfortunate day, poor Cheney was prevailed upon to indulge a brother sportsman, and let him take the dog out with him for a few hours. The hunter soon returned, but the hound never came back. Under his master's eye, he had been taught

never to follow a deer beyond a certain limit;
but now, long confinement had given him such
a zest for the sport, that he crossed the fatal
bounds. The mountain-ridge of a more friendly
region was soon placed between him and his
master — the deer took to the treacherous
streams infested by the Still-hunters, and the
generous hound and his timorous quarry met
the same fate from the rifles of their prowling
enemy.

CHAPTER XVIII.

_____

CRUSTING MOOSE.

"CRUSTING" is the term applied to taking large game amid the deep snows of winter, when the crust of ice which forms upon the surface after a slight rain is strong enough to support the weight of a man, but gives way at once to the hoofs of a moose or a deer; while the animal, thus embarrassed, is easily caught and despatched with clubs. In our northern states more game is destroyed in this way than in any other; and you may read in the newspapers every winter some account of the inhabitants of a whole village turning out and butchering hundreds of deer when thus entrapped. Only a few years since, it was said that more than a thousand were so destroyed in the township of Catskill in one season. All true sportsmen, however, hold " crusting deer" in contempt and abhorrence—for the venison is generally not in season at the time of year when it is thus procured; and this mode of taking it belongs rather to the butcher than to the hunter.

Crusting moose is rather a different thing, as it requires both skill and courage on the part of the hunter, and the animal has a chance at least of escape or resistance. Still, as the law will not, or cannot protect this noblest of all forest game from destruction in this manner, it must at no distant day become extinct within the boundaries of New York. The broad west has no moose-ground so celebrated as that in our northern counties, and when you leave the sources of the Hudson, you must travel westward to those of the Mississippi before you find the gigantic moose as numerous as they were in our forests but a few years since. The woods of Maine, however, are probably richer in this noble game than any within the United States' territories.

The moose who is both more shy and more sagacious than the deer, has his favourite haunts in the depths of the forest. He moves about, not like the elk, in roving gangs, but stalks in lonely majesty through his leafy domains; and when disturbed by the hunter, instead of bounding away like his kinsman of the forest and prairie, he trots off at a gait which, though faster than that of the fleetest horse, is so easy and careless in its motion, that it seems to cost him no exertion. But though retreating thus when pursued, he is one of the most terrible beasts of the forest when wounded and at bay; and the Indians of the north-west, among some tribes, celebrate the death of a bull-moose, when they are so fortunate as to kill one, with all the songs of triumph that they would raise over a conquered warrior.

The deepest snows of winter of course offer the best occasion for moose-hunting. The sagacious animal, so soon as a heavy storm sets in, commences forming what is called a "Moose-yard," which is a large area, wherein he industriously tramples down the snow while it is falling, so as to have a place to move about in, and browse upon the branches of trees, without the necessity of wandering from place to place, struggling through the deep drifts, exposed to the wolves, who, being of lighter make, hold a carnival upon the deer in crusting-time. No wolf, however, dare enter a moose-yard. He will troop round and round upon the snow-bank which walls it, and his howling will, perhaps, bring two or three of his brethren to the spot, who will try to terrify the moose from his 'vantage ground, but dare not descend into it.

But, when the hunter, prowling about on his snow-shoes, discovers a moose-yard, he feels so sure of his quarry, that he will sometimes encamp upon the spot, in order to take the game at his leisure; and, when there have been several hunters in company, I have heard of their proceeding patiently to fell the neighbouring trees, and form a lofty fence around the yard, which enabled them to take the animal alive, when subdued by long confinement and starvation. An opportunity of doing this occurred near M'Intyre last winter, when a yard, with three moose in it, an old cow-moose and two yearlings, was discovered and surrounded by a band of hunters. Some of the party were desirous of taking them alive, as one of the proprietors of this extensive property—a gentleman of great public spirit—wishes to make an attempt to domesticate the animal, and, if possible, introduce the use of it to agricultural purposes. This is an exceedingly interesting and hardly doubtful experiment, for the moose has been frequently tamed, and, unlike the common deer, can be halter-broken as easily as a horse.

The hunters, however, were too excited with their good luck to listen to any suggestion of the kind—few of them had ever killed a moose. Their rifles were in their hands, and they were bent upon having a shot at the game, which dashed to and fro, snorting and whistling, within the snowy bounds of the yard. The whoops and shouts of their enemies, redoubled by the echoes from the adjacent mountains, made them furious at being thus beset; and, at each discharge of a gun, they would plunge at the assailing marksman so desperately, that he would be compelled to take refuge behind the nearest tree. The scene became thus so exciting, that all order was lost among the huntsmen. Each fired as fast as he could load, hardly waiting to take aim, lest some quicker-sighted comrade should bear off the prize. The moose, though repeatedly wounded, would charge again and again into the snow-banks around them, and drive their enemies from the brink, retiring, at each turn, to a corner of the yard where they were least molested, and there rally at once for another charge. Faint with the loss of blood, however, they were successively discomfited and borne down by the hunters, who, retreating upon the crust when pursued, would turn upon the moose the moment they tried to retrace their steps, and assail them with axes and bludgeons while floundering in the snow to recover the vantage ground of the yard. The two yearlings, with their dam, after making a most gallant resistance, were ultimately despatched.

Such was the description which I had one day from a veteran hunter, while lying round a fire discussing a venison steak cut from a fine buck, whose death had been compassed after the curious fashion described as follows.

CHAPTER XIX.

WITHING A BUCK.

AFTER a week of fine trout-fishing, alternated by such picturesque rambles as I have attempted to describe, we could not leave the sources of the Hudson without devoting our last day to a deer-hunt, which had only been hitherto deferred from Cheney's hounds being absent with a brother hunter.

Taking an early breakfast, my friend and I, accompanied by John Cheney, another forester of the name of Linus Catlin, and our hospitable host, separated at the inlet of Lake Sandford, to take our different stations. Cheney, with three hounds, was to rouse the deer from his lair upon an adjacent mountain; Catlin was to take post in his skiff, behind one of the islets of the lake; and the rest of us were to watch in the canoe, under the shelter of a bold promontory, opposite which the deer was expected to take the water.

Before entering his boat, Catlin, who appeared to be one of those quiet fellows that say little and do much, having no gun with him, proceeded to cut down a birchen sapling, and strip it of all its branches except two, the elastic wood of which he twisted together, so as to form a large noose upon the end of the pole. As he was laying this weapon in the stern of his skiff, and preparing to push off, his preparations did not seem to meet the approbation of his friend Cheney.

"What, Linus, you are not a-going to withe the deer?"

"And why not?" answered Catlin, taking his seat, and placing the oars in the rowlocks.

"Because I never see any good in withes: a man that can't tail a deer oughtn't to hunt him."

"Why, John, you couldn't hold a fat buck by his tail long enough to cut his throat with your hunting-knife."

"Can't I? I'd like to see the time! Well, if I know'd I could never tail another, as I have thousands, the cretur might go afore I'd be the man to drown him with a withe!"

The quiet Linus only replied by pushing off into the current and dropping down the stream, and we immediately followed, while Cheney, whistling to his dogs, plunged into the forest and disappeared.

The boats kept near each other for some time, and we landed together upon a sunny point to deposit a basket of bread and vegetables, an iron pot, and some other culinary apparatus which we had brought with us, under the confident promise of John that we should surely have a venison dinner in the woods that day, if he had to drive a dozen deer before we could kill one. Our craft being lightened of her lading, Catlin pulled for the islet which was yet a mile off down the lake, and we, after watching his oars flashing in the sunshine for a few moments, embarked anew and paddled round a headland; when running the canoe under the trees, whose morning shadows still hung over the lake, we stretched ourselves upon the grass, listening and looking with the most eager attention for the first intimation of approaching sport.

There was a slight ripple upon the lake,

which was not favourable to our seeing the deer should he take the water at any great distance from us; and the incessant call of the jay, with the ever-changing cry of the loon, created so many noises in the woods, generally so still, that the opening of the hounds might have escaped us unheard.   These early sounds, however, soon ceased as the sun came marching up above the mountain tops, and spread the silver waves from the centre of the lake far and wide, into all its sheltered bays and wood-embowered friths.   The faint ripple of the waters upon the rocky shore was the only murmur left.

My companions were conversing in a subdued voice, and I was lying a little apart from them revelling in the singular beauty of the scene, and trying to fix in my memory the peculiar outline of a ridge of mountains opposite, when I heard the faint crashing of a bough upon the other side of the lake, and running my eye along the water, discovered a noble buck, with fine antlers, swimming beneath the bank. My comrades caught sight of him a moment afterwards, and we all waited with eager anxiety to see him put out far enough for us to row round him, and cut him off from the shore. But the buck had evidently no idea of making a traverse of the lake at this time. He was far in advance of the hounds, and had taken the water at this place not from being hotly pursued, but only to throw them off the scent, and then double on his own track. He, therefore, kept swimming along the shore, close under the steep bank, looking up at it every now and then, as if in search of a "runway" which would carry him back again into the depths of the forest. This runway was in a little cove immediately opposite to us, and though it was almost impossible now to cut him off from reaching it, yet the moment we saw his object, we determined to make the effort.

The position of each in the canoe had of course been previously arranged; we accordingly crept into our seats, and pushed out into the lake, without making a sound that could attract the attention of the deer. The little islet of Inch-Hamish lay but a few yards out of our course, and we slid along as quietly as possible, until we could get under cover of this, and then gave way with all our strength. The lean craft glanced like an arrow through the rippling waters. We were all three familiar with the use of oar or paddle, and the buck would have had no chance of escape from that canoe had we been a hundred yards nearer. Our hopes were high in the brief moments that the islet shut him from view, but he had just reached the shore when we shot from its cover. We now threw up our paddles in despair, and paused to take a fair view of him as he escaped from the lake. It was beautiful to see him lift his arching neck from the water when he first touched the bottom; and his whole form was brought to view while he made a few steps through the shallow waves, as leisurely as if no pursuers were near. Throwing his antlers, then, upon his shoulders to clear the boughs above him, he bounded over a fallen tree near the margin, and disappeared in the forest.

Looking now to the point where he had entered the lake, we saw one of the hounds standing out on a rock, with nose uplifted to catch the vanished scent of his quarry. The dog saw us pulling for the runway, and, dashing into the lake, swam for the point to which we were steering, and reached it just as our boat grated upon the beach. A moment sufficed to put him again upon the scent. He opened with a joyous yell—his mouthing soon became deeper, and more distant—it neared again—and the two other hounds, who, while following some other trail, had now, for the first time, struck his, joined in the chorus. The echoes in the upper part of the lake are the finest that I ever heard; and as the morning breeze had now lulled, they were all awakened by this wild music. The deer was evidently making for the inlet; and, indeed, before we could pull out far enough to command a view of the point where he would probably cross, he had made the traverse, and we only caught a glimpse of the dogs thrashing through the wild grass upon a tongue of land upon the opposite side of the inlet.

"You may give up that buck," said our host; "he has gone over to Lake Henderson, and the best thing we can do is to start another."

Almost as he spoke, a clear whoop rang through the forest, and soon after we saw

John Cheney waving us to the shore we had just left.

" Tormented lightning ! what are ye doing there, when the deer is going down the lake ?"

" Down ! why he has just crossed at the upper end, and gone over to Lake Hender-son."

" I tell you he hasn't. No deer will go there when the water's so high that he would be en-tangled in the bushes before he could swim beyond his depth. I know the natur of the cretur; and that deer has gone round to the lower end of the lake, to cross back to the mountain, where I started him."

With these words Cheney waded into the water without waiting for us to approach nearer the shore, jumped into the canoe, seized a paddle, and away we sped again over the waves. The event proved that he was right. The buck after crossing at the inlet, made a circuit of several miles, and before we could pull half way down the lake, took the water at a runway opposite to the islet, behind which Catlin was watching in his skiff.

Cool and experienced in the sport, this hunter never broke his cover until the deer got fairly out into the lake, when he launched out and turned him so quickly, that the buck made for the island which his pursuer had just left. Linus, however, was too quick for him, and threw his withe over the deer's antlers before he could touch the bottom with his feet. But the buck was a fellow of great weight and vigour, and feeling himself thus entangled, he made a lateral spring into deeper water, which dragged the hunter out of the boat in an instant. Linus fortunately seized one of the oars, which, being rigged with swivels instead of rowlocks, still kept him connected with the skiff. But his situation was a very precarious one; the buck becoming the assailant, struck at him with his forefeet, and got him again fairly under water. He rose this time, however, with the oar between himself and his antagonist, and while clutching the gunwale of the boat with one hand, seized the withe which had escaped from his grasp, in the same moment that the buck made a pass at him with his horns, which ripped up the bosom of his shirt, and was within an inch of goring him to death. But before the desperate animal could repeat the thrust, the hunter had gained the skiff, now half full of water, and seizing the first missile that came to hand, he dealt the buck a blow upon the head, which, followed up by a slash from his hunting-knife put an end to the encounter.

The conflict was over before we could reach the combatants ; but the carcass was still warm when we relieved the leaky boat of Catlin by lifting the buck into our canoe; and his eye was so bright, his skin so smooth and glossy, and his limbs, not yet stiffened in death, folded so easily beneath him, that it was difficult to imagine life had departed.

When we landed at the spot before selected, it required the united strength of the whole party to lift the buck up the steep bank, and suspend him upon the timbers, which Cheney prepared, *secundum artem*, for scientific butchery. The eloquent Bucklaw, by whose learned discourse upon this branch of " the gentle science of venerie," the reader has been enlightened, when reading Scott's " Bride of Lammermoor," could not have been a more thorough practitioner of the art than John Cheney.

A group worthy of Inman's pencil was collected around the roaring fire, by which the dripping Catlin was drying himself; while Cheney, with the fat buck before him, and the dogs licking the blood at his feet, as ever and anon he paused in his operation, and turned round to us, to point out some graceful line of fat with his hunting-knife, would have formed the prominent features of the picture.

The potatoes, in the mean time, were roasted whole or sliced up with various savory matters, which were put into the kettle to boil; and though we had omitted to bring tumblers with us, Cheney's axe hollowed out and fashioned some most ingenious drinking-cups, which were ready by the time divers choice morsels of venison had been grilled upon the coals. There were a few drops at the bottom of an old flask of cognac for each of us; we had Mackinaw-blankets, stretched upon balsam branches, to recline upon; there was no call of duty or business to remind us of the lapse of hours; and stories and anecdotes of former huntings in these mountains, with practical discussions as to what part of a deer afforded the most savory venison, prolonged the repast till sunset.

The haunch of the buck wrapped in its clean skin, was left untouched for future feasting. " Well, John," said I, as I tried in vain to lift it into the boat, by the short, fat tail, " how could you ever have taken such a fellow as this by ' tailing him,' as you call it?"

" It's all knack—it's being used to the thing only. Not but that I always said that withing is a good way."

" No, no, John!" we all exclaimed, " you said just the reverse."

" Well, perhaps I did, and without meaning to discredit Linus, who, for certain, has been

the man among us this day, I still say that
withing only does for those that don't know
how to tail a deer. And now let's take the old
hounds in the boats and pull homewards."

CHAPTER XX.

THE DEPARTURE.

THE hunters with whom we had enjoyed our last day's sport upon Lake Sandford, accompanied us some forty miles through the woods, when we started next day upon our homeward journey. John Cheney, like the rest, trudging along on foot, found an opportunity of shooting several partridges by the way, picking them from the trees with his pistol with as much case as an ordinary sportsman could have effected with a fowling-piece (admitting the thick cover to give the bird such a chance of

life as to warrant a *sportsman* to take him sit-
ting). After killing three or four partridges,
however, John could not be prevailed on to
shoot at more. I several times called his atten-
tion to a good shot, but he always answered
shaking his head. " It's wrong, it's wrong, sir,
to use up life in that way—here's birds enough
for them that wants to eat them, and that saddle.
of venison on the buckboard will only be wasted,
if I kill more of these poor things."

About noon we halted by a brook which ran
through the forest near a clump of maples
which grew so widely apart as to let the sun-
shine down upon a grassy spot, where we
spread our table upon a fallen tree, and
kindling a fire proceeded to cook our dinner.
All found something to do, while this was in
preparation; one attended to the comforts of the
horses, another kept the fire supplied with fuel,
some shot at a mark with Cheney's pistol,

while worthy John himself, watched with the most sedulous care over the venison and partridges, which he roasted after a fashion peculiarly his own, and which, with four or five large trout that we had brought from the lake, and the customary accompaniment of roast potatoes and wheaten bread, all being flavoured with good humour and keen mountain appetites, made the repast a delicious one.

The day was fine, the air clear and remarkably bland for the season, and I don't know how long we should have protracted our woodland revel, as Cheney exercised his skill and ingenuity serving up every moment some tempting morsel of venison, pressing my friend and myself particularly to eat, as " we didn't know when again we might have a real nateral dinner in the woods, and it was a comfort to him to see gentlemen from the city take things in the woods as if they liked them."

No town-adoring cockney, nor patriotic villager, nor proud Castellan, could imagine himself more thoroughly identified with all the honours and glory of his distinct and especial dwelling-place, than does this genuine forester with every thing that appertains to the broad woods through which he ranges. Cheney was now, as he told me when walking by my side, after resuming our journey, going out of the woods for the first time in three months, to visit his father, who lived some sixty miles off. He was very old, and John had not seen nor heard from him for some time previously to his last visit to the settlements which we were now approaching, and from which his father lived still another day's journey distant. He seemed quite anxious as to the tidings he might hear about his venerable parent, and talked of remaining to spend a month with him. Such

was the complexion of the hunter's feelings
when we came out of the forest at nightfall
upon what is called the Schroon-road, where
we found a good inn to receive us.   Here, my
friend and I, after securing a conveyance which
should enable us to follow down the course of
the Hudson instead of returning home through
Lake Champlain, invited Cheney to take a seat
in our vehicle, which would carry him some
thirty miles on his next day's journey.   He was
so eager to see his father, that the proffer was
at once accepted, and all our mutual arrange-
ments were completed for the morrow.   But
just as we were on the point of starting, and
had shaken hands with our hearty host of Mac-
Intyre and his party, Cheney was hailed by a
brother hunter, who, rifle on shoulder, trudged
up to the inn door upon the road we were
about to travel.

" Hullo, Bill!" cried the filial John, advancing to shake hands with him. " Come up from Ti', eh? and how's the old man?"

" Right well, I tell ye," replied Bill; he's killed six bear this fall, and thinking the creturs must be pretty well routed out among our mountains, I've struck over the ridge to see what I can find among your'n."

" Tormented lightning! six bear!" quoth John. " Why, the raal old chap; his grain is as tough and springy as ever. Well, Bill, if you'll hold on till I can speak a word to these gentlemen in the waggon, I'll turn round with you, and back into our woods again."

Saying this, Cheney came up to us, and repeating what we had just overheard as the reason for changing his intentions, he shook hands with us, and we parted upon our separate journeys.

We reached Lake George that night, our

road winding side by side with the Hudson for many miles, passing several picturesque lakes, crossing mountain ridges commanding the most superb bird's-eye views, or descending into valleys, where the painter might find an ever-varying novelty for the exercise of his art; but as the reader is perhaps already fatigued with these loose sketches, and as the prominent figure which gave them animation has disappeared from the scene, we will here conclude our notes upon THE SOURCES OF THE HUDSON.

WILD SCENES

ON

THE WISCONSAN.

CHAPTER I.

NIGHTS IN AN INDIAN LODGE.

"*Neshin Wikiewun,*" exclaimed White-plume, after kindling our fire in the deserted shantee of some roving hunter which we found in one of these deep ravines, through which the brooks of the north-west discharge themselves into the Wisconsan. "A good house," said he, rubbing his hands, and looking around with an air of satisfaction.

"Aneendee," growled Che-che-gwa (*the Rat-*

tlesnake) with Indian sententiousness, while his less dignified friend sliced off a couple of steaks from the moose he had just killed, and left the Canadian to prepare the supper, which was soon despatched by all four of us.

It was still early in the evening, and though somewhat fatigued, as I was not at all sleepy, I should have had a pretty tedious time of it, after the Rattlesnake had coiled himself to rest, if left alone with so laconic a companion.

But the White-plume, who had been a great traveller in his day, and was noted for his talkativeness and story-telling, seemed seized with a more than usual fit of loquacity. The other Indian appeared at first much inclined to repose, but his disposition to sleep was gradually dispelled by the vivacity of his comrade. He soon raised himself on his elbow and yielded

attention to the waggish sallies of the other.
Finally, sitting erect, he carefully filled his pipe
with kinnekinic, and, placing his back against
the rough timbers of the lodge, seemed pre-
pared for a long siege, as his friend entered
upon one of those rambling legends of which
the Indians are so fond.   The story-teller also,
clearing his throat, asked for "some milk from
the 'Mokomuan's' *black cow !*" and emptying
the whiskey-bottle, which the Canadian handed
him, at a draught, he pursued his tale without
further interruption, except from the guttural
expression of satisfaction which now and then
escaped from the deep chest of his companion,
or the loud snoring of my guide, whose slum-
bers were as noisy as if he were sleeping
against time.

My knowledge of the language used by the
story-teller was so slight, that the meaning of
his words often escaped me altogether; and it

was only from his frequent repetition of the same ideas, enforced by the most animated and expressive gestures, and, perhaps, from my having before heard of the wild tradition upon which it was founded, that I was at all able to follow him in the narration. It would be affectation in me to attempt to give the style, and mode of expression, in which the tale I am about to relate was conveyed to me, but the main tissue of it was as follows.

CHAPTER II.

THE GHOST-RIDERS.

A LEGEND OF THE GREAT AMERICAN DESERT.

" Away!—Away! My breath was gone,
I saw not where he hurried on!
'Twas scarcely yet the break of day
And on he foam'd—Away!—Away!—
And my cold sweatdrops fell like rain,
Upon the coursers bristling mane;
But snorting still, with rage and fear,
He flew upon his far career."

Mazeppa.

THE hunters of the far west who trap for beaver among the defiles of the Oregon Mountains, regard no part of their long journey, from the borders to their savage hunting-grounds, where the fur-bearing animals are still found in the greatest profusion, with more aversion than that which leads over the great desert, where the tributaries of the Padouca, the Konzas, and the Arkansaw rivers, are half absorbed by the arid sand. Lewis and Clarke, Major Long, and other scientific explorers of this desolate region, suffered much from the want of water while passing through it on their way to the Rocky Mountains; and they often mention the disheartening effect it had upon their followers, when, after traversing the scorching plain for weeks, it still lay stretched in unbroken and monotonous vastness before them. This portion of country, which extends along the base of the Rocky Mountains as far as we have any acquaintance with their range, is said to have an average width of six hundred miles. In the north, the surface is occasionally characterized by water-worn pebbles and hard gravel, but the predominant characteristic is sand, which, in many instances, prevails to the entire exclusion of vegetable mould. At the South, the arid plains are profusely covered with loose fragments of volcanic rocks, amid whose barren bosom no genial plant has birth; and, indeed, throughout the whole region, large tracts are often to be met with, which exhibit scarcely a trace of vegetation. In some few instances, sandy hillocks and ridges make their appearance, thickly covered with red cedar, of a dwarfish growth; but in general, nothing of vegetation appears upon the uplands, but rigid grass of spare and stunted growth, prickly pears profusely covering extensive tracts, and weeds of a few varieties, which, like the prickly pears, seem to thrive the best in the most arid and steril soils.

The Indians, who inhabit this extensive region, are composed of several roving tribes, who, unlike the nations to the east and west of them, have no permanent villages, nor hunting grounds which they claim as peculiarly their own. They hunt the buffalo and antelope, and, dwelling only in tents of leather, migrate from place to place in pursuit of the herds of those animals; and so extensive is their range, that while they exchange their skins for blankets and strouding, with the British traders on the Cheyenne river of the north, they also trade their mules and horses, for vermilion and silver ornaments, with the Spaniards of Mexico on the Colorado of the south. The Arapahoes, Kaskaias, Kiaways, and Tetaus, which are the chief of the desert hordes, are ferocious and predatory in their habits, and are continually at war with various tribes of the Missouri Indians, who inhabit the fertile countries which lie between them and our western frontier. The grizzly bear, the king of the American wilds, shares these dreary domains with the savages, hardly less ferocious than himself, and roams the west in quest of living prey. Here, too, the illusive mirage of the desert cheats the parched traveller with its refreshing promise, and the wanderers in these solitudes often tell of those monstrous shapes and unnatural forms, which, like the spectre of the Brocken, reflected on the heated and tremulous vapour, are magnified and distorted to the eye of the appalled and awe-stricken traveller.* Strange fires, too, are said

* As the day advanced, and the heat of the sun began to be felt, such quantities of vapour were seen to ascend from every part of the plain, that all objects at a little distance appeared magnified and variously distorted. Three elks, which were the first that we had seen, crossed our path at some distance before us. The effect of the mirage, with our indefinite idea of the distance, magnified those animals to the most prodigious size. For a moment we thought we saw the mastadon of America moving in those vast plains which seem to have been created for his dwelling-place."—*Major Long's Expedition to the Rocky Mountains.*

K 2

to shoot along the baked and cracking earth, and the herds of wild horses that can be seen trooping along the horizon, seem at times to be goaded on by gigantic and unearthly riders, whose paths are enveloped in wreaths of flame.*

* Luminous appearances, like those mentioned in the text, are also said to be common in some of the mining districts west of the Mississippi. Dr. Edwin James, of the army, the accomplished naturalist and traveller, received several accounts of them from the residents in that region, though neither he nor any of his party witnessed any such phenomena. A settler told them of two itinerant preachers, who had encountered an indescribable phenomenon, at a place about nine miles east of Loutre lick. " As they were riding side by side at a late hour in the evening, one of them requested the other to observe a ball of fire attached to the end of his whip. No sooner was his attention directed to this object, than a similar one began to appear on the other end of the whip : in a moment afterwards, their horses and all objects near them were enveloped in a wreath of flame. By this time the minds of the itinerant preachers were so much confounded, that they were no longer capable of observation,

The scientific explorer readily calls philosophy to his aid in examining these strange appearances : learning explains the phenomena of which he is himself a witness, and reason rejects the preternatural images, which he only knows from the representations of others. But the nomadic tribes, who make their dwelling upon the desert, or the uneducated adventurer, who wanders thither from some more smiling region, are differently affected. The monstrous shapes, and unearthly appearances, that present themselves to his excited vision, are regarded through the medium of superstitious awe. The wild imagination of the Indian, and the credulous fancy of the Creole and Canadian hunter,

and could, therefore, give no further account of what happened." He also stated as a fact, authenticated by the most credible witnesses, that a very considerable tract of land near by, had been seen to send up vast columns of smoke, which rose through the light and porous soil as if it had been the covering of a coalpit.

people these mysterious solitudes with actual beings ; while the grotesque figures, drawn upon the mocking mirage, after presenting themselves frequently to the eye, assume at length an individuality and a name ; and it is said that the Indians and Canadian wanderers become at last so familiar with the images represented, as even to pretend to recognise the features, and swear to the identity of shapes which are continually changing, and which probably never present themselves more than once to the same person. Among those most often mentioned, there are none whose identity has been more completely established, and whose names are whispered with deeper awe, than those of the GHOST-RIDERS. The Canadian Engagé always crosses himself when he utters the name, and the Otto, or Omaw-whaw warrior, who may have skirted the desert in a war party, against the Cheyennes, or the Pawnee-Loup, who has crossed it in his battles with the Crow and Kiawa Indians, invariably places his hand upon his Meta-waüann, or repository of his personal manitto, when he speaks of these fearful apparitions.

Those who affect to have seen these strange dwellers of the desert, describe them as two gigantic figures, representing a man and woman locked in each other's arms, and both mounted on one horse, which is of the same unearthly make as themselves. Some pretend to have been near enough to discover their features, and these assert that the countenance of the man, though emaciated and ghastly, and writhed with the most fearful contortions, by an expression of shrinking horror, can plainly be identified as the face of a white man; while the features of the woman, though collapsed and corpse-like, are evidently those of an Indian female. Others insist that no one can ever have been near enough to the phantoms to remark these peculiarities ; for the Ghost-Riders, say they, are for ever in motion, and they scour the desert with such preternatural velocity, as to mock the scrutiny of human eyes. They appear to be goaded on for ever by some invisible hand, while the phantom charger that bears them overleaps every obstacle, as he flies on his mysterious and apparently aimless career.

There is a tradition among the Indians accounting for the origin of these fearful apparitions, to which universal credence is given. It is a story of love and vengeance—of gentle affections won by gallant deeds, and Eden-like happiness blasted by unholy passion—of black-hearted treachery and ruthless violence, that met with a punishment more horrible even than itself.

And thus the story runs :

Upon the western borders of the great desert already described, and somewhere about the

head-waters of the Padouca and Arkansaw
rivers—where they approach each other among
those broken sandstone ledges which lift their
gray parapets, and isolated columnar rocks of
snowy whiteness, from copses of hazel and
shrubby oaks—there stood, many years since,
the lodge of Ta-in-ga-ro;—" *The-first-thunder-
that-falls.*" The hunter, though no one knew
whence he came, appeared to be upon friendly
terms with all the allied tribes of the desert,
and he was said to have recommended himself
to them on his appearance in those wilds, by
bringing a dozen scalps of different tribes of the
Missouri Indians at his saddle-bow, when he
first presented himself in the skin tents of the
roving Kaskaias. So rich an offering would
have placed the chief at the head of an inde-
pendent band of his own, had he wished to be-
come a " partisan," or leader of warriors; but
the habits of Ta-in-ga-ro were unsocial and se-

cluded, and the only object that claimed the solicitude, or shared the sympathies of the bold stranger, was a beautiful female—the sole companion of his exile.

The name of the hunter was evidently of Omaw-whaw origin, but there was nothing about his person to mark him as belonging to that distant nation, and it was equally difficult to identify the partner of his wandering with any neighbouring tribe.   Some, from the fairness of her complexion, insisted that she must belong to the Rice-eaters (*Menomonés*), or White Indians of the north, who dwell near the country of the Long-knives; others, that she must be a *Boisbrulé*, or daughter of a Sioux mother by some Sakindasha (British) trader; but no one, after a while, troubled themselves about the origin of Zecana, or *The Bird*, as she was called in the Yauckton language.   Indeed the lonely couple lived so completely by themselves, in a spot but seldom visited, that they were soon forgotten among a people so scattered as the dwellers of the desert. The only object of Ta-in-ga-ro appeared to have been, to find a home where he could place his wife in safety; and the broken mounds, and hillocks, and angular tables of sandstone, now heaped upon the soil, like the plates of ice often piled upon each other in the eddies and along the banks of rivers, and now raising themselves in solitary pyramids and obelisks, along the grassy vales in which he sought an asylum, made this the country, of all others, wherein the outlaw might find a secure fastness—especially when the whole breadth of the desert lay between him and his people. Secure amid these wild and picturesque retreats, the sole care of the exile was to keep a few wild horses in training near his lodge, and to hunt the game that was necessary for the subsistence of his small household. The soul of Ta-in-ga-ro appeared to be completely wrapt up in the being who had united her fate with his. He seldom allowed her to go out of his sight, and when the disappearance of the buffalo and antelope from his immediate neighbourhood extended the range of the chase, Zecana always accompanied him on his more distant expeditions. Indeed, the love which the hunter bore to his wife, was not like the ordinary affection of an Indian to his squaw: it resembled more the devotion which distinguishes those who, in some tribes, are coupled out as friends, to be nearer to each other than children of the same father, in all the concerns that mark the pathway of life.—It was like the mystic tie which unites together the fated brothers of " The Band of the Brave." *

* *Nanpashene*—The Dauntless, or " Those who never retreat." The different members of this singular and romantic association are generally coupled out in pairs; and incredible instances are told of the exclusive devotion

The genial months of summer had passed away, and the first moon of autumn still found the exile and his bride dwelling in their sequestered valley. His success in the chase had enabled Ta-in-ga-ro to exchange a pack of skins for a few simple comforts, with a Spanish trader on the Mexican border, aud by merely shifting his lodge to the mountain recesses near, when the winter called for a more sheltered situation, he was easily enabled to strike the wild goats of the Oregon highlands, and by trapping for beaver among the adjacent glens, supply all the wants of himself and Zecana. It was necessary, however, in disposing of the latter, to be frequently brought in contact with the Spaniard; and his unwillingness to leave his wife unprotected, induced Ta-in-ga-ro often to take her

to each other of the friends thus united—a devotion that extends even to death when made terrible by all the horrors of Indian torture.

with him on his visits to the trading-post. The consequences were such as are continually occurring on our own frontier, in the intercourse between the licentious whites, who are bound by no ties except those of interest and passion, and the confiding and simple-hearted Indians.

The Spaniard, whose cabin was already shared with two wives, taken from the adjacent tribes with whom he traded, soon conceived a partiality for the fairer features of the northern girl; and, with that disregard of moral obligations, which is but too characteristic of his order, when the welfare of one of the aborigines is concerned, he determined that she should become the victim of his unbridled passions. His advances were received by Zecana with indignation and scorn; but notwithstanding the disgust which his persevering in them awakened, she feared to tell her husband of the insults she received lest his impetuous disposition should embroil him with all the renegado whites, villanous half-bloods, and degraded Indians, that usually hang round a trading-post, and become the pliant creatures of its master. The return of Spring, too, was near, and Zecana thought that its earliest blossoms would find her once more alone with her lover, enjoying the sequestered privacy of their summer retreat together; and, confident in her own purity and strength, she contented herself with repelling the advances of the trader in silence. But the wily and profligate Spaniard, was not to be cheated so easily of his victim; and after meditating a variety of designs, he at last brought both cunning and force to the accomplishment of his purpose. He succeeded in luring the unsuspecting Indian into an agreement, by which a pack of skins was to be delivered within a certain period. In order that Ta-in-ga-ro might be completely unshackled in his efforts to procure them, and rove as far as possible in his dangerous quest, the trader prevailed upon him to leave his wife in his guardianship, while her husband went upon an expedition into the inmost recesses of the Rocky Mountains. The hunter, according to the custom of the Indians departed upon his errand, without giving Zecana the slightest intimation of his distant mission, or of the arrangements, which he had made for her care during his absence.

In one of the most romantic valleys on the eastern side of the mountains, at the foot of that snow-capped peak, which is called after the first white man that ever planted his foot on the summit,* there is a large and beautiful fountain, whose transparent water, highly aërated with exhilarating gas, has procured it the name of "The Boiling Spring," from the white hunters, who trap for beaver in this

* Edwin James's U. S. A.

lonely region. This fountain is one of the first
you meet with after crossing the Great Desert,
and its grateful beverage not less than its sin-
gular situation, causes it to be regarded with
deep veneration by the roving natives of the
mountain and the plain. The Indian hunter
when he drinks from the rocky basin, inva-
riably leaves an offering in the refreshing bowl;
and the clean bottom is paved with the beads
and other ornaments which the aborigines
have left there as sacrifices or presents to the
spring.

By the side of this fountain, one sultry
April noontide, reposed an Indian hunter.
His mantle of blue and scarlet cloth, beaded
with white wampum, was evidently of Spa-
nish manufacture and indicated perhaps the
gay and predatory rover of the south-west;
but the long-plaited and ribbon-twined locks
of the Tetan, or Kaskaia, were wanting: and

the knotted tuft on his crown with the war-
eagle's feather as its only ornament, charac-
terized more truly the stern and less volatile
native of the north; while the towering form
and prominent aquiline nose were combined
with other features and proportions which more
particularly distinguished the Pawnees and
other tribes of the Missouri Indians. It was,
in fact, impossible to say to what nation the
hunter belonged. The best blood of the noblest
band might channel unmingled with any baser
current in his veins; but whatever might be the
totem of his tribe, it was evident that he now
held himself identified with no particular clan—
and was, perhaps, indeed an outlaw from his
people. The expression of dauntless resolution
that dwelt around his firmly-cut mouth, and the
air of high command discoverable in his
piercing eye, revealed, however, that the hunter
was no common man—that, in fact, whatever

might now be his pursuits, he was once a warrior and a chieftain.

Weary with the chase, and exhausted by the noontide heat, Ta-in-ga-ro was reposing upon the rich greensward, which carpeted the spot. He had thrown off the gay Mexican blanket, or cloth mantle, as it might rather be called, and was occupied in stripping the beads from the woven garters of his metasses for an offering to the divinity of the place. One after another, the bits of wampum were dropped by him into the bubbling well, over which he leaned. But each, as it struck the bottom, was thrown again to the surface, by some boiling eddy, and after dancing for a moment on the brim, it topped over the lips of the fountain, and disappeared in the stream which swept down the valley. The heart of an Indian is the abode of a thousand superstitions; and Ta-in-ga-ro, though more enlightened than most of his race, was still, so far as fancy was concerned, a genuine child of the wilderness. The sudden onset of a score of Blackfeet he had met without dismay, and their charging yell would have been flung back with his own whoop of defiance; but the soul of the intrepid savage sank within him as he beheld the strange reception of his reverential rite. Danger and death he feared not for himself, but there was another whose existence was wound up in his own; and misgiving thoughts of her condition floated wildly through his brain at this moment. A strange mist swam before his dizzied sight, and he saw, or deemed that he saw, the reproachful countenance of Zecana reflected in the mysterious pool. The appalled lover sprang like lightning to his feet, and riveted his piercing gaze intently upon the fountain. But the apparition was gone. The wampum-strewed bottom was all that met his eye within the sacred bowl, and he knew not whether the mocking semblance, just presented on its surface, was distorted by pain, or whether the motion of the unstable mirror changed those lineaments from their wonted sweetness. A startling train had been given to his ideas, however, which fancy rudely followed up without the aid of new images to quicken her power. A sudden resolve and instant execution was the result. The call of the chief brought his horse in a moment to his side; another served to readjust his few equipments, and leaping into his seat, he at once bade adieu to the scenes, where he had hardly yet commenced his new employment, leaving his fur-traps, and all they might contain to the first fortunate hunter that should chance to light upon them.

Ta-in-ga-ro had a journey of some length before him along the base of the mountains; but at last the "Spanish Peaks" hove near, and the impatient voyager soon after appeared before the trading-post of the Spaniard. He found it occupied by a small force of provincial soldiers, who had been ordered thither on account of some hostile movements of the neighbouring Cumanches; and a goodnatured Mexican, who was one of the sentinels on duty, apprized him that Zecana was there no longer, and warned him that imprisonment and death would be the certain consequence, should he present himself before the commandant. The anxious husband waited not to learn whether the trader was still at the station; but thinking that Zecana might have sought a refuge in his own home, during the existing difficulties upon the border, he struck the spurs into his jaded horse, and wheeling from the inhospitable gate, his lessening form soon disappeared over the rolling prairie.

Never had the road seemed so long to the

retreat where he had known so many happy hours, and where, in spite of some misgivings at his heart, he still hoped to realize many more. After winding his way for some time among the singular pieces of table-land which rise in such formal mounds from those plains, he descended at last into the little vale where his lodge was situated.. All looked as still and sheltered as when last he left it; and his heart rose to his lips when, reclining beneath the dwarf willows which bent over the stream near his door, he saw the loved form of Zecana. There was something unpleasant to him, however, in the singular listlessness of her appearance. The tramp of his horse appeared not to startle her; and when, at last, his figure met her eye, she looked at him as carelessly as if wholly unconscious of his presence. She appeared to be busied in watching the ingenious labours of a group of prairie-dogs, one of whose neat villages was clustered around a small mound near the spot where she sat; and as the little animals would move in and out of their burrows and sport in the warm sunshine, she sung to them snatches of strange airs, such as had either originated among her own people or been caught in other days from some wandering Mexican or Canadian trader. The chieftain threw himself from his horse, and stood over the insane female in agonized horror. The wild words that she murmured appeared to have no allusion to him; and, though in her fallen and emaciated features he could still recognise the face of her whom he had loved, yet the being before him could hardly be identified with his own Zecana. But the strange superstition of his race in relation to those afflicted with the loss of reason, began soon to influence his mind, and, dropping on one knee before the maniac, he listened as solemnly to her ravings as if he had the art of a *ouabineau,* or wizard, to interpret them. They were incoherent and wandering, but they seemed ever and anon to hover near some revelation too horrible even to pass the lips of insanity. The Indian sprang from the ground as if a bullet had pierced his heart when the conviction of their import first flashed upon his brain, while the soul-piercing cry he uttered summoned back for a moment the reason of the desolated woman before him. But the gleam of mind was instantly lost in a darker eclipse than that from which the voice of her lover had evoked it. She gave him a look of anguish, more piteous even than the ravings of her previous distraction—and then —while her lips seemed convulsed with the effort — she shrieked forth the name of the Spaniard, in the same instant that a knife, which she clutched from her husband's belt laid her a gory corpse at his feet.

It would be impossible to describe the emotions of Ti-an-ga-ro at the spectacle which had just passed, like some dreadful vision, before his eyes. The very soul within seemed blasted with horror and dismay at the frightful desolation that had overtaken his happy home. The casket in which he had garnered up his hopes —the being in whom he had merged his existence — lay an irretrievable ruin, a desecrated corpse, before him! And he that had wrought this stupendous injury—he the author of this fiendish destruction — was the trusted friend of his bosom, the appointed guardian and protector of all it prized on earth or in heaven!

The lapse of hours found the wretched husband still standing in mute stupefaction where the knowledge of his calamity had first burst upon his agonized senses. But some new feeling seemed now to be at work within him; a wild and sudden impulse gleamed fearfully over his fixed and haggard countenance. He became an altered being—changed on the instant—changed in heart, soul, and character, as if the spell of an enchanter had passed through his brain. Till now, he had been, either more or less, than an Indian. The plastic hand of love had moulded him into a different creature from the stern and immoveable children of his race. The outlawed warrior had loved Zecana; he had loved her, not as the sons of pleasure, the slaves of sordid toil—not as men enervated by the luxuries, and fettered by the interests, the prejudices, the soul-shackling bonds of civilization—not as the artificial creature of society can only love. He loved with a soul that knew no dividing cares — that was filled with no hollow dreams of pomp and power. He loved with a heart that was tenanted by one only passion. He worshipped her with a mind that bowed to no image beneath the sun save that which was graven on his own bosom. Nor was Zecana unworthy such a passion. Gentle, as the antelope that skimmed the green savannas near, she was still a being, fond, warm, and doting; and the deepest passions of her woman's nature had been called into action by the wild devotion of her lover. The flower of her young affections had budded and matured to life, like the quickly-blowing blossoms of an arctic spring, while the fruits it bore were rich, and full, and glowing, as those which a tropic summer warms into existence. And, though no conflicting feeling had ever come athwart the fulness of their love, think not that the ties of association were wanting to knit the memory of every look and word of hers to the heartstrings of Ta-in-ga-ro. The radiant face of nature speaks ever to the Indian of the being that on earth he most adores. Her sigh will whisper from the leafy forest; her smile will brighten on the blossom-tufted prairie; the voice that murmurs in the running stream syllables her name in tuneful eloquence for ever. And they were happy. The brook that sang beneath the willows near their lodge—the flowers that kissed its current—the bird that warbled on the spray above them, were all the world to them — those lonely lovers. And now this bower of bliss was blasted—this home of peace and simple joys was desolated—ruined and desecrated, as if the malice-breathing fiat of some unhallowed and fabled monster had gone forth against the happiness of its owner.

The pulse of no living being beat with sympathy for the master of that lonely wreck—but the soul of Ta-in-ga-ro was sufficient to itself. The indomitable pride of an Indian chief filled its inmost recesses with new resources for battling with his fate. Love and sorrow—like the snowdrift which smooths the rocky casing of a volcano—melted in a moment before the fires that glowed within his flinty bosom, and his original nature asserted itself in every fibre of his frame. His mien and his heart alike were altered. His features petrified into the immobility of a savage, while his brain burned with a thirst for vengeance, which only gave no outward token because its fiendish cravings were unutterable through any human organ.

Calmly now, as if nothing had occurred to ruffle the wonted placidity of his disposition, Ta-in-ga-ro proceeded to occupy himself, for the rest of the day, in the few concerns that required his attention. The still warm body of

Zecana, after being carefully wrapped in a buffalo-skin, was disposed of for the time in the sungiwun, or *caché*, wherein his few valuables were usually kept — and, after carefully adjusting every thing to ensure its concealment, he occupied himself in taking care of his favourite horse — which, after the late arduous journey, required both attention and refreshment. When these necessary duties were fulfilled, the solitary, at the approach of evening, tranquilly lighted his pipe, and, passing several hours under its soothing influence, with as much equanimity as if nothing had occurred to interrupt his customary enjoyment, he at last wrapped himself in his wolf-skin robe, and was soon sleeping as soundly as if a dream of human ill had never thrown a shadow over his slumbers.

It was two nights after this that the Spanish trader lay securely asleep within the guarded walls of his station. His repose was apparently as unmolested as that which has just been ascribed to Ta-in-ga-ro; and at the foot of his bed sat the dusky form of the Indian warrior, watching the sleep of his enemy with as mild an eye as if he were hanging upon the downy slumbers of an infant. All was as quiet as the tenantless lodge of the lonely watcher. The chamber, or cabin, stood on the ground-floor, in an angle of the blockhouse. It was guarded by sentries, both within and without the station; and how this strange visitant had penetrated within the walls no human being has ever known; but there, by the flickering light of a low fire, could be seen the wily and daring savage, sitting as calm, cool, and collected, as if patience were all that was required to effect the purpose that had brought him thither.

The tramp of armed men was now audible

near the gate of the fort, while the customary relief of sentinels was taking place. The slight commotion incident to the occasion soon ceased, and all around the post became again perfectly silent.

A considerable space of time now elapsed, and the Indian still maintained his statue-like position. At last he sank noiselessly from the couch to the floor, and placing his ear to the ground, listened for a while—as if assuring himself that all was as he wished. His measures were then instantly taken: he first loosed the wampum-belt from his person, and possessed himself of a long cord, or *lariat*, which he had either brought with him or found in the chamber of the Spaniard; placing now his scalping-knife in his teeth, he glided like a shadow to the head of the bed, and at the same moment that the noose of the *lariat* was adroitly thrown over the neck of the sleeping trader with one hand, the belt of beaded woollen was forced into his mouth with the other, and his waking cries effectually stifled. The ill-starred Spaniard made but a short struggle for release; for the arms of the sinewy savage pinioned him so closely, that he saw in a moment his efforts were in vain, and the threatening motion of his determined foe, in tightening the noose when his struggles were more vigorous, intimidated him into deferring the attempt to escape to some more promising opportunity. He submitted to be bound in silence; and the Indian swathed his limbs together till he lay utterly helpless, an inanimate log upon the couch whereon he had been reposing.

Having thus secured his prize, Ta-in-ga-ro went to work with the same imperturbability to place it beyond the danger of recapture. He first displaced a portion of the bark roof of the rude chamber, and, lifting his unresisting captive through the aperture, carefully placed his burden beside the wooden chimney of the primitive structure, where it projected above the timber-built walls of the station, and threw its shadows far over the area of the fort. Returning then to the room from which he had just emerged, he took an arrow thickly feathered from the combustible pods of the wild cotton-tree, which grows profusely along the river bottoms of this region, and lighting it by the dying embers before him, he swung himself once more above the rafters, and, standing in the shadow of the chimney, launched the flamingshaft far within the window of a cabin which opened upon the central square of the station, immediately opposite to the shantee of the trader. The fiery missile performed its errand with speed and fidelity—the sleeping apartment of the commandant was instantly in a blaze, and the ill-disciplined sentinels, eager to make up for their want of vigilance by present officiousness, rushed from their posts to shield their officer from the danger which had so suddenly beset him. The exulting savage availed himself of the commotion, and the fettered trader was lowered instantaneously on the outside of the fort. One dosing sentry only, who had hitherto been unobserved in the deep shadow of the wall, witnessed the daring act, and he started aghast at the inanimate form which was placed so abruptly at his feet; but the Indian dropped like a falcon on his prey beside it, and a half-uttered cry of astonishment died away in a death-groan as the knife of the descending savage buried itself in the chest of the unfortunate soldier. The disappearance of the trader was not observed amid the pressing concern of the moment. The fire spread rapidly among the inflammable buildings, and the incendiary, who had a couple of horses waiting for him in a slight ravine which traversed the prairie, mounted by the light of the blazing cabins, and was far on his journey before the flames which had been kindled from his captive's chamber were extinguished.

Arriving at his own lodge, by several short turns through the broken country, known only to himself, Ta-in-ga-ro unbound the trader from his horse, and, keeping his hands still tied behind him, attentively ministered to his wants, while refusing to reply to a single question, or to heed the pleadings of the anxious Spaniard for liberty. At length, being fully refreshed, the Indian left him for a few moments to his reflections, while he went to select a large and powerful charger from a herd of half-domesticated horses that were grazing near. The animal was soon caught and tethered by the door of the cabin. Ta-in-ga-ro then proceeded to strip his captive, and compelling him to mount the horse, he secured him to the wooden saddle by thongs of elf-skin, attached to the surcingle, which girt it in its place. The wretched man trembled with apprehension, and, with a choking voice, offered all he was worth in the world, to be redeemed from the fate to which he now believed he was to be devoted. But the doomed profligate had not yet begun to conceive the nature of the punishment, to which he was destined, or his pleadings for immediate death would have been as earnest, as his prayers for life were now energetic.

"Slave of a Pale-face!" thundered the Indian —while the only words that had yet passed his lips, betrayed a momentary impatience to the craven cries of the other. "Think not that I am about to commit *thee alone* to the desert!" A murmur of thanks escaped the faltering tongue of the Spaniard, but died away in a cry of horror, as the Indian placed a gory and disfigured corpse astride the horse before him.

When he recovered from the swoon, into which the recognition of Zecana's features had thrown him, the unhappy trader found himself bound to the stark and grim effigy of her, that was once so soft and beautiful. So closely, too, was he bound, that the very effort to free himself, only rendered nearer the hideous compact. Trunk for trunk, and limb for limb, was he lashed to his horrible companion. His inveterate foeman stood ready mounted beside him, and waited only to feast his eyes with the first expression of shrinking horror evinced by the trader, when he should regain his consciousness. A blow from his tomahawk then severed the halter by which the horse of the Spaniard was tethered; and the enfranchised animal, tossing his mane in fury as he snuffed the tainted burden, bounded off in full career, followed by the fleet courser of the vindictive savage.

Instinct taught him to make at once for the Great Desert, on whose borders lay the little prairie from which he started ; and on he went with the speed of an antelope. The dreary waste of sand was soon gained, and the limbs of the steed seemed to gather new vigour, as they touched once more his native plains. But not so with his hapless rider. The fierce sunbeams, unmitigated by shade or vapour, beat down upon the naked person of the Spaniard, while the moisture that rolled from his naked body, seemed to mould him more intimately into the embraces of the corpse, to which he was bound. Night, with its blistering dews, brought no relief, and seemed only to hasten the corruption, to which he was linked in such frightful compact. The cessation of motion, at this time, when the horse, now accustomed to his burden, was recruiting upon the rough grasses, which forms the subsistence of his hardy breed, seemed even more horrible than the flight by day. The gore that oozed from the limbs of the trader, stiffened around the cords which bound him, while his struggles to release himself, when the Indian was no longer by his side, served only, by further excoriating his skin, to pollute the surface beneath it with the festering limbs, which were twining around him. Sleep was allowed to bring no intermission to his sufferings. His head would indeed droop with languor and exhaustion, and his eyes would close for a moment in grateful forgetfulness of his situation. But the next moment, his untiring and ever-vigilant enemy was before him. A cry, like the curses of a damned spirit, pealed in his dreaming ears; the startled charger bounded off in affright: and the break of dawn still found the remorseless pursuer howling in his track.

And day succeeded to day, and still those ill-matched riders speeded on their goadless journey. At length the pangs of hunger which were soon added to the other tortures of the fated Spaniard, became too excruciating for endurance. His thirst being always with ingenious cruelty quenched by the proffered cup of the savage, when their horses stopped to drink, the vitality of his system was still as exacting as ever. The gnawing torments to which his body was now subjected, surpassed even those with which its more delicate senses were agonized. In vain did he try to stifle the cruel longing that consumed him—in vain did he turn with loathing and abhorrence from the only subsistence within his reach. An impulse stronger than that of mere preservation wrought within his frenzied bosom. An agony more

unendurable than that which affected his re-
volting senses, consumed his vitals. A horrid
appetite corroded every feeling and perception,
that might have stayed the vulture-like eager-
ness, with which he came at last to gloat upon
the hideous banquet before him. A demoniac
craving, like that of the fabled ghouls of eastern
story, impelled him to ——

But why protract these harrowing details of
superhuman suffering? The awful vengeance
exacted from the foul-hearted and treacherous
trader, like all things mortal, had its end. But
the implacable Indian still hovered near, and
feasted his eyes with the maddening anguish
of his victim, until his last idiotic cry told that
reason and nature were alike subdued, that
brain and body were alike consumed by the
fearful, ceaseless, and lingering tortures which
ate them away by inches.

The subsequent fate of Ta-in-ga-ro has never

been known. Some say, that he still dwells, a harmless old man, in the wandering tents of the Cheyennes; others that he leads a predatory band of the ferocious and untameable Blackfeet; but there are those who insist that he has long since gone to the land of spirits— and these aver that when the GHOST-RIDERS are abroad, the grim phantom of the savage warrior may be seen chasing them over the interminable waste of the GREAT AMERICAN DESERT.

CHAPTER III.

MEDICINE SONG OF AN INDIAN HUNTER.

A FEBRUARY thaw had set in, and as the rising of the brooks compelled us to move our camp from the ravine in which we had slept for the last week, the chase was abandoned earlier than usual, in order that, after choosing a new location, we might have time to make ourselves comfortable for the night. A clump of trees on the upland offered the most suitable spot, as a few evergreens were scattered among them, and the loose heaps of stone which lay upon the edge of the prairie, might be made useful in more ways than one, should we determine to remain long in the same place, and be at any pains in constructing our lodge. An accidental pile of these, against which the Canadian at once commenced building the fire, furnished the leeward side of our new cabin; and a couple of upright crotches being planted in the ground opposite, two saplings were laid transversely from them to this rude wall; the other sides were then enclosed with dried brush, and when a few cedar boughs had been laid across the top, we found ourselves in possession of very comfortable quarters. The Crapeau then commenced picking a wild turkey and some prairie chickens, which were the only spoils of our day's hunt, while one of the Indians went off to bring some parched corn from the caché near our old camp.

He had not been gone more than ten minutes before I heard the crack of a rifle, and the Plume, who was already engaged before the fire mending his moccasins, sprang to his feet, and seizing his tomahawk rushed out of the cabin, exclaiming, " Ah-wes-sie hi-ah-wah-nah bah-twa-we-tahng-gah ? Mukwaw ewah bah-twa-we-tahng-gah."* And true enough, I had not followed him a hundred rods before we saw needji Mukwaw desperately wounded beneath a tree, while Che-che-gwa was coolly loading his rifle within thirty paces of his sable enemy. The moon was shining as bright as day, and there being still a little snow upon the ground where the bear was lying, his huge black limbs were drawn in full relief upon its white surface. The poor animal seemed unable to move, but though the groans he sent forth were really piteous, yet he ground his teeth with such rage that it seemed undesirable to venture too near him; especially as, though his hinder parts

* " A beast comes calling—what beast comes calling? —a beast comes calling."

were paralyzed from the shot having taken effect in his spine, his forepaws were still almost as dangerous as ever. The claws of these were now continually thrust in and out with a convulsive motion as he writhed about and tore the ground with wrath and agony. Formidable as he appeared, however, the Plume did not wait for his tribe's-man to throw away another shot upon him, but rushing up with his uplifted tomahawk, he paused within a few paces of his mark, and, poising the weapon for a moment, hurled it with unerring aim at the head of the ferocious brute. The whizzing hatchet cleft his skull as it had been a ripe melon, and buried itself in the bark of the tree behind him.

" Ah c'est bon, Needje-nanbi; vere good, sauvage," shouted the Canadian, coming up with a half-picked grouse in his hands, and his mouth full of feathers; " the bourgeois will tell his people what a great hunter is La Plume Blanche." But the Indian only answered by running up to his dead enemy, and taking him by the paw and shaking it with a ludicrous and reverential gravity, he asked his pardon for having killed his uncle. Che-che-gwa at the same time unsheathed his scalpingknife, and drawing it across the throat of the animal, he filled his hand with blood, exclaiming as he poured it upon the ground toward the four cardinal points:

" Ma-mo-yah-na miskwee, mamoyahna. Hi-a-gwo ne-ma-na-ho-gahn-nah-we-he-a! Whe-a-ya?"*

The fat steaks that were soon broiling before our fire, made no mean addition to our supper;

---

* That which I take is blood—that which I take— Now I have something to eat.

the birds, indeed, were not touched by my companions, who, I thought, would never tire of cutting piece after piece from the huge carcass that hung in the doorway. At last they seemed filled to repletion, and in capital humour from the brilliant winding up of the day's sport. Even Che-che-gwa became quite talkative and facetious, and broke out into a half-dozen songs, all laudatory of himself as a great hunter. As for White-Plume, he dubbed his tomahawk, incontinently, "A Medicine;" while together they made up a sort of duet, which if hammered into English verse might rhyme to this effect:

They fly on—you know the clouds
   That fling their frowns o'er rock and river:
They fly on—you know the clouds
   That flee before the wind for ever!

But I—though swift as them he rushes ;
  Or though like them he scowls in wrath,
Am one whose charmed weapon crushes
  Whoever dares to cross his path.*

" Yes," continued Che-che-gwa, still maintaining a kind of chant, when the song was ended, " though it were a bear concealed under the ground, I could find him."

    * Nonogossiu nahga ahuaquœ,
      Nonogoss'u nahga ahuaquœ,
      Messahgoonah au ain-ne-moy-au
      En enowug an ain nemo-woœ
Neen bapah-msssaghau negoche ahweisie neen-gah-kwatin ahwaw, Heo-wiu-nah hannemowetah neengetemahhah bochegahaue Moetah neengetemahhahnah.

LITERALLY.

1st *Voice.*—They fly on—you know the clouds.

2nd *Voice.*—They fly on—you know the clouds.

   Both. { Truly I esteem myself
        { As brave men esteem themselves.

1st *Voice.*—Fly about, and if any where I see an animal I can shoot him.

2nd *Voice.*—Any thing I can kill with it (this medicine —his tomahawk) even a dog I can kill with it.

" Yes," pursued his comrade, in the same sort of recitative, " aided by the Mani-toag, and armed with the weapons of Nannabozho, what animal shall be able to escape from the hunter ?"

Nannabozho, as the reader must know, is the chief of the Mani-toag or genii of fairy lore, among the Indians of the lakes. The more learned in these matters pretend to identify him (under the name of " The Nannabush of the Algoukins") with the Iswara of India, and the Saturn of ancient Italy. Mr. Schoolcraft considers him as " a sort of terrene Jove," who could perform all things, but lived on earth, and excelled particularly in feats of strength and manual dexterity.

The introduction of his name induced me now to ask some account of this worthy personage from my companions : and among a number of desultory anecdotes I elicited the following nursery tale from Che-che-gwa, which is given as nearly in his own words as possible, a literal translation from the Chippewa or Ojibbeway dialect.

CHAPTER IV.

NANNABOZHO: HOW HE CAME TO MAKE THIS EARTH.

AN OJIBBEWAY LEGEND.

ONCE upon a time, a great many years ago, when Nannabozho was at war with Mibanaba, or the Manitoag of the water, it happened on one very warm day, that several of these spirits came out of a lake to bask upon the beach. They were followed by a train of animals of various kinds, each the largest of its species, waiting upon them. When they had all lifted themselves from the water, and gained the shore, the two chiefs of the band appointed sentinels to keep watch while the rest should sleep.

" Nannabozho, their great enemy," said they, "was always vigilant, and this would be a good time for him to steal upon them and injure them."

The otters were, therefore, ordered to act as watchers, while the others gave themselves up to repose ; and soon the whole company, both spirits and animals, were sleeping on that shore.

Now the weather, which was at first excessively warm, became gradually hotter and hotter, and the otters, after keeping awake for awhile, were at last overcome with languor ; and when they saw all around them basking so comfortably on the sand, these sentinels, too, nodded on their posts, and were soon dreaming with the rest.

The chiefs finding the otters could not be depended upon, next commanded the loons to keep watch; they were permitted to swim about in order to keep themselves awake, but they were ordered not to go far from the group of sleepers.

Now, it chanced that at this time Nanna-bozho was travelling about in search of these very Manitoag, nor was it long before he found out where they were. He knew at once what precautions they had adopted for their safety, but he was determined to destroy some of them before they could leave the place where he found them. Having carefully examined the position in which they were lying, he caught up his puggamaugun, or war-club, and sprang toward them. But the loons were on the watch, and the moment Nannabozho came in sight, they gave a scream that awakened the whole band of sleepers. The chiefs were, of course, first upon their feet, while the rest of the Manitoag, and all the animals, rose in equal alarm. But when they looked around, there was no enemy to be seen, for Nannabozho had fled instantly, and hid himself in the long grass through which he had stolen toward the shore.

The chiefs said it was a false alarm, and after a while all again betook themselves to re-pose.

When Nannabozho saw that all around was quiet once more, he raised himself slowly from the ground, and was again about to rush upon them, when again did the loons give warning of his approach the moment he appeared in sight.

It seems that the loon, who, some say, is a

manitou, has the power of sleeping with but one eye at a time, and when most overcome by slumber, he can always keep one eye open to watch for an enemy, while the other takes its necessary repose. But now, when they awakened a second time, and saw no enemy near, the chiefs were angry with the loons for giving a false alarm; and the otters, who were jealous of them for pretending to be more sharpsighted than themselves, said that it was not Nannabozho who hovered around, for if it had been they would have seen him as well as the loons.

After much disputing, at last the otters were believed, and all, excepting the loons, once more closed their eyes in sleep.

Nannabozho was pleased with this.

The weather was still very warm, and he wished it might become yet warmer. It was so.

Then Nannabozho crept forward, and took

his station close by the group of sleepers, and the very moment the loons gave their warning cry, he wished he might be turned into an old stump, and straightway the wish was granted.

A rough bark raised itself in a moment all round his body, which stiffened into the hard fibres of a tree; his toes separated, and twisting among the loose soil, spread into roots on every side, while his hair became matted into ancient moss, that clung to the brown stump as if, moist and green as now, it had always mantled its decayed top.

The enemies of Nannabozho were completely at a loss when, having again shaken off their drowsiness at the signal of the loons, they cast their eyes about the place. They looked in every direction, but there was nothing to be seen near, save the stump of a shattered tree, which apparently had once flourished upon the edge of the water.

The loons told the chiefs that there was no stump there when they first came to the shore, but that it was Nannabozho himself who had taken this semblance. Some believed them and others did not; and to settle the question, the chiefs ordered the great water serpents to go and twine themselves around him, and try and crush him to death, if, indeed, it were Nannabozho.

These serpents then straightway glided out of a slimy pool in which they had coiled themselves to rest, and twisting their folds around the stump, they knotted their bodies together so as to press with all their might against every part of it. But it was all to no purpose. Nannabozho kept a strong heart, and did not betray the pain he suffered by the least sign or sound.

The fire serpents were next ordered to try if they could not destroy him. They had been basking upon the hottest part of the beach until each scale had become like a coal of fire; and as their scorching folds, coil after coil, were twisting around him, Nannabozho suffered the greatest tortures. The stump became black from the heat that was applied to it; but though the wood smoked as if about to burst into a blaze, yet the slime which the water serpents had left upon it prevented it from actually taking fire. No one but Nannabozho could have kept quiet under the pain which these serpents inflicted. The stump had a little the shape of a man, and the serpents had a good place to twist around the part which represented the neck. Several times Nannabozho, finding himself choking, was upon the point of crying out, when the snakes would loosen themselves to apply their efforts in some other place. After repeated attempts in this way, the serpents at last desisted from their endeavours, and told the chiefs that it was not Nannabozho, for it was impossible that he could endure so much pain.

The hostile spirits, however, were not yet satisfied, and the chiefs commanded the great red-nailed bears* to go and scratch the stump wfth their long claws. Nannabozho was all but torn to pieces by these ferocious creatures, but was still able to support the agony he endured.

The bears at last gave up, as the serpents had done, and went back and told that it was not Nannabozho, for he, they said, was a coward, and could not quietly endure so much pain. It was then decided that it was not Nannabozho, and all went quietly to sleep as before.

* *Ma-mis-ko-gah-zhe Mukwaw.*—The great red-nailed bear lives in woods and rocky places, and, according to Dr. James, is more dreaded by theIndians than even the *Manitou-mukwaw,* or great grizzly bear of the prairies.

Nannabozho wished they might sleep very sound; and it was so: then he assumed his natural shape, and began cautiously to approach the sleepers. He stepped lightly over the bodies of the animals, and passing by all the lesser Manitoag, he placed himself near the heads of the two chiefs. Planting his foot, then, upon the throat of the one nearest to him, he dealt a blow with his war-club, which crushed the head of the other. Another blow, and his companion was likewise dead.

But now that the deed was done, Nannabozho found himself surrounded by dangers, and nothing but his swiftness of foot gave him any chance of escape from his revengeful foes, who were, immediately, in full cry after him. But soon, the spirits finding they could not overtake him by running, adopted a new device for getting Nannabozho in their power. They commanded the water to rise and flow after him; and straightway the lake began to swell until its waves rushed along his path so rapidly that it seemed impossible to escape them. Nannabozho did not know what to do in this emergency; but at last, just as the water was about overwhelming him, he saw a crane, and determined to claim his assistance.

"My brother," said Nannabozho, "will you not drink up this water for me?"

The crane replied, "What will you give me in return?"

"I will give you the skin of one of the chiefs that I have killed," answered Nannabozho.

The crane was satisfied with the promise, and he commenced drinking up the water. He drank, and he drank until he had nearly drank it all, when he was unable longer to stand up.

His body had swollen to an immense size, and as he went toddling along on his thin shanks with his long neck, bobbing about, he presented such a ludicrous appearance that Nannabozho burst out a laughing to see brother Crane make such a figure. Nannabozho, indeed, must have been mad with merriment, for when he saw the crane's body become bigger and bigger, while his skin was stretched so, that he could not bend his legs as it tightened around his joints—he could not withstand the temptation of pricking the bloated mass. He drew his bow, and the arrow went through the crane's body. But quickly was he punished for his wanton sport. At once the waters began to rise again, and so fast did the big waves increase, that Nanna-bozho was compelled to ascend the highest mountain he could find, and still the waters followed him there. He then climbed the highest tree on the mountain. But the flood kept rising and rising: the branches on which he stood were soon dipping in the waves, which at last rolled completely over his head.

Just as they swept finally over him, Nannabozho chanced to look up, and saw the shadow of an object floating near him; he stretched out his arm and seized it. It proved to be a piece of wood buoyant enough to sustain him, and he placed himself upon it.

Nannabozho now floated about for some time. The water encompassed him on every side. It had covered up every thing. The rocks, hills, and trees, had all disappeared. The flood seemed to ripple against the sides of the sky all around, and whichever way he looked, there was nothing to be seen but a never-ending succession of waves, that had nothing but the wind to play against.

At last he saw a musquash swimming about

alone, and he asked him to go down to the earth, and bring him a little of it. The animal obeyed, and plunged toward the bottom, but it was soon seen on the surface of the water perfectly dead. Nannabozho, however, did not yet despair. He immediately after saw a beaver paddling toward him, and as soon as the beaver got near enough to hear, he said to him—

" My brother, will you not dive and get me some earth ?"

The beaver dived, but did not appear for a long time. The beaver, it seems, when he dives, can carry down so much air entangled in his coat, that, when compelled to stay long under water, he can thrust his nose into his fur and breathe for some time. At last, he appeared again upon the surface nearly dead with exhaustion; he brought up a very little piece of mud on the flat end of his tail, which he gave to Nannabozho. Nannabozho scraped every particle of it carefully together, and placed it in the palm of his hand to dry. When it had become perfectly dried he blew it out into the water, and straightway a portion of the earth upon which we now live, was created. The dust, too, in the hand of Nannabozho, kept increasing the longer he blew, until more and more of the earth was made; and at last the whole world was finished just as large as it now is.

———

When Che-che-gwa had finished his legend, I could not help asking him whence came the plants and animals which had sprung into existence since the days of this Chippewa Deucalion. These, he answered, had been subsequently created in various ways. Many of the larger trees had been produced from the piece of wood upon which Nannabozho had floated in the deluge; and several shrubs, brought up by the loons in diving, had taken root again upon the shores to which they drifted. A shell lying upon the strand, was transformed into the racoon, and many of the other animals had come into existence in a similarly miraculous manner; while different kinds of birds had their origin in some metamorphosis like that of the pious but fainthearted youth, who, when his ambitious father wished him to go on the war-path, pined away and was changed into a robin;* his guardian spirit permitting him to cheer his parent with songs to console him for the glory that had

* See " Life on the Lakes," by the author of " Legends of a Log-cabin." New York. 1836.

thus departed from his family. The habits of
the whippoorwill, who, like the robin de-
lights to linger near the lodge of the hunter,
were accounted for in the following simple
manner.

CHAPTER V.

WAW-O-NAISA; OR, THE ORIGIN OF THE WHIPPOORWILL.

THE father of Rauche-wai-me, the Flying Pigeon of the Wisconsan, would not hear of her wedding Wai-o-naisa, the young chief who had long sought her in marriage; yet, true to her plighted faith, she still continued to meet him every evening upon one of the tufted islets which stud the river in great profusion. Nightly through the long months of summer did the lovers keep their tryste, parting only after each meeting more and more endeared to each other.

At length Wai-o-naisa was ordered off upon a secret expedition against the Sioux: he departed so suddenly that there was no opportunity of bidding farewell to his betrothed; and his tribesmen, the better to give effect to his errand, gave out that the youth was no more, having perished in a fray with the Menomones, at the Winnebago portage. Rau-che-wai-me was inconsolable, but she dared not show her grief before her family; and the only relief she knew for her sorrow, was to swim over to the island by starlight, and calling upon the name of her lover, bewail the features she could behold no more. One night the sound of her voice attracted some of her father's people to the spot; and, startled at their approach, she tried to climb a sapling in order to hide herself among its branches; but her frame was bowed with sorrow, and her weak limbs refused to aid her. "*Waw-o-naisa*," she

cried, " *Waw-o-naisa !*" and at each repetition
of his name, her voice became shriller, while in
the endeavour to screen herself in the under-
wood, a soft plumage began to clothe her deli-
cate limbs which were wounded by the briers,
and lifting pinions shot from under her arms
which she tossed upward in distress ; until her
pursuers, when just about to sieze the maid,
saw nothing but the bird, which has ever since
borne the name of her lover, flitting from bush
to bush before them, and still repeating, " Waw-
o-naisa"—" Waw-o-naisa."

CHAPTER VI.

MEDICINE SONG OF AN INDIAN LOVER.

RETURNING from an unsuccessful hunt about dusk on the succeeding day, we found, upon entering the lodge, that the wolves had paid it a visit during our absence on the previous night. The *pukwi,* or mats, which had formed quite a comfortable carpeting for the humble chamber, were torn to pieces; and the voracious animals had devoured whatever articles of skin or lea-ther they could lay their teeth upon. A pair of moccassins belonging to the Rattlesnake, the carrying-straps of the Canadian, and a shot-pouch of my own, had all been spirited off in this audacious burglary.

" *Wah!*" ejaculated Che-che-gwa, with a ludicrous intonation of dismay, as he followed me into the shantee.

" *Wha-nain-ti-et* "—" Whose dog is this?" —echoed White-plume, thrusting his head over the shoulder of the other, as his companion paused on the threshold to observe the extent of the mischief. " *Kitchi-que-naitch* "—" It is very well "—added he, drily, upon observing that a large piece of moose meat, suspended from the rafters, had escaped the long-haired pilferers.

I could not but sympathize with him in the self-gratulation, for I remembered once, while spending a day or two with a settler in Michigan, having gone supperless to bed when equally sharp set, after a severe day's hunt, owing to a similar neighbourly visit. The prairie-wolf, though a much less ferocious and powerful animal than the wood's-wolf, makes up in sagacious impudence for his want of size and strength. On the occasion alluded to, one of these fellows had climbed into the window of a shantee, and actually carried off a whole saddle of venison which had been prepared for cooking, before the settler and myself had started, soon after dawn, on our day's tramp.

White-plume now deposited his rifle in a corner of the lodge, and leaving the Canadian to put our disarranged household to rights, he proceeded to the *sunjewun*, or caché, which was made in the bank of a rivulet near the door, and soon returned with a gourd of bear's fat and a sack of hard corn. The latter, when pounded and duly mixed with the snowy lard, made a crisp and inviting dressing for the moose meat, and enabled the Frenchman, who acted as cook, to turn out some *côtelettes panées*, that for flavour and relish would not have discredited the *cuisine* of Delmonico. I confess, however, that my appreciation of the luxurious fare was not enhanced by the dexterity with which White-plume would, ever and anon, thrust the ramrod of his short north-west rifle into the dish, and flirt the dripping slices into his expectant mouth; nor was the marksman-like precision with which Che-che-gwa launched his scalping-knife into the kettle, that served us for both frying-pan and platter, less refined and elegant. It was not their fault, however, that we had no silver forks at table; and they certainly committed no greater breach of decorum in their eating, than certain travellers affect to have seen on board some of our Atlantic steamers.

" *Caw   ke-we-ah   m'   woi-gui-nah-needji* "—
"Will you not eat, my friend ?"—observed
White-plume more than once, offering me a
morçeau from the point of his chopstick.   In
spite of the example of Lord Byron and Sir
John Malcolm — accepting the reeking pilau
from the greasy knuckles of Turk and Persian
—I thought myself at liberty to decline the
proffered civility, inasmuch as I was not par-
taking of the particular hospitality of the
Indian, but felt myself as much at home in
the entertainment as he was himself.

The customary pipe succeeded, and there
being no more "fire-water"—*skuta-warbo*—
in the flask of the Canadian, we added an
additional quantity of tobacco to the willow-
scrapings from the kinnekinic bag, in order to
make the smoking mixture more potent.   The
fumes of the inebriating weed very soon began

to act upon the excitable system of White-plume, and he regaled us with a number of songs, which were anything but musical. There was but one of them that appeared to me to have any thing poetical, either in sentiment or imagery, to recommend it. It was a *Mezi-nee-neence*, or "Medicine Song," of a lover, in which he is supposed to have some magical power of knowing the secret thoughts of his mistress, and being able to charm her to him from any distance. In English, it might run as follows :

I.

Who, maiden, makes this river flow?
The Spirit—he makes its ripples glow—
But I have a charm that can make thee, dear,
Steal o'er the wave to thy lover here.

II.

Who, maiden, makes this river flow?
The Spirit—he makes its ripples glow—
Yet every blush that my love would hide,
Is mirror'd for me in the tell-tale tide.

III.

And though thou shouldst sleep on the farthest isle,
Round which these dimpling waters smile—
Yet I have a charm that can make thee, dear,
Steal over the wave to thy lover here.*

In the fragments of rude and often insipid poetry with which the singer followed up this specimen of his art, there were occasional allusions which interested me, and for which I at-

* 1. O-wa-nain ba-me-ja-waunga? Manito o-ba-meje-waun-ga
    Me-nee-sing, a-be-gwain neen-ge-wun-naitch Che-ha-ga-toga Me-ne-sing a-be-gwain Whe-he-yah!

2. O-wa-nain ba-me-ja-waunga? Manito o-ba-me-je-waunga
    Neen-dai-yah gutche-hah hi-e-qua-waw-hah, neen-noan-dah-waw sah-ween a-ye-ke-tote whe-i-ah-hah Whe-he-yah.

3. Waus-suh wa-keem-me-ga ora-bah-gwain, whe-a whe-hah-a
    Yag-gah-ming-go na-bah-qua, neen-ge-wun-naitch Che-hah-ga-toga.

tempted to get an explanation. But it was almost impossible to obtain a direct answer, for White-plume, though a great talker for an Indian, had no faculty for conversation—that is, there was no such thing as exchanging ideas with him; and even when I asked him the names of particular things, in order to increase my slight vocabulary of his language, his replies were equally rambling.

Among other objects, the evening star, which glows with remarkable effulgence in the clear frosty atmosphere of these regions, attracted my eye, as its silver rays, pouring through an opening of our lodge, exhibited even more than their wonted virgin purity, when contrasted with the red glare of our fire. He mumbled over some unpronounceable epithet, when I asked the name of it, which was wholly lost upon my ear. But the question gave a new and more steady turn to his wandering ideas; and with

the occasional assistance of my Canadian inter-
preter, I was able to follow him out in a very
pleasing story, founded upon an Indian super-
stition, connected with the planet. The tale
will, of course, lose much on second-hand repe-
tition, for no writer has, as yet, succeeded in
his attempt to infuse the true Indian character
into his narrative, when he speaks in the person
of a red man. The figurative phraseology of
the luxurious Asiatic, and the terse conciseness
of expression that survives in some relics of the
poetry of the ancient Northmen, are sometimes
so curiously reconciled and blended in the lan-
guage of our aborigines, as to defy even the
most ingenious and gifted pen to imitate it. I
cannot, perhaps, better begin the narrative,
than by recalling Major Long's account of the
barbarous Indian ceremony, which gave rise to
the historical incident which is here commemo-
rated.

CHAPTER VII.

PETALESHAROO, OR THE LAST OFFERING TO THE GREAT STAR.

" So light to the croupe the fair lady he swung,
So light to the saddle before her he sprung !
' She is won ! we are gone, over bank, bush, and scaur ;
They'll have fleet steeds that follow,' quoth young
    Lochinvar."

SCOTT.

THE Pawnee-Loups, or *Ske-re* as they called themselves not many years since, and within the memory of persons now living, exhibited the singular anomaly, among the North American aborigines, of a people addicted to the re-

P 2

volting superstition of making propitiatory offerings of human victims upon the altars of idolatry. *Mekakatungah,* " The Great Star," was the divinity to whom the sanguinary worship had been, from time immemorial, ascribed. The barbarous ceremony was performed annually. The Great Star was supposed to preside over the fruits of the earth ; and on each return of the season of planting, the life-blood of a human being was poured out in libation upon the soil. A breach of this duty, the performance of which they believed was required by the Great Star, it was supposed would be succeeded by the total failure of their crops of maize, beans, and pumkins, and the consequent privation of the supply of vegetable food, which formed half the subsistence of the tribe. To obviate a calamity so formidable, any person was at liberty to offer up a prisoner, of either sex, of whom, by his prowess in war, he had become possessed; and the horrid rite was accompanied by all the solemn ceremonies which characterize the superstitious idolatry of an ignorant and barbarous people. The devoted individual was placed under the care of the *Ouabineaux*, or magi of the tribe, who anticipated all his wants, while they cautiously concealed from him the real object of their sedulous attentions, which was to preserve his mind in a state of cheerfulness, with the view of promoting obesity, and thereby render the sacrifice more acceptable to their Ceres.

When the victim was pronounced sufficiently fattened for immolation, a suitable time was appointed for the performance of the rite, that the whole nation might attend. When the appointed day of his fate arrived, he was clothed in the gayest and most costly attire, and led out to the spot where he was to suffer. Here he was bound to a cross, in presence of the assembled multitude, and a solemn dance was performed around him. A number of other ceremonies followed, and then the warrior whose prisoner he had been, stepped forth into the open space, and assumed the inglorious task of his execution. Generally a single blow with the tomahawk despatched the victim; but if the first throw failed to cleave his head, the speedy death of the person immolated was insured by a shower of arrows from a band of archers, who were always in attendance. The abolition of this revolting custom was brought about in the manner here related.*

* The account of this singular and sanguinary superstition, as well as the interesting historical incident which follows it, and the description of the dress and personal appearance of the heroic Indian who abolished the barbarous rite, will be found in " Major Long's Expedition to the Rocky Mountains," with but little variation from the text. The portrait of the youthful and handsome Petalesharoo is preserved in the Indian Gallery at Washington.

The season of planting was at hand: the Pawnee-Soups, in order to call down a blessing upon their labours in the field, prepared for their wonted sacrifice to the cruel divinity, who they believed, presided over the genial fruits of the earth. There was more than the usual bustle in the principal village of the tribe. The faces of some of the seniors wore a look of anxiety, and the young people, for several days preceding the ceremóny, could be seen grouped together before the scattered lodges, with an air of curiosity and impatience, seldom observable in their little community. The fact was, that there chanced to be at this moment, not a single captive in the band, to offer up in sacrifice. The last that had been taken—a pretty Tetau girl, of the name of Lataka—had escaped the horrible fate which awaited her, by perishing, as was thought, in a fray which had occurred at nightfall, soon after her arrival in the village. The young partisan, Petalesharoo, the son of the old Knife-chief Latelesha, had interfered at the moment that the maid was about to be consigned to the hands of the magi, to be by them prepared for their annual rite, and in the confused broil which ensued, the prisoner disappeared, and was represented by the principal magician to have perished by falling, while her hands were yet bound, into a stream near the village, during the commotion which took place upon its immediate banks. The old crones in gossiping from lodge to lodge, had circulated a story, that the officious interference of Petelasharoo was caused by his being suddenly enamoured of the captive damsel; and they were very much incensed at the idea that the stripling might be the instrument, possibly, of cheating them out of their yearly festival, in which, unless tradition has belied them, they took no passive part. But it was more generally believed, that the act was prompted by less exceptionable motives, on the part of the young chief; that it was, in short, nothing more nor less than a manifestation of his determined purpose to put an end to a custom, which he had already attempted, by argument, to do away with, and which, it was known, that his less daring father was but too solicitous to root out from among his people.

As the time now approached when the GREAT STAR would expect his victim, and not a single captive was to be had, the incident of the previous autumn was called up afresh to memory.

There was a great deal of murmuring and discontent among the tribesmen, and nothing but the personal popularity of the warrior, who had taken so prominent a part in the occurrence, would have prevented some violent outbreak of popular feeling; day after day elapsed, and no captive appeared to supply the place of the victim that Petalesharoo had snatched from the sacrifice. Several warriors, who had been out on war parties, returned one after another to the village. They almost all claimed to have struck the dead body of an enemy, and some could show more than one scalp at their belt, but no one brought in a live prisoner. There was yet one more to come back, and, though " The Running Fox" had no great repute as a brave, yet the whole hopes of the tribe were now fixed upon his address alone. He had not left the village, until after almost all the other warriors that were out had returned from the war-path; but there was strong confidence in the success of his expedition, because he had been seen in close consultation with the magi before he departed, and a favourable result was said to have been propitiated, by their having a *Mezi-nee-nence*, or medicine hunt, together. Indeed, the chief magician had given out that the Fox would certainly return with the wished-for prey. The Great Star, he said, had promised him that a victim should be forthcoming; and he had invited Petalesharoo to meet him at a lonely place, remote from the village, when he said that the young man might witness how the God he served would keep his promise.

It was a close and sultry night, and nothing but the swarms of moschitoes, which were continually rising from the wet prairie, could have induced one to tolerate the fire that was blazing on an isolated table-rock, in the midst of a lonely savannah. The singularly exposed situation, however, of this fire, which shone like a beacon over the waste, would seem to imply that it could hardly have been kindled for mere purposes of comfort or convenience—for cooking the rude meal of a hunter, or for driving off the insects that might molest his slumber—and the two swarthy figures that were crouched beside it, though evidently belonging to that wild race, who find their chief subsistence in the chase, were characterized by some marks which indicated that they were not exclusively devoted to the pursuits of common savages.

The eldest of the two, whose attenuated features, projecting forehead, and screwed, sinister-looking mouth, imparted a mingled expression of fanaticism and knavery to his countenance, was perfectly naked, with the exception of an *azeeaun,* or apron of congar skin, secured by a curiously-ornamented belt, about the middle of his person; but his limbs and body were so completely covered with various devices, tattooed in strong black lines upon his copper-coloured skin, that, to a slight observer, he would appear to be dressed out in some elaborate and closely-fitting apparel. The prominent device in the tattooing, was an enormous double-tailed serpent, whose flat head appeared to repose upon the chest of the Indian, while his scaly folds were made to twine themselves around his extremities, with a fidelity to nature that was equally ingenious, grotesque, and hideous.

The high, uncouth shoulders, long skinny arms, and squat figure of this person as he sat stooping over the fire, with his legs folded under him, were strikingly contrasted with the fine proportions, the rounded and agile limbs, and lion-like port of a young warrior, who was reclining along the rock on the opposite side of the fire. The features of the youth were naturally of an open and generous, almost a careless cast; but they now wore a troubled expression of impatience and curiosity, occasionally wrought up to anxiety and awe. At times, as the sub-

siding of an ember would make the fire flash
up and fling its fitful light far over the plain,
the young man would spring eagerly to his feet,
and throw a restless glance upon the shifting
gloom around him, as if he expected some one
to emerge from its shadow. His companion,
however, calmly maintained his sitting posture,
and seemed only to busy himself in occasion-
ally turning over a collection of roots, seeds,
pap-pous, and powders, which were deposited
upon a piece of wolf-skin before him, and which
he never touched without mumbling over some
of those strange phrases, which are only found
in the mouths of necromancers and magicians,
and which are said to be unpronounceable by
any but a true medicine-man.

"I tell thee, Wahobeni," said the youth at
last, flinging himself upon his bison-skin, as if
his patience was at length wholly exhausted, "I
tell thee, the Fox will never more return. The

master of life wills not that this accursed rite should ever again be performed by his red children."

"The words of the young chief are less than his years," replied the senior. "The Great Star must have his offering. The season of planting is at hand, and unless the spirit of fruits be propitiated, there will be no maize in the lodges of the She-re."

"Think'st thou, magician, that should even the crafty fox produce his victim, my father will allow the ceremony to proceed? I tell thee, no! Satelesha sheds no blood, save that which is poured out in battle."

"The sire of Petalesharoo is a great chief; but he has no power over his people, to step between them and the god of their worship. The heart of the Knife-chief is no more with his tribe, and his son hath learned to speak with the tongue of the pale-face."

The eyes of the young man flashed fire, while clutching his tomahawk, he made a sudden movement as if about to brain the magician. But the impulse was instantly checked, and he resumed his former position, with only a slight ejaculation of contempt at the reproach of an old man whom he despised.

"The spirit will keep Wahobeni from bad things," said the medicine-man, observing the movement. "Wahobeni is a great magician. the Great-under-ground-wild-cat* is his friend, and he walks with serpents along the ground. Myself—know me, my son, the servant of the Great Star. Believe my words, when I interpret the will of my master. Behold the parched and cracking earth! Behold the crowded thunders in yon blackening sky, which even now

---

* Gitche-a-nah-mi-e-be-zew—"The Devil yard-long-tailed."

refuse to break the clouds and let the showers through! Behold—"

A sudden flash lit up the waste, and gave an unearthly glare to the forbidding features of the magician, as the bolt went rattling by.

"*Manito Sah-iah*—There is a God!" exclaimed the youth, as he reverently took a handful of tobacco from his pouch, and threw the offering upon the fire. "The master of life himself replies to thy impious mummery, Wahobeni. The God that answered thee but now, is the only one that can send blossoms and fruits to the gardens of our tribe."

The medicine-man was silent; and the young chief, folding his arms thoughtfully, contented himself with this brief rebuke. But the stolidity of a bigot, and the cunning of a hypocrite, were too subtly and actively blended in the composition of the other, to allow him to feel more than a moment's confusion, or to rob him

of the resources with which a life of successful
imposture had stored his mind.   The few broad
drops which succeeded the single thunder-clap,
were not followed by the shower that seemed
impending; and the magician cast a malignant
glance of triumph at the youth, when, after ad-
justing the machinery of his trade in some new
form upon the skin before him, and passing his
hands repeatedly over his bat-skin skull-cap,
the clouds suddenly parted, and the evening
star shone forth redly above the horizon.
"The Great Star blushes for my son," said he,
stretching forth his bony arms towards the
planet. "The God of planting scowls in wrath
upon his minister, who listens to the ravings of
a boy.   The Running Fox *will* keep his promise,
and the Ske-re will make their annual offer-
ing."

"Not so—not so, old man," replied the youth
firmly; and then, while a sudden change came

over his features, " Not unless a Jebi steps from its grave, and the shadows of men's souls (*ojee-chaugomen*) are sent on earth to mock your bloody ceremony." And the young man placed his hand convulsively upon his sacred metawaun, while his eyes, dilating with horror, became fixed upon a well-known face, which, even as he spoke, peered above the ledge of the rock opposite to where he sat.

" And what," rejoined the medicine-man calmly, as if unobservant of the agitation of the speaker—"what if the Great Star in kindness to his red children, should call back one of those who have already passed the *je-be-ku-nong* (road of the dead), to enable Wahobeni to fulfil the sacrifice for which, till now, a victim has never been wanting. I tell thee, son of Latelesha, that a shaft of maize has never yet hung forth a tassel above the ground, that was not watered with the blood of an enemy. But now the warriors of the Ske-re are squaws—there are no captives in their lodges, and the Great Star who wills that there must be a victim, will send one of his own choosing from among those who have already passed the swinging tree, and attained the gardens of the happy."

With these words the magician rose, and stamping upon the ashes, he shook some combustible powder from the cougar skin that enveloped his loins. A dozen forks of yellow smoke curled up in shreds from the fire, and seemed to wreath themselves with the coils of the serpent that was twined round his body—each bursting into flame, before it reached his head. There was a sudden flood of lurid light about the place, and when its bewildering glare subsided, the form of the Tetan maiden was fully disclosed to the awe-struck gaze of her lover, as she stood with her hand locked in that of the terrible being before him.

A thousand conflicting feelings tugged at the heart-strings of the noble youth—a thousand changing images of love and fear, hope and horror, shot in maddening confusion across his brain. His senses reeled in the effort to rally their flying powers; and Petalesharoo, the dauntless partisan of the Pawnee-Loups—he, whose heart had never quailed—whose nerves had never shrunk in the wildest horrors of savage warfare swooned at the feet of the sinking damsel.

The day of the sacrifice to the Great Star had arrived. It was a beautiful morning in April, when the misguided children of the wilderness were assembled at the call of the magi, to celebrate the anniversary of their cruel deity.

The scene of their infernal orgies, was a tall grove upon the edge of the prairie, an islet of timber, which viewed at a distance, seemed rather to repose upon, than to spring from, the broad green surface. It was a grand festival day with the Pawnee-Loups, and the wonted military watchfulness of this warlike tribe was dispensed with, upon the occasion of general relaxation—the usual sentinels of the camp were scattered round in groups among the rest of the people—and their horses, which generally were tethered, ready saddled near the lodges of the guard, were now scattered over the prairie with the other cattle of the tribe. There were two chargers only, that did not seem to share the general liberty; and these stood fully equipped, pawing the ground as if impatient of confinement, behind a small copse not far from the scene of the sacrifice. One of them, a light and graceful palfrey, was tied to a sapling which grew upon the spot, while the reins of the other were held by as gallant a cavalier as ever crossed a saddle. He was a young man of not more than three-and-twenty, of the finest form, tall and muscular, and of a most prepossessing countenance. His head-dress of war-eagle's feathers descended in a double series over his back, like wings, to his saddle-croup: his shield was highly decorated, and his long lance was ornamented with a plaited casing of red and blue cloth. The steed he backed was every way worthy of such a rider.

It was the partisan, Petalesharoo and his charger, *Leksho*, the Arrow. The large dark eye of the young warrior wore an expression of seriousness and concern, but little in unison with the festivities of the day. And ever and anon, he turned to look along the edge of the thicket, and grasped the handle of his toma-hawk, as if as restive as the champing courser beneath him. But his lips were compressed in resolution rather than anger, and the nervous bracing of his feet in the stirrups, gave an air of high determination to his whole figure.

At length, the different groups of Indians were collected around one central spot, where a cross was erected upon a slight elevation in the prairie, and the captive Lataka was led forth among them, to be offered up as a sacrifice to the Great Star. Her youth and beauty were lost upon the sterner part of the assemblage; but her gorgeous apparel, rich with wrought ornaments of the precious metals, and gay with the woven texture of beads and feathers of the most elaborate and costly workmanship, drew a murmur of admiration from those of her own sex, who mingled with the crowd.*　The multi-

---

* The gala dresses of the Indians in some tribes, are very costly. The minute embroidery of wampum and porcupine quills, and the profusion of silver ornaments, with the high value placed upon the war-eagle's feathers, and other favourite materials, make a full festival suit command a price of several hundred dollars

tude were generally overawed by the solemnity
of the occasion, and preserved a decorous
silence, as the principal Meta, with his train of
Ouabineaux, led on the captive. A few, how-
ever, would thrust their heads over the shoul-
ders of their neighbours, and fix their savage
eyes as eagerly upon the victim, as if, by read-
ing her feelings in her face, they could enjoy in
anticipation, the horrid festival. But Lataka
was an Indian maiden, and her soul was too
proud to let the enemies of her tribe guess the
feelings which swelled in her bosom, as she
moved, with the step of an empress, to the spot
on which she was to be immolated. The Oua-
bineaux now, under the direction of the Meta,
entered at once upon their barbarous office;
and rudely seizing the fragile girl, her limbs
were bound to the stake almost before she dis-
covered the full extent of the fate that awaited
her. Still not a murmur was made by the

Indian maiden—not a sob nor a sigh escaped the lips, that quivered in the effort to repress the thrilling emotions of the moment. Her eye wandered mildly around the dusky circle of faces, as if seeking rather for sympathy than rescue—as if she wished only for some one being to appreciate the fortitude with which she could offer up her life. The grim gaze of a motionless multitude was all that met her view. There was no one there, who could have an emotion kindred to her own. There was no one there who could care for Lataka; and raising her eyes to heaven, she commended her spirit to the Wacondah, who cares for all.

And now the solemn dance commenced around the prisoner, slowly and silently at first, but gradually increasing in rapidity, as with savage yells, they encouraged each other, until the fiendish faces of her executioners whirled around her in one continuous chain of glaring and demoniac glances. The motion ceased, and the chief of the magi stepped into the open space to make his sacrificial prayer to the Great Star.

Myself—myself. Behold me, and see that I look like
    myself.

I sit down in the lodge of the Metai—the lodge of the
    spirit.

I am a magician ; the roots of shrubs and weeds make me
    a magician.

Snakes are my friends.

I am able to call water from above, from beneath, and
    from around.

I come to change the appearance of this ground. I make
    it look different in each season.

Notwithstanding you speak evil of me, from above are my
    friends, my friends.

I can kill any animal, because the loud-speaking thunder
    helps me—I can kill any animal.

Thus have I sat down, and the earth above and below
    has listened to me sitting here.

The eye of Lataka had been cast heavenward during the utterance of this prayer, and when it was concluded she merely murmured the plaintive, *Dadainsh-ta-a*, "Oh! alas! for me," and resigned herself once more to her cruel fate. The master of the infernal rite then turned round to give the signal for her tortures to begin, and the deep roll of the Indian drum commanded silence while he spoke again for the last time. The murmur of the multitude was hushed, and the melancholy dirge died away in the distant prairie.

The Meta had raised his arm to give the fatal signal; when forth from the thicket, like an arrow from the bow of the thunder-god, shot the warlike form of Petalesharoo. With one hand he couched his quivering lance, and waved his gleaming tomahawk high above his head with the other. His bridle floated loose on the neck of his charger. On—on he came like a bolt from heaven, while his charging cry speedily made a lane for him through the multitude, as his courser bounded into the midst of it. A blow from his tomahawk severed the thong, which bound Lataka, in an instant, and before his startled and astounded tribesmen could recover from their surprise, he had gained anew his greenwood covert, with the sinking form of the rescued damsel. A moment sufficed to place her on the fleet palfrey, that bowed his neck to the beautiful rider—in another they were speeding like the wind over the smooth prairie, while before his disappointed and baffled countrymen could mount in pursuit, Petalesharoo had placed a broad strip of forest between them; and the infuriated yells of the baffled multitude died upon the breeze which whispered nought but hope and confidence to the flying lovers.

The Pawnee and his bride enjoyed the blessings of summer in another land. But before the snows of the next season had come again, his tribesmen had invited him back to

the lodges of the Ske-re. Nor since that day
have they ever offered up a human victim to
the Great Star.

CHAPTER VIII.

THE MISSIONARY BRIDE.

" Young bride,
No keener dreg shall quiver on thy lip
Till the last ice-cup cometh."

MRS. SIGOURNEY.

THE leading circumstances of the following narrative may possibly be known to more than one of my readers ; but, if now recognised, notwithstanding the altered guise in which they are here given, I trust that they are still so presented to the public as to infringe upon no feeling of domestic privacy.

In the spring of 18—, the Rev. Mr. B——, of ——, in Connecticut, received a letter from his old friend and college chum, the Rev. E—— T——, who had been for some time established as a missionary in one of the islands of the Pacific, soliciting the fulfilment, on the part of his friend, of a most delicate and peculiar office for him. The request of T——, who, having been long isolated from the world, had arrived at the age of forty without marrying, was nothing more nor less than that B—— would choose a wife for him, and prevail upon the lady to come out to her expectant husband by the first opportunity. Strange as it may seem, Mr. B—— found but little difficulty in complying with the request of his friend. The subject of missions at that time filled the minds of the whole religious community; and, in some sections of the Union, a wild zeal wrought so powerfully in the breasts of individuals, that they were eager to abandon their homes and their country, and sunder every domestic tie, in order "to do their Master's bidding" in strange and inhospitable lands. Nor was this a mere burst of enthusiasm, that was to pass off with other fashions of the day—for its fruits are still constantly maturing; and now, as then, there are not a few instances of young females of re-respectability and accomplishments educating themselves for the avowed purpose of becoming the wives of missionaries. With these preliminary remarks I will at once introduce the reader to the subject of the following sketch, with whom I became acquainted in the manner here related.

I had been enjoying a week's shooting at Quogue, on Long Island, when, wishing to return to New York by steam-boat through the sound, I engaged a seat one morning in the stage-coach for Sag Harbour, which sometimes stopped for dinner at mine host's, Mr. Pierson Howell. In the present instance it was delayed merely long enough to receive my luggage and myself. The only other passenger was a female, whom, notwithstanding the effectual screen of her long cottage bonnet, I knew to be pretty, from the quizzical look my landlord put on as he shook hands with me at parting after I had taken my seat by her side.

The day was warm; and we had not driven far before, without appearing officious, I had an opportunity of obtaining a glimpse of my companion's face, while leaning before her to adjust the curtains on her side of the coach. It was beautiful — exceedingly beautiful. Not the beauty which arises from regularity of feature, or brilliancy of complexion—though in the latter it was not deficient, but that resistless and thoroughly womanish charm which lies in expression solely. It evinced that feminine softness

of disposition which is often the farthest re-
moved from weakness of character, though, by
the careless observer, it is generally confounded
with it; and which, though sometimes it may
mislead one in judging of the temper of the
possessor, yet almost invariably, like the ore-
blossom upon the soil that is rich in mines
beneath, bespeaks the priceless treasure of an
affectionate and noble heart. The reader, who
would realize the attractions of the countenance
before me, need only call up their most winning
expression in the features he most admires.

I gradually fell into conversation with my
companion, and, stopping at South Hampton
to change horses, her first remark upon our
again taking our seats, was, that she feared we
should not get into Sag Harbour until after
dark, when she would be unable to find *the ship*
which was expected to sail in the morning. As

I knew that no ships but whalers lay at that time in Sag Harbour, I could not at first possibly conceive what a young and delicate female could have to do aboard of such a vessel; and then, the idea suggesting itself that she might be the daughter or sister of the captain, who came to bid him farewell for his two years' cruise, I asked her if she expected to remain on board the ship till she sailed.

"Oh yes, sir," was the reply; " I go out in her."

"What! to the South Sea?" rejoined I. "You have relations on board, though, I suppose?"

"No, sir, I don't know any one in the ship; but I have a letter for the captain, which, I think, will procure me a safe voyage to the —— Islands."

"The —— Islands! Is it possible you have

friends in so remote a place as the —— Islands?
They must be dear friends, too,—pardon me,—
to carry you unprotected so far."

" My hu-us-band is there," she answered
with some embarrassment, though the growing
twilight prevented me from seeing whether the
confusion extended from her voice to her coun-
tenance. The peculiarity in the young lady's
manner, as she pronounced the word " hus-
band," piqued my curiosity; but, as it would
have been impertinent to push my inquiries
further, I did not urge the subject, but merely
remarked, that her youth had prevented me
from taking her for a married woman.

" Nor am I married yet," was the reply.
" And, indeed," she continued, with a slight
tremour in her voice, " I have never seen the
man who is to be my husband." An expres-
sion of unfeigned surprise, of a more lively
interest, perhaps,—for I have said " the maid

was fair," and we had now been some hours *téte-à-tête*,—escaped me: I scarcely remember what followed, but before we had reached the inn-door, the ingenuous girl had given me a full account of herself and her fortunes. She was an orphan child, and had been bred up in great seclusion in a clergyman's family in Western New York. She was, in a word, the young enthusiast whom the Rev. Mr. B—— had chosen as a wife for his Missionary friend, and prevailed upon to encounter a six months' voyage through stormy latitudes, for the purpose of connecting herself for life with a man she had never seen. I did not express a sympathy, that would be useless in her situation, much less did I give vent to the indignation with which her story filled me: her fanatical friends, who permitted a young, a beautiful, and delicate female, to take so wild a step, had, perhaps, after all, acted from the best of motives. Indeed, the poor thing herself, though not exactly proud of having been chosen to the station she was about to fill, seemed determined to enter upon it with all the exalted feeling of one who fulfils a high duty, and who is on the certain road to a preferment which most of her sex might envy. It would certainly have been a very equivocal kindness to interpose another view of the subject, and disturb the honest convictions of propriety which could alone have sustained her in a situation so trying.

I accompanied Alice Vere—for such I learned her name to be—to the vessel; and, after bidding her a kind farewell, I took an opportunity, while passing over the side, to whisper a few words to the captain, which might induce him to believe that she was not so friendless as she appeared to be, and secure her whatever attention it was in his power to offer. In the morning, having a few moments to spare before breakfast, I again strolled down to to the pier; but the whaler had hoisted sail with the dawn, and a brisk wind had already carried her out into the sound: nor was it till years after that I heard the name of Alice Vere, and learned the issue of her voyage; though the name, and the features, and voice of her who bore it, did, I confess, long haunt me. It was too pretty a name, I thought, to be changed lightly; and, somehow, when I heard it I could not for the life of me ask that into which it was to be merged for ever. The sequel of her story I learned from a friend, whose vessel being driven from her course in coming from the East Indies, stopped at the —— Islands to water, where he casually heard the fate of the Missionary girl.

The tender and imaginative temperament of Alice Vere, though perhaps it impelled her to make the sacrifice for which she was schooled by those who called themselves her friends, but badly fitted her for the cold destiny to which she was condemned. The imagination of any woman, isolated upon the great deep for six long months, with nothing to think of but the stranger husband to whose arms she was consigned, could not but be active, whatever her mental discipline might be. But with a girl of fancy and feeling, who had taken a step so irretrievable when surrounded by approving and encouraging friends, what must have been her emotions in the solitude of her own cabin, when such an influence — such a sustaining atmosphere of opinion — was wholly withdrawn. Doubt and fear would at first creep into her mind; and, when these disheartening guests could no longer be controlled by factitious notions of duty, fancy would throw her fairy veil around their forms, and paint some happy termination of a prospect so forbidding. And thus it was with Alice Vere. Anxiety soon yielded to hope; her future husband and her future home filled her mind with a thousand dreaming fancies. She was no romance reader, and therefore could not make a *hero* of the future partner of her bosom; but a saint he indeed might be, a saint too, not less in form than in godliness, for the association of physical and moral beauty is almost inseparable in the minds of the young and the inexperienced. She imagined him, too, as one who, though not " looking from Nature up to Nature's God," for " God must be first and all in all with him," would still be one whose mind would look from the Creator to his works, with a soul to appreciate all their excellences. The fancied portrait of her future husband was laid in simple though impressive colours, but the background of the picture was filled with all the splendours of a tropical clime, of groves such as the early

Christians wandered through in Grecian Isles, and skies such as bent over Him who taught beneath them in the golden orient. True, she was to be exiled for ever from the sheltered scenes and quiet fireside of her youth; but, would she not be content to rove for ever with one only companion whose soul could fully sympathize with hers in scenes so fresh and so Elysian?

With a mind softened, if not enervated, by these day-dreams, not less than by the bland and voluptuous clime in which they had been for some days sailing, our young enthusiast could scarcely suppress a scream of delight, when, upon coming on deck one morning, she found that the ship had cast anchor in the beautiful bay of——, where her wildest visions of tropical scenery seemed more than realized. The water around the ship was as clear as the mountain-streams of her native country; and the palm-trees and cocoas that bent over it, lifted their slender columns, and waved their tufted heads against a sky more purely bright than any she had ever beheld ; while clouds of tropical birds, of the most dazzling plumage, sailed along the shore, or sported around the vessel, as if wholly regardless of man.

A number of the natives had launched their light barks from the shore, filled with bread, fruit, and other acceptable luxuries to those who have been long at sea. Alice was watching their approach with girlish interest in the novelty of the scene, when a boat from the opposite side of the crescent-shaped harbour made the ship, and, almost before she was aware of its approach, a striking figure, dressed after the clerical fashion of her own country, in a full suit of black, presented himself at the companion way, and, leaping on deck, instantly hurried towards her. She turned round —

looked at him intently for a moment — made one faltering step towards him, and fainted in his arms.

The gentleman laid her carefully upon a flag that chanced to be folded near ; and, still supporting her head upon one knee, gazed upon her features with looks of surprise and anxiety, which soon yielded to complete bewilderment as she addressed him upon coming to herself.

"Thank God !" she exclaimed, gradually reviving ; "thank God ! thank God !—how can I ever have deserved this ?" and, bending her face forward, she impressed a reverential kiss upon his hand, and then covered her face in confusion.

My readers have all read of *love at first sight*, and some, perhaps, have heard of instances of it among their acquaintance. The sceptics to the doctrine, however, I imagine, far outnumber those who really believe in it. It is the latter, therefore, whom I will beg to recollect all the circumstances which preceded this singular scene; when they cannot deem it unnatural that the wrought-up feelings of an ardent and sensitive girl should thus burst forth upon first meeting in her affianced husband, her appointed friend and protector in a strange land, him that religion and duty taught her that she *must* love, —upon meeting in him all that her dreams of happiness for long, long months of anxious solitude had pictured. I ought to add, however, that the interchange of several letters between Miss Vere and her betrothed before leaving her native shores, had, while partially removing the awkwardness of their first meeting, supplied perhaps that " food for young thoughts " which, in a nature artless and enthusiastic as hers, might engender the most confiding affections even for an object she had never seen.

"And is this beautiful island to be our home?—Are these my husband's people around us?—Oh! how I shall love every thing that belongs to this fair land! But why do you not speak to your poor wanderer?—Alas! alas! can I ever deserve all these blessings?"

The embarrassment of the gentleman seemed only to increase as the agitated girl thus poured out her feelings. He begged her to be calm, and seemed most nervously solicitous to restrain her expressions; and the captain approaching at that moment, he made a hurried and indistinct apology for his abruptness; and, withdrawing his arm from her waist as she regained her feet, moved off to seek the mate in another part of the vessel.

"Ah! Mr. Supercargo, I mistrusted we should find you at this island!" exclaimed the mate, turning round, and shaking hands with him, as the gentleman touched his shoulder upon joining this officer near the capstan. "All well at home, Mr. F—. Here's a letter from your wife."

The other tore open the letter, and devoured it with evident delight, and then shaking hands again with the officer, exclaimed,

"Thank you, thank you; all are well at home, as you tell me. But how in the world came that beautiful insane creature in your vessel?"

"A mad woman! The devil a bit of a mad woman or any other woman have we on board, except Mrs. T——, the wife of Parson T—— that is to be."

"The wife of Mr. T——?"

"Why, yes, as good as his wife. She's a gal from York State we are carrying out to be spliced to old Dead-eyes."

The gentlemanlike supercargo seemed struck with concern; in fact, the true state of the case flashed upon his mind in a moment. The deep mourning which he wore out of respect for one of his employers, whose ship he was that day to visit, had evidently caused him to be mistaken for a clergyman; and the excited imagination of the lonely girl had prompted her to see in him the future guardian of her friendless condition. Nothing, however, could be done: an attempt at explanation would but betray her secret to the coarse natures by which she was surrounded. Her lot in life, too, was cast; his sympathy could avail her nothing, and a few days' voyage would consign her to the care of him who might legitimately receive the proofs of tenderness which he had so innocently elicited in his own behalf. He called for his boat, and passing slowly and dejectedly over the side of the vessel, pulled for the shore.

Alice Vere had in the mean time retired to the cabin, where she expected her lover—it was the first time she had even *thought* the word—

to join her. Her own feelings had so crowded
upon her mind during the brief interview, that
they had prevented her from observing his;
and the luxury of emotion in which she now
indulged, and in which she thought there was
not one consideration human or divine to make
it wrong for her to indulge, prevented her from
observing the lapse of time. Simple and single-
hearted, with a nature whose affluent tender-
ness piety could regulate and delicacy could
temper, though neither could repress, she
poured the flood of her pent-up feelings in
what seemed their heaven-appointed channel;
in a word, she was gone an age in love while
numbering the minutes of her acquaintance
with her lover. His noble and manly figure,
his alert and elastic step in approaching
her, and the kindly look of feeling and intelli-
gence his features wore, a look of intense in-
terest, which she, poor girl, little dreamt was

prompted by concern for another, of whom he was about to ask her;—nay, even the hurried tones of his agitated but still most musical voice, all, all were stamped upon her heart as indelibly as if their impress had been the work of years.

The water rippling along the vessel's side first roused her from this delicious revery, and the mate, who was a rough but kind-hearted seaman, at that moment came below to make an entry in his log.

"Well, miss," he cried, "with this breeze we'll soon bring up at the parson's door; and right glad to be rid of us you'll be, I guess, when we get there. Only thirty-six hours more, and you'll be home."

"This island, then, is not Mr. T——'s residence?"

"This?—Oh no. There used to be a Britisher here, but they have got no missionary man upon it now."

"And does Mr. T—— have to go thus from island to island in the performance of his duty? —or did he only come so far from his people to meet me?" she asked with some embarrassment.

"*Come!*" exclaimed the seaman, not a little puzzled; "why, law bless your soul, Parson T—— has not been here, at least that I know on."

"Surely he's now on board," cried Alice, alarmed, yet hardly knowing why: "surely I saw him speaking to you on deck?"

"To *me*, missus!—I never cared to exchange two words with old Dead-eyes, axing your pardon, since I knowed him. Speaking to me! Why, that—that was—why, —— my eyes! you have not taken young Washington F——'s handsome figure for old Ebenezer T——'s mouldy carcass?"

The rude, but not unfriendly mate, had hardly uttered the sentence before he cursed himself to the bottom of every sea between the poles, for the use he had made of his tongue. Alice fell lifeless upon the cabin-floor. The seaman shouted for assistance; and then, as he and the better-bred captain, who, as the father of a large and estimable family, was a more fitting nurse for the forlorn maiden, applied one restorative after another, she recovered animation at intervals. Fit succeeded fit, however; and then, as the wind rose, and a brewing tempest called all hands on deck, the captain could only place her kindly in her berth, in the hope that the new excitement at hand might possibly be of service to his patient.

The ship was driven widely out of her course. Alice was long indifferent to every thing around;

but as the storm lasted for several days, and finally threatened to destroy the stout craft in which she sailed, the near prospect of the death for which she had but now been longing, called all her religious feelings into action. She felt that she was the child of destiny: her gentle piety would not allow her to wish for a sudden and violent death, though the peace of the grave was what she most desired. She prayed, then, not for life, but from an escape from its horrors; alike from those which raged in the angry elements around her, and those which warred so fearfully in her own bosom.

Weeks elapsed before the vessel reached the haven, of which she had once been within a few hours' sail. The missionary girl had apparently recovered from all bodily indisposition, and her features were again as calm as ever; but they wore the calmness of rigidity, not of peace. It was a sacrifice of herself to Heaven which she had meditated originally. "And why," exclaimed she mentally, "why should I shrink from the offering now, when Providence has enabled me to make it richer and more abundant—to make my soul's triumph more complete, as its trial is more bitter and severe!" Still, when the isle of her destination hove in view, it was with a shudder that she first looked upon the shore, and thought of the fate that there awaited her.

Woman's heart is a strange, a wayward thing. In many a bosom its strongest chords are never touched by the hand to which it is yielded. It is often bestowed with faint consent on him who seeks it—bestowed in utter ignorance of the power of loving—the wealth of tenderness it hoards within itself. " Circumstance, blind contact, and the strong necessity of loving," will afterwards mould it to its fate, and prevent any repining at its choice; but when once its hidden strings have vibrated, and given out their full music,— when once its inmost treasures have been disclosed to its owner, counted over, and yielded up with a full knowledge of their worth, to another,—when "the pearl of the soul" has been once lavished in the mantling cup of affection, it revolts from all feebler preferences, and is true, even in death, to *its one only love.*

The missionary soon came on board to claim his bride. He was a plain and worthy man, with nothing to distinguish him from the members of his profession in our country, who, mistake the promptings of zeal for the inspiration of a special calling, and who, without minds matured by experience or enlightened by education, leave the plough or the shopboard to become the instructors of those who, with feelings as sincere as their own, and understandings far more exercised in knowledge of good and evil, are expected to bow to their narrow teachings, and to receive them, not as humble soldiers of the Cross needing guidance like themselves, but as the captains and leaders of the church militant, armed in full panoply,—a living bulwark against its foes.

Alice Vere had but little experience in society; but the quickening power of love had lately called all her dormant perceptions of taste and feeling into play, and a very brief interview sufficed for her to read the character of her destined husband. She felt that she could never love him. Respect him she did, as she would have done the humblest brother of her faith; and had she never known what love was, her regard would perhaps not have been withholden in time; for every woman loves the father of her children, if he be not a creature to be abhorred. But if there be an agonizing thought to a girl of delicacy and sensibility, it is the idea of becoming a bride under such circumstances as surrounded poor Alice Vere—the thought that her heart shall beat against the bosom of a stranger, when its every pulse throbs for another. Still a high, imperious duty, as she believed, constrained her, and she prepared to resign herself to her fate.

The nuptial day arrived. It had been arranged that the master of the vessel, on board of which Alice, wistfully lingering, had begged to remain, should perform the ceremony (agreeably to the laws of the state of New York, by which marriage is merely a civil contract, requiring only a formal declaration of the parties before competent witnesses). Mr. T—— himself commenced the ceremony by a prayer, which, as giving solemnity to the occasion, was perhaps most proper in itself; but it was painfully long, and seemed to refer to almost every thing else but the immediate subject of interest. At length the bride, whose languid limbs refused to sustain her so long in a standing position, sank into a seat, and the missionary, glancing a look of reproval at her, abruptly concluded his harangue. The worthy seaman was more expeditious in getting through with his share of the office. He merely asked the parties severally if they acknowledged each other as man and wife. The missionary made his response in the affirmative with a slow and grave distinctness; but Alice faltered in her reply. A tumult of feelings seemed oppressing her senses for a moment; she looked to the untamed forest, whose boughs waved unfettered on the shore, to the broad main that spread its free waves around her, and the wild bird that sported over its bosom,

" Then she turn'd
To him who was to be her sole shelterer now,
And placed her hand in his, and raised her eye
One moment upward, *whence her strength did come.*

The certificates, which had been previously
drawn up, being then signed and witnessed, the
missionary concluded with another homily; and
the crew, who had been allowed to collect upon
the quarterdeck during the ceremonial, dis-
persed over the vessel.

It was now sunset, and, as a heavy cloud
which threatened rain brooded over the island,
the captain politely insisted that Mr. T——
should not think of returning to the shore, but
take possession of his own private cabin. The
rain soon after beginning to fall in torrents,
drove those on deck below. Here the mates
claimed the privilege of having a jorum of
punch to drink the health of the bride, and the
captain being willing to unite with them, Alice

was compelled to retire to the new quarters which had been just provided for her; while the festive seamen insisted upon keeping their clerical guest for a while among themselves. Their mirth soon became so uproarious as to mock the tempest without, when a sudden squall struck the vessel, carrying her over, even as she lay at anchor under bare poles, upon her beamends. The seamen, followed by the missionary, rushed to the deck, where the glare of the lightning, as they looked to windward, revealed to them a female figure standing upon the taffrail, with arms outstretched towards a huge wave that lifted its over-arching crest above her, and threatened to ingulf the vessel. A cry of horror escaped the revellers, the bridegroom breathed a prayer as he clung to the rigging for safety; and then, as the descending sea righted the vessel, a suffocating moan was heard above the surge that swept the body of Alice Vere like a drift of foam across her decks.

The morning came at last, the sun rose serenely, the bright waves rippled joyously beneath the stern of the vessel, and their reflected light playing through the sloping windows of the cabin, glanced upon the unpressed couch of the Missionary Bride. None could even tell how she had made her way to the deck in the midst of the tempest; yet none have ever whispered the sin of self-destruction against the lovely, the lonely, the ill-fated ALICE VERE.— Let this " ower-true" tale bear a sad and solemn warning.

CHAPTER IX.

THE INN OF WOLFSWALD.

"Tramp—tramp on the oaken floor!
   Heard ye the spectre's hollow tread?
He marches along the corridor,
   And the wainscot cracks beside thy bed
As he tracks his way through the jarring door,
   Which the wild night-blast has opened."
               The Yankee Rhymer.

My horse had cast a shoe; and, stopping about sunset at a blacksmith's cabin in one of the most savage passes of the Alleghanies, a smutty-faced, leather-aproned fellow, was soon engaged in enabling me again to encounter the flinty roads of the mountains, when the operation was interrupted in the manner here related :—

" Pardon me, sir," cried a middle-aged traveller, riding up to the smithy, and throwing himself from his horse just as the shaggy-headed Vulcan, having taken the heels of my nag in his lap, was proceeding to pare off the hoof preparatory to fitting the shoe, which he had hammered into shape, and thrown on the black soil beside him. " Pardon me, sir," repeated the stranger, raising his broad-brimmed beaver from a head remarkable for what the phrenologist would call the uncommon development of "ideality," revealed by the short locks which parted over a pair of melancholy gray eyes, "matters of moment make it important for me to be a dozen miles hence before nightfall, and you will place me, sir, under singular obligations by allowing this good fellow to attend to my lame beast instantly."

The confident and not ungraceful manner in which the stranger threw himself upon my courtesy sufficiently marked him as a man of breeding, and I, of course, complied at once with his request by giving the necessary order to the blacksmith. His horse was soon put in travelling trim, and, leaping actively into the saddle, he regained the highway at a bound. Checking his course for a moment, he turned in his stirrups to thank me for the slight service I had rendered him, and, giving an address which I have now forgotten, he added that if ever I should enter ——'s valley, I might be sure of a cordial welcome from the proprietor.

An hour afterward I was pursuing the same road, and rapidly approaching the end of my day's journey. The immediate district through which I was travelling had been settled by Germans in the early days of Pennsylvania—a scattered community that had been thrown somewhat in advance of the more slowly-extended settlements. In populousness and fertility it could not be compared with the regions on the eastern side of the mountains; but the immense stone barns, which, though few and far between, occasionally met the eye, not less than the language spoken around me, indicated that the inhabitants were of the same origin with the ignorant but industrious denizens of the lower country.

One of these stone buildings, an enormous and ungainly edifice, stood upon a hill immediately at the back of the Wolfswald Hotel,—a miserable wooden hovel, where I expected to pass the night,—and, while descending the hill in rear of the village, I had leisure to observe that it presented a somewhat different appearance from the other agricultural establishments of the kind which I had met with during the day. The massive walls were pierced here and there with narrow windows which looked like loop-holes, and a clumsy chimney had been fitted up by some unskilful mechanic against one of the gables, with a prodigality of materials which made its jagged top show like some old turret in the growing twilight. The history of this grotesque mansion, as I subsequently learned it, was that of a hundred others scattered over our country, and known generally in the neighbourhood as " Smith's," or " Thompson's Folly." It had been commenced upon an ambitious scale by a person whose means were inadequate to its completion, and had been sacrificed at a public sale when half-finished, in order to liquidate the claims of the mechanics employed upon it. After that it had been used as a granary for a while, and subsequently, being rudely completed without any reference to the original plan, it had been occupied as an hotel for a few years. The ruinous inn had, however, for a long period been abandoned, and now enjoyed the general reputation in the neighbourhood of being haunted, for ghosts and goblins are always sure to take a big house off a landlord's hands when he can get no other tenant.

" We have not room pfor mynheer," said mine host, laying his hand on my bridle as I rode up to the door of a cabaret near this old building; while three or four waggoners, smoking their pipes upon a bench in front of the house, gave a grunt of confirmation to the ungracious avowal of the German landlord. I was too old a stager, however, to be so summarily turned away from an inn at such an hour; and, throwing myself from my horse without further parley, I told the landlord to get me some supper, and we would talk about lodging afterwards.

It matters not how I got through the evening

until the hour of bedtime arrived. I had soon ascertained that every bed in the hostelry was really taken up, and that unless I chose to share his straw with one of the waggoners, who are accustomed to sleep in their lumbering vehicles, there was no resource for me except to occupy the lonely building which had first caught my eye on entering the hamlet. Upon inquiring as to the accommodation it afforded, I learned that, though long deserted by any permanent occupants, it was still occasionally, notwithstanding its evil reputation, resorted to by the passing traveller, and that one or two of the rooms were yet in good repair, and partially furnished. The good woman of the house, however, looked very portentous when I expressed my determination to take up my abode for the night in the haunted ruin, though she tried ineffectually to rouse her sleeping husband to guide me thither. Mine host had been luxuriating too freely in some old whiskey brought by a return waggon from the Monongahela to heed the jogging of his spouse, and I was obliged to act as my own gentleman-usher.

The night was raw and gusty as with my saddle-bags in one hand, and a stable-lantern in the other, I sallied from the door of the cabaret, and struggled up the broken hill in its rear to gain my uninviting place of rest. A rude porch, which seemed to have been long unconscious of a door, admitted me into the building; and tracking my way with some difficulty through a long corridor, of which the floor appeared to have been ripped open here and there in order to apply the boards to some other purpose, I came to a steep and narrow staircase without any balusters. Cautiously ascending, I found myself in a large hall which opened on the hill-side, against which the house was built. It appeared to be lighted by a couple of windows only, which were partially glazed in some places, and closed up in others by rough boards nailed across in lieu of shutters. It had evidently, however, judging from two or three ruinous pieces of furniture, been inhabited. A heavy door, whose oaken latch and hinges, being incapable of rust, were still in good repair, admitted me into an adjoining chamber. This had evidently been the dormitory of the establishment, where the guests, after the gregarious and most disagreeable fashion of our country, were wont to be huddled together in one large room. The waning moon, whose bright autumnal crescent was just beginning to rise above the hills, shone through a high circular window full into this apartment, and indicated a comfortable-looking truckle-bed at the further end before the rays of my miserable lantern had shot beyond the threshold.

Upon approaching the pallet I observed some indications of that end of the apartment being still occasionally occupied. The heavy beams which traversed the ceiling appeared to have been recently whitewashed. There was a small piece of carpet on the floor beside the bed; and a decrepit table, and an arm-chair, whose burly body was precariously supported upon three legs, were holding an innocent *tête-à-tête* in the corner adjacent.

" I've had a rougher roosting-place than this," thought I, as I placed my lantern upon the table, and, depositing my saddle-bags beneath it, began to prepare myself for rest.

My light having now burned low, I was compelled to expedite the operation of undressing, which prevented me from examining the rest of the apartment; and, indeed, although I had, when first welcoming with some pleasure the idea of sleeping in a haunted house, determined fully to explore it for my own satisfaction before retiring for the night, yet fatigue or caprice made me now readily abandon the intention just when my means for carrying it into execution were being withdrawn; for the candle expired while I was opening the door of the lantern to throw its light more fully upon a mass of drapery which seemed to be suspended across the further end of the chamber. The total darkness that momentarily ensued blinded me completely; but in the course of a few moments the shadows became more distinct, and gradually by the light of the moon, I was able to make out that the object opposite me was only a large old-fashioned bedstead prodigally hung with tattered curtains, I gave no further thought to the subject, but turning over, composed myself to rest.

Sleep, however, whom Shakspeare alone has had the sense to personify as a woman, was coy, in coming to my couch. The old mansion wheezed and groaned like a broken-winded buffalo hard pressed by the hunter. The wind, which had been high, became soon more boisterous than ever, and the clouds hurried so rapidly over the face of the moon that her beams were as broken as the crevices of the ruined building through which they fell. A sudden gust would every now and then sweep through the long corridor below, and make the rickety staircase crack as if it yielded to the feet of some portly passenger. Again the blast would die away in a sullen moan, as if baffled on some wild night-errand; while anon it would swell in monotonous surges, which came booming upon the ear like the roar of a distant ocean.

I am not easily discomposed; and perhaps none of these uncouth sounds would have given annoyance if the clanging of a window-shutter had not been added to the general chorus, and effectually kept me from sleeping. My nerves were at last becoming sensibly affected by its ceaseless din, and wishing to cut short the fit of restlessness which I found growing upon me, I determined to rise, and descend the stairs at the risk of my neck, to try and secure the shutter so as to put an end to the nuisance.

But now, as I rose from my bed for this purpose, I found myself subjected to a new source of annoyance. The mocking wind, which had appeared to me more than once to syllable human sounds, came at length upon my ear distinctly charged with tones which could not be mistaken. It was the hard-suppressed breathing of a man. I listened, and it ceased with a slight gasp like that of one labouring under suffocation. I listened still, and it came anew, stronger and more fully upon my ear. It was like the thick suspirations of an apoplectic. Whence it proceeded I knew not;

but that it was near me I was certain. A suspicion of robbery — possibly assassination — flashed upon me; but was instantly discarded as foreign to the character of the people among whom I was travelling.

The moonlight now fell full upon the curtained bed opposite to me, and I saw the tattered drapery move, as if the frame upon which it was suspended were agitated. I watched, I confess, with some peculiar feelings of interest. I was not alarmed, but an unaccountable anxiety crept over me. At length the curtain parted, and a naked human leg was protruded through its folds; the foot came with a numb, dead-like sound to the floor; resting there, it seemed to me at least half a minute before the body to which it belonged was disclosed to my view.

Slowly, then, a pallid and unearthly-looking figure emerged from the couch, and stood with its dark lineaments clearly drawn against the dingy curtain beside it. It appeared to be balancing itself for a moment, and then began to move along from the bed. But there was something horribly unnatural in its motions. Its feet came to the floor with a dull heavy sound, as if there were no vitality in them. Its arms hung, apparently, paralyzed by its side, and the only nerve or rigidity in its frame appeared about its head : the hair, which was thin and scattered, stood out in rigid tufts from its brow, the eyes were dilated and fixed with expression of ghastly horror, and the petrified lips moved not, as the hideous moaning which came from the bottom of its chest escaped them.

It began to move across the floor in the direction of my bed, its knees at every step being drawn up with a sudden jerk nearly to its body, and its feet coming to the ground as if they were moved by some mechanical impulse, and were wholly wanting in the elasticity of living members. It approached my bed, and mingled horror and curiosity kept me still. It came and stood beside it, and, childlike, I still clung to my couch, moving only to the farther side. Slowly, and with the same unnatural foot-falls, it pursued me thither, and again I changed my position. It placed itself then at the foot of my bedstead, and moved by its piteous groans, I tried to look calmly at it;—I endeavoured to rally my thoughts, to reason with myself, and even to speculate upon the nature of the object before me. One idea that went through my brain, was too extravagant not to remember. I thought, among other things, that the phantom was a corpse, animated for the moment by some galvanic process in order to terrify me. Then, as I recollected that there was no one in the village to carry such a trick into effect— supposing even the experiment possible—I rejected the supposition. How, too, could those awful moans be produced from an inanimate being? And yet it seemed as if every thing about it were dead, except the mere capability of moving its feet, and uttering those unearthly expressions of suffering. The spectre, however, if so it may be called, gave me but little opportunity for reflection. Its ghastly limbs were raised anew with the same automaton movement; and, placing one of its feet upon the bottom of my bed, while its glassy eyes were fixed steadfastly upon me, it began stalking towards my pillow.

I confess that I was now in an agony of terror.

I leaped from the couch and fled the apartment. The keen-sightedness of fear enabled me to discover an open closet upon the other side of the hall. Springing through the threshold, I closed the door quickly after me. It had neither lock nor bolt, but the closet was so narrow, that by placing my feet upon the opposite wall, I could brace my back against the door so as to hold it against any human assailant who had only his arms for a lever.

The sweat of mortal fear started thick upon my forehead as I heard the supernatural tread of that strange visitant approaching the spot. It seemed an age before his measured steps brought him to the door.   He struck;—the blow was sullen and hollow, as if dealt by the hand of a corpse—it was like the dull sound of his own feet upon the floor. He struck the door again, and the blow was more feeble, and the sound duller than before. Surely, I thought, the hand of no living man could produce such a sound.

I know not whether it struck again, for now its thick breathing became so loud, that even the moanings which were mingled with every suspiration became inaudible. At last they subsided entirely, becoming at first gradually weaker, and then audible only in harsh, sudden sobs, whose duration I could not estimate, from their mingling with the blast which still swept the hill-side.

The long, long night had at last an end, and the cheering sounds of the awakening farm-yard told me that the sun was up, and that I might venture from my blind retreat. But if it were still with a slight feeling of trepidation that I opened the door of the closet, what was my horror when a human body fell inward upon me, even as I unclosed it. The weakness, however, left me the moment I had sprung from that hideous embrace. I stood for an instant in the fresh air and reviving light of the hall, and then proceeded to move the body to a place where I could examine its features more favourably. Great heaven! what was my horror upon discovering that they were those of the interesting stranger whom I had met on the road the evening before.

The rest of my story is soon told. The household of the inn were rapidly collected, and half the inhabitants of the hamlet identified the body as that of a gentleman well known in the country. But even after the coroner's inquest was summoned, no light was thrown upon his fate, until my drunken landlord was brought before the jury. His own testimony would have gone for little; but he produced a document which in a few words told the whole story. It was a note left with him the evening before by Mr. ——, to be handed to me as soon as I should arrive at the inn. In it the stranger briefly thanked me for the slight courtesy rendered him at the blacksmith's, and mentioning that, notwithstanding all precaution, his horse had fallen dead lame, and he

should be obliged to pass the night at Wolfs-
wald, he would still further trespass on my
kindness, by begging to occupy the same apart-
ment with me. It stated that, owing to some
organic affection of his system, he had long
been subject to a species of somnambulism, re-
sembling the most grievous fits of nightmare,
during which, however, he still preserved suf-
ficient powers of volition to move to the bed
of his servant, who, being used to his attacks,
would of course take the necessary means to
alleviate them. The note concluded by saying
that the writer had less diffidence in preferring
his request to be my room-mate, inasmuch as,
owing to the crowded state of the house, I was
sure of not having a chamber to myself in any
event.

The reason why the ill-fated gentleman had
been so urgent to press homeward was now
but too apparent; and my indignation at the

drunken innkeeper, in neglecting to hand me his note, knew no bounds. Alas! in the years that have since gone by, there has been more than one moment when the reproaches which I then lavished upon him have come home to myself; for the piteously appealing look of the dying man long haunted me, and I sometimes still hear his moan in the autumnal blast that wails around my casement.

END OF VOL. I.

WHITING, BEAUFORT HOUSE, STRAND.

Wild Scenes
in the
Forest and Prairie

Volume II

Charles Fenno Hoffman

LITERATURE HOUSE / GREGG PRESS
Upper Saddle River, N. J.

Republished in 1970 by
LITERATURE HOUSE
an imprint of The Gregg Press
121 Pleasant Avenue
Upper Saddle River, N. J. 07458

Standard Book Number—8398-0784-8
Library of Congress Card—76-104485

WILD SCENES

IN THE

FOREST AND PRAIRIE.

BY C. F. HOFFMAN, Esq.

AUTHOR OF "A WINTER IN THE FAR WEST."

IN TWO VOLUMES,

VOL. II.

LONDON:

RICHARD BENTLEY, NEW BURLINGTON STREET,

Publisher in Ordinary to Her Majesty.

Price Sixteen Shillings.

———

1839.

CONTENTS OF VOL. II.

WILD SCENES

ON

THE WISCONSAN.

CHAPTER X.

THE DEAD CLEARING.

" Unapprehensive thus, at night
  The wild deer looking from the brake
To where there gleams a fitful light
  Dotted upon the rippling lake,
Sees not the silver spray-drop dripping
From the lithe oar, which, softly dipping,
  Impels the wily hunter's boat ;
But on his ruddy torch's rays,
  As nearer, clearer now they float,
The fated quarry stands to gaze ;
  And, dreaming not of cruel sport,
Withdraws not thence his gentle eyes,
  Until the rifle's sharp report
The simple creature hears, and dies."

The Indian Ambuscade.

SCHROON LAKE is the largest, and perhaps

the finest, body of water among the myriad lakes which form the sources of the Hudson. "The Schroon," as it is called by the country people, has, indeed, been likened by travellers to the celebrated lake of Como, which it is said to resemble in the configuration of its shores. It is about ten miles in length, broad, deep, and girt with mountains, which, though not so lofty as many in the northern part of the state of New York, are still picturesque in form, while they enclose a thousand pastoral vallies and sequestered dells among their richly-wooded defiles.

In one of the loveliest of these glens, near a fine spring, well known to the deer-stalker, there flourished a few years since, a weeping willow, which, for aught I know, may be still gracing the spot. The existence of such an exotic in the midst of our primitive forest would excite the curiosity of the most casual observer of nature, even if other objects adjacent did not arrest his attention, as he emerged from the deep woods around, to the sunny glade where it grew. On the side of a steep bank, opposite to the willow, the remains of an old fireplace were to be seen; and blackened timbers, with indications of rough masonry, could be discovered by turning aside the wild raspberry-bushes that had overgrown the farther side of the knoll. These ruins betokened something more than the remains of a hunting-camp; and the forester who should traverse an extensive thicket of young beeches and wild cherry-trees, within a few hundred yards of this spot, would be at no loss to determine that he had lighted upon the deserted home of some settler of perhaps forty years back;—a scene where the toil, the privation, and the dangers of a pioneer's life had been once endured, but where the hand of improvement had wrought in vain, for the

forest had already closed over the little domai
that had been briefly rescued from its embrace
and the place was now what in the language c
the country is called a " dead clearing."

The story of this ruined homestead is a ver
common one in the private family annals of th
state of New York, which has always been ex
posed to the perils of frontier warfare, an
which, for twenty years, at the close of th
seventeenth century, and throughout the whol
of that which followed it, was the battle-field c
the most formidable Indian confederacy tha
ever arrayed itself against the Christian power
on the shores of this continent. The brcke
remains of that confederacy still possess larg
tracts of valuable land in the centre of our mos
populous districts; while their brethren of th
same colour, but of a feebler lineage, have bee
driven westward a thousand miles from ou
borders. And when this remnant of the Irc

quois shall have dwindled from among us, their
names will still live in the majestic lakes and
noble rivers that embalm the memory of their
language. They will live, too, unhappily, in
many a dark legend of ruthless violence, like
that which I have to relate.

It was in the same year when Sullivan's army
gave the finishing blow to the military power of
the Six Nations, that a settler, who had come
in from the New Hampshire grants to this part
of Tryon County (as the northern and western
region of New York was at that time called),
was sitting with his wife, who held an infant to
her bosom, enjoying his evening pipe beside
his hearth. The blaze of the large maple-wood
fire spread warmly upon the unpainted beams
above, and lighted up the timbers of the shanty
with a mellow glow that gave an air of cheer-
fulness and comfort to the rudely-furnished
apartment. From the gray hairs and weather-

beaten features of the settler, he appeared to be
a man considerably on the wrong side of forty,
while the young bright-haired mother by his
side had not yet passed the sunny season of
early youth. The disparity of their years, how-
ever, had evidently not prevented the growth
of the strongest affection between them. There
was a soft and happy look of content about the
girl, as she surveyed the brown woodsman,
now watching the smoke-wreaths from his pipe
as they curled over his head, now taking his
axe upon his lap, and feeling its edge with a
sort of caressing gesture, as if the inanimate
thing could be conscious of the silent compli-
ment he paid to its temper, when thinking over
the enlargement of the clearing he had wrought
by its aid during the day. Nor did the eye of
the young mother kindle less affectionately
when the brawny pioneer, carefully depositing
the simple instrument, which is the pride of an

American woodsman, behind the chimney turned to take the hand of the infant, which she pressed to her bosom, and shared at the same time with her the caresses which he bestowed on the child.

" That boy's a raal credit to you, Bet. But I think, if he cries to-night, as he has for the last week, I must make a papoose-cradle for him to-morrow, and swing him somewhere outside of the shanty, where his squalling can't keep us awake. Your face is growing as white as a silver birch, from loss of sleep o'nights."

"Why, John, how you talk! I'm sure Yorpy never cries;—never, I mean, worth talking of."

As the mother spoke, she pressed the unhappy little youngster somewhat too closely to her bosom, and he awoke with one of those discordant outbreaks of infant passion with which the hopeful scions of humanity sometimes test the comforts of married life.

" Baby — why, baby — there — there now! what will it have ?—does it want to see brother Ben ? Hush—hush—he's coming with something for baby! Hush, now, darling!—Will it have this ?"

" Why, Bet, my dear," said the father, " don't give the brat Ben's powder-horn to play with; for thof he does like you as much as he did my first missus, his own mother and flesh and blood, the lad doesn't love to have his hunting-tools discomboborated. God's weather! where can the tormented chap be staying ?—he ought to be home by this time." With these words he walked to the door, and stood for a moment commenting upon the mildness of the night, and wondering why Ben did not return. But the mother was too much engaged in soothing the infant, by rocking him to and fro in her arms, to reply.

" Now don't, don't, gal," continued the kind-hearted woodsman, turning from the door, which he left open; "you'll tire yourself to death. Let me take him—there, now—there," said he, as she relinquished the child to his arms; and, addressing the last words to the poor, perverse little thing, he walked up and down the room with it, vainly trying to lull its gust of passion or peevishness.

"Hush! you little varmint, you!" said the father at last, growing impatient; "hush! or I'll call in the Indians to carry you off—I will."

The settler was just turning in his walk, near the open threshold, as he uttered the ill-omened words, when a swarthy hand reaching over his shoulder, clutched the child from his arms, and brained it against the doorpost, in the same moment that the tomahawk of another savage struck him to the floor. A dozen painted demons sprang over his prostrate body into the centre of the room. The simple scene of domestic joy, but a moment before so sheltered

and homelike, was changed on the instant.
The mummied nursling was flung upon the
embers near the feet of its frantic mother, who
slipped and fell in the blood of her husband,
as she plucked her child from the coals, and
sprang towards the door. It was a blow of
mercy, though not meant as such, which dis-
missed her spirit, as she struggled to rise with
her lifeless burden. The embers of the fire
soon strewed the apartment, while the savages
danced among them with the mad glee of the
devil's own children, until the smoke and blaze,
ascending to the roof-tree, drove them from the
scene of their infernal orgies.

The next day's sun shone upon that moul-
dering ruin as brightly as if unconscious of the
horrors which his light revealed. So complete
had been the devastation of the flames, that
little but ashes now remained; and the blue
smoke curled up among the embowering trees
as gently as if it rose only from a cottager's

hospitable fire. The oriole, perched upon a cedar-top, whistled as usual to his mate, swinging in his nest upon the pendent branches of a willow which had been planted by the ill-fated settler near a spring not far from his door; while the cat-bird from the brier-thicket replied in mocking notes blither and clearer than those he aimed to imitate. The swallow only, driven from her nest in the eaves, and whirling in disordered flight around the place, seemed in sharp cries to sympathize with the desolation which had come over it.

There was one human mourner, however, amid the scene. A youth of sixteen sat with his head buried in his hands upon a fallen tree hard by. So still and motionless he seemed, that his form might almost be thought to have been carved out of the gray wood, with which his faded garments assimilated in colour. It would not be difficult to surmise what passed in the bosom of the young forester, as at last, after rising with an effort, he advanced to the funeral pyre of his household, and, turning over the dry embers, disengaged a half-burned cloven skull from among them. He threw himself upon the grass, and bit the ground with a fierce agony that showed some self-reproach must be mingled with his sorrow.

" My father ! my father !" he cried, writhing in anguish; "why—why did I not come home at once, when I heard that the Black Wolf had gone north with his band !" A burst of tears seemed to relieve him for a moment; and then, with greater bitterness than ever, he resumed, " Fool — thrice accursed fool that I was !—I might have known that he would strike for these mountains, instead of taking the Sacondaga route, where the palatine yægars were out and on the watch for him. To die so like a brute in the hands of a butcher—without one

word of warning—to be burned like a wood-
chuck in his hole—stricken to death without a
chance of dealing one blow for his defence!
My father! my poor father! Oh, God! I
cannot bear it!"

But the youth knew not the self-renovating
spirit of life's springtime, when he thought
that his first sorrow, bitter as it was, would
blast his manhood for ever. A first grief never
blights the heart of man. The sapling hickory
may be bowed—may be shattered by the storm,
but it has an elasticity and toughness of fibre
that keep it from perishing. It is only long
exposure to a succession of harsh and biting
winds that steals away its vigour, drinks up its
sap of life, and sends a chill at last to the roots
which nourished its vitality.

That day of cruel woe, like all others, had an
end for the young forester; and, when the
waning moon rose upon the scene of his

ruined home, her yellow light disclosed the boy
kneeling upon the sod wherewith he had co-
vered up the bones of his only earthly relatives.
She, too, was sole witness to the vow of undy-
ing vengeance which he swore upon the spot
against the whole race of red men.

There are but too many traditions surviving
in this region to prove the fulfilment of this
fearful vow. But I leave the dire feats of
" Bloody Ben," by which name only is the
avenger now remembered, to some annalist
who finds greater pleasure than I do in such
horrible details. My business, here, is only to
describe the first deed by which he requited
the murderous act of the Indians.

The seasons had twice gone their round since
destruction had come over the house of the
settler, and his son had never yet revisited the
spot, which, with the exuberant growth of an
American soil, had partly relapsed into its

native wildness, from the tangled vines and thickets which had overgrown the clearing. The strong arm of the government had for a while driven the Indians beyond the reach of private vengeance; but now they were again returning to their favourite hunting-ground north of the Mohawk, and around the sources of the Hudson. Some even had ventured into Albany to dispose of their packs and skins, and carry back a supply of powder and other necessaries of the hunter of the wilderness. It was two of these that the orphan youth dogged from the settlements, on their way through the northern forests, to the spot where his oath of vengeance had been recorded. The sequel may best be told in the words of an old hunter under whose guidance I made my first and only visit to the Dead Clearing.

" It was about two o'clock of a hot August afternoon, that Ben, after thus following up their

trail for three days, came upon the two Injuns
jist where the moose-runway makes an opening
in the forest, and lets the light down upon yon
willow that still flourishes beside the old hem-
lock.   The Injuns were sitting beneath the
willow, thinking themselves sheltered by the
rocky bank opposite, and a mass of underwood
which had shot up round the top of an oak,
which had been twisted off in a tornado in
some former day, and then lay imbedded in
weeds beneath the knoll.   But, a few yards
from this bank, in that thicket round the roots
of yon mossy old beech, Ben found a shelter,
from which, at any moment, he could creep up
and cover either with his fire from behind the
knoll.   But, as he had only a one-barrel piece,
it required full as cool a hand as his to wait
and take both the creeturs at one shot.   Bloody
Ben, though, was jist the chap to do it.   Like
enough he waited there or manœuvred round

for an hour to get his chance, which did come
at last, howsumdever. The Injuns, who, in
their own way, are mighty talkers, you must
know,—that is, when they have really some-
thing to talk about,—got into some argerment,
wherein figures, about which they know mighty
little, were concerned. One took out his
scalping-knife to make marks upon the earth
to help him : while the other trying to make
matters clearer with the aid of his fingers, their
heads came near each other jist as you may
have seen those of white people when they get
parroiching right in earnest. So they argufied
and they counted, getting nearer and nearer as
they became more eager, till their skulls,
almost touching, came within the exact range of
Ben's rifle : and then Ben, he ups and sends
the ball so clean through both, that it buried
itself in a sapling behind them. And that, I
think, was pretty well for the first shot of a lad

of eighteen; and Bloody Ben himself never confessed to making a better one afterwards."

The tourist, who should now seek the scene of this adventure, would, perhaps, look in vain for the graceful exotic that once marked the spot. The weeping willow, which was only a thrifty sapling when the Indians met their death beneath its fatal shade, was changed into an old decayed trunk, with but one living branch when I beheld it; and a ponderous vine was rapidly strangling the life from this decrepit limb. The hardy growth of the native forest had nearly obliterated the improvements of the pioneer. The wild animals, in drinking from the spring hard by, had dislodged the flat stones from its brink; tall weeds waved amid the spreading pool; and the fox had made his den in the rocky knoll upon whose side once stood the settler's cabin of THE DEAD CLEARING.

WILD SCENES

ON

THE SACONDAGA.

CHAPTER I.

THE HUNTING-GROUNDS OF THE MOHAWKS.

I HAVE wandered about "considerably" in my time—some five or six thousand miles perhaps—over the northern parts of the Union on either side of the mountains, and all for the sake of seeing Nature in what poets call "her wild retreats:" of beholding her in those unmolested fastnessess where, like a decorous female as she is, she may freak it about in dishabille without being subjected to that abashing scrutiny which always awaits her when architects and landscape-gardeners assist at her toilet in those places where wealth compels her sometimes to hold her court.   Like all the rest of her sex, she is capricious enough in her choice of what she likes, and leads her admirers many an idle dance with but slight reward; while her choicest favours often await him who stumbles upon her at her retiring moments, in spots where he would least expect such good fortune.   Certes, I have never found her more propitious than within a day's journey of Saratoga, among lakes, mountains, and forests; where, notwithstanding the vicinity of one of the gayest haunts of dissipation, my only rivals for her favours were a sportsman or two who had stumbled upon these retreats as I did.

It was many years since when in early youth I went upon my first hunting excursion in that unsettled region, about the sources of the Sacondaga river, generally known as "Totten and Crossfield's Purchase," never in very great repute at land-offices, and selling at that time for sixpence an acre. The deer were then so abundant that they were often destroyed by the few settlers for their skins alone; and wolves, and bears, and panthers, prowled the thick forest unmolested, save by a few Indians who once or twice throughout the year would straggle in from the Iroquois reservation on the Canadian frontier. This district was in old times a favourite hunting-ground of the Mohawks, and the salmon-trout that abound in the head waters of the Hudson would still sometimes tempt them at the spearing season in July; the moose, which is still occasionally shot in this district, used generally to lure them thither in the winter season.

There was one old Mohawk, yclept Captain Gill, who alone kept there all the year round, and was a sort of sylvan sultan of the whole region about. His daughter, Molly Gill, who led a kind of oyster life (though no one would have mistaken her for a peri) in their wigwam on the outlet of Lake Pleasant, used to make his moccasins, gum the seams, sew up the rips of his birchen canoe, and dress his venison for him, while the captain roved far and near in search of whatever might cheer the home enlivened by these two only inmates—a tender fawn cutlet, a trinket sent by some goodnatured settler to Molly, or a stoup of vile whiskey secreted in the captain's hunting-pouch for his especial refreshment and delight.

Gill, notwithstanding this unhallowed league with bad spirits, was a capital guide upon sporting excursions whenever the larger kinds of game were the object; and a college chum whom we called "The Barrister," from his having just entered on the study of the law, took as much pleasure as myself in wandering about among the mountains, or cruising from lake to lake, and camping out on their banks with the old Mohawk for our *decus et tutamen.*

A hunting-party of Iroquois Indians from St. Regis was at that time in the country; and uniting with these we turned out a pretty stout band upon our greater excursions; our company being often strengthened by a queer original, hight Major Jake Peabody, and several other white hunters that may still be living somewhere along that border.

As I took no notes of our different "tramps," it is impossible now to trace their various routes through rocky glens and over sagging morasses, amid the labyrinth of lakes that are linked together by innumerable streams and waterfalls among these mountains; and I may be sufficiently inaccurate while trying to recall some of the tales and anecdotes with which our party used to while away the evenings between the hours of making our camp-fire and the moment of retiring to repose: but neither shall prevent me from attempting to sketch some of these scenes from recollection, and relating the legends connected with them as I now remember them.

Embarking one morning on a small lake called Konjimuc by the Indians, we entered its outlet, and floated many hours down a stream scarcely a pistol-shot in breadth, where, from the rapidity of the current, the steering-paddle alone was necessary to keep our canoes on their course. The brook wound generally through a wooded morass, where the dense overhanging foliage excluded even a glimpse of the neighbouring mountains; at times, however, it would sweep near enough to their bank to wash a wall of granite, from which the hanging birch and hemlock would fling their branches far over the limpid tide; and then again it would expand into a broad, deep pool, circled with water-lilies, and animated by large flocks of wild-fowl, that would rise screaming from the black tarn as we glided out from the shadow of the forest and skimmed over its smooth surface. Innumerable streams, the inlets and outlets of other lakes, mingled their waters in these frequently-occurring ponds, and about sunset we struck one so broad that we determined to change our course, and, heading our shallops now against the current, we soon found ourselves upon the outlet of a considerable lake. The water gradually became deeper and more sluggish, and then a pull of a few hundred yards with a sudden turn in the forest, shot us out upon one of the most beautiful sheets of water I ever beheld.

It was about four miles in length, with perhaps half that breadth; the shores curved with the most picturesque irregularity, and swelled high, but gradually, from the water; while their graceful slopes were held in strong contrast by a single islet which shot up in one bold cliff from the centre, and nodded with a crown of pines, around which an eagle was at that moment wheeling.   There were then, I believe, but two farms upon the banks of Lake Pleasant, a couple of small "clearings" on the brows of opposite promontories, each covered with grain-fields, whose brown stubble smiled in the light of the setting sun—the only cultivated spots in an unbroken wilderness.   Every where else the untamed forest threw its dusky shadow over the lake, while beneath the pendant branches, which in some instances swept the wave, a beach as white as the snowy strand of the ocean glistened around the clear blue water.

The sun was setting in heavy, though gorgeous clouds, which at each moment lost some of their brightness in a volume of vapour that rolled along the mountains; and by the time we reached the upper end of the lake, the broad drops that began to descend warned us to hurry on our course and gain a shelter from the coming storm. We had reached the inlet of the lake, which was only a narrow, crooked strait, a few hundred rods in length, connecting it with another sheet of water that covered about the same surface as that over which we had passed, the promontory between affording, as I afterwards experienced, a commanding view of both the sister lakes. Our destination was the farthest side of the upper lake, and the management of a canoe was no boy's play when we left the sheltered strait and launched out upon the stormy water. The shores were bold and rocky, and as the wind had now risen to a tempest, the waves beat furiously upon them. The rain blew in blinding sheets against us, and it was almost impossible, while urging our way in its teeth, to keep our canoes from falling off into the trough of the sea; in which case they would inevitably have been swamped.   Our flotilla was soon separated and dispersed in the darkness.   A pack of hounds had been distributed among the different boats, and some of the younger dogs, alarmed by the shouting and confusion, would raise a piteous howl at parting company with the rest.   We called long to each other as the lightning from time to time revealed a boat still in hail; but our voices were at last only echoed by the dismal wailing of the loon, whose shriek always rises above the storm, and may be heard for miles amidst its wildest raging.

The night was far spent before we all again united at our place of destination; the different boats straggling in one by one so slowly, that those who first arrived passed an hour in great anxiety for the fate of the last that made a harbour.

Sacondaga, the lake we were on, the fountain-head of the river of that name, is shaped, as an Indian hunter phrased it, "like a bear's paw spread out with an island between the ball of each toe;"* and the different bays and islets, resembling each other to an unpractised eye, might, on a dark night, mislead even the skilful voyageur in making any given point on the shore: more than one of our canoes must have coasted the greater part of it before they were all successively drawn up on the beach at the place we had fixed on for our rendezvous.

" God's weather ! but this is quite a night," quoth Major Jake, peering out upon the storm which was still raging an hour afterward.

" Yes ! I may say that the Flying Head is

* It is called " Round Lake " by the land-surveyors, probably *quasi lucus*, &c.

abroad to-night," replied the old Mohawk, in
good round English, as he lighted his pipe and
looked contentedly around the bark shantee,
wherein each of our company, having cheered
himself with a hearty supper of dried venison,
was lounging about the fire in every variety of
attitude. The remark seemed to attract the
attention of no one but myself; but when I
asked the speaker to explain its meaning, my
mongrel companions eagerly united in a request
that " the captain would tell them all about the
varmint of which he spoke, be it *painter* (pan-
ther) or devil." Gill did not long hesitate to
comply; but the particulars, not to mention the
phraseology of his narrative, in the years that
have since elapsed, have almost escaped me;
and I may fail, therefore, in preserving the
Indian character of the story while trying to
recall it here.

CHAPTER II.

KO-REA-RAN-NEH-NEH, OR THE FLYING HEAD.

[A Legend of Sacondaga Lake.]

" It hath tell-tale tongues ;—this casing air
    That walls us in—and their wandering breath
Will whisper the horror every where,
    That clings to that ruthless deed of death.
And a vengeful eye from the gory tide
Will open, to blast the parricide."

The Yankee Rhymer.

THE country about the head waters of the great Mohegan (as the Hudson is sometimes called), though abounding in game and fish, was never, in the recollection of the oldest

Indians living, nor in that of their fathers'
fathers, the permanent residence of any one
tribe. From the black mountain tarns, where
the eastern fork takes its rise, to the silver
strand of Lake Pleasant, through which the
western branch makes its way after rising in
Sacondaga Lake, the wilderness that inter-
venes, and all the mountains round about the
fountain-heads of the great river, have from
time immemorial been infested by a class of
beings with whom no good man would ever
wish to come in contact.

The young men of the Mohawk have indeed
often traversed it, when, in years gone by, they
went on the war-path after the hostile tribes of
the north; and the scattered and wandering
remnants of their people, with an occasional
hunting-party from the degenerate bands that
survive at St. Regis, will yet occasionally be
tempted over these haunted grounds in quest

of the game that still finds a refuge in that mountain region. The evil shapes that were formerly so troublesome to the red hunter, seem in these later days to have become less restless at his presence; and, whether it be that the day of their power has gone by, or that their vindictiveness has relented at witnessing the fate which seems to be universally overtaking the people whom they once delighted to persecute—certain it is that the few Indians who now find their way to this part of the country are never molested except by the white settlers who are slowly extending their clearings among the wild hills of the north.

The "FLYING HEAD," which is supposed to have first driven the original possessors of these hunting-grounds, whosoever they were, from their homes, and which, as long as tradition runneth back, in the old day before the whites came hither, guarded them from the occupancy of every neighbouring tribe, has not been seen for many years by any credible witness, though there are those who insist that it has more than once appeared to them hovering, as their fathers used to describe it, over the lake in which it first had its birth. The existence of this fearful monster, however, has never been disputed. Rude representations of it are still occasionally met with in the crude designs of those degenerate aborigines who earn a scant subsistence by making birchen-baskets and ornamented pouches for such travellers as are curious in their manufacture of wampum and porcupine quills; and the origin and history of the Flying Head survives, while even the name of the tribe whose crimes first called it into existence has passed away for ever.

It was a season of great severity with that forgotten people whose council-fires were lighted on the mountain promontory that divides Sacondaga from the sister lake into which it discharges itself.*

A long and severe winter, with but little snow, had killed the herbage at its roots, and the moose and deer had trooped off to the more luxuriant pastures along the Mohawk, whither the hunters of the hills dared not follow them. The fishing, too, failed; and the famine became so devouring among the mountains, that whole families, who had no hunters to provide for them, perished outright. The young men would no longer throw the slender product of the chase into the common stock, and the women and children had to maintain life as well as they could upon the roots and berries the woods afforded them.

* A hamlet is now growing up on this beautiful mountain-slope, and the scenery in the vicinity is likely to be soon better known from the late establishment of a line of post-coaches between Sacondaga Lake and Saratoga Springs.

The sufferings of the tribe became at length so galling, that the young and enterprising began to talk of migrating from the ancient seat of their people; and as it was impossible, surrounded as they were by hostile tribes, merely to shift their hunting - grounds for a season and return to them at some more auspicious period, it was proposed that if they could effect a secret march to the great lake off to the west of them, they should launch their canoes upon Ontario, and all move away to a new home beyond its broad waters. The wild rice, of which some had been brought into their country by a runner from a distant nation, would, they thought, support them in their perilous voyage along the shores of the great water, where it grows in such profusion; and they believed that, once safely beyond the lake, it would be easy enough to find a new home abounding in game upon those flowery plains which, as they had heard, lay like one immense garden beyond the chain of inland seas.

The old men of the tribe were indignant at the bare suggestion of leaving the bright streams and sheltered vallies, amid which their spring-time of life had passed so happily. They doubted the existence of the garden-regions of which their children spoke; and they thought that if there were indeed such a country, it was madness to attempt to reach it in the way proposed. They said, too, that the famine was a scourge which the master of life inflicted upon his people for their crimes—that if its pains were endured with the constancy and firmness that became warriors, the visitation would soon pass away; but that those who fled from it would only war with their destiny and that chastisement would follow them, in some shape, wheresoever they might flee. Finally, they added, that they would rather perish by inches on their native hills—they would rather die that moment, than leave them for ever, to revel in plenty upon stranger plains.

" Be it so—they have spoken!" exclaimed a fierce and insolent youth, springing to his feet and casting a furious glance around the council as the aged chief, who had thus addressed it, resumed his seat. " Be the dotard's words their own, my brothers—let them die for the crimes they have even now acknowledged. We know of none; our unsullied summers have nothing to blush for. It is they that have drawn this curse upon our people—it is for them that our vitals are consuming with anguish, while our strength wastes away in the search of sustenance we cannot find—or which, when found, we are compelled to share with those for whose misdeeds the Great Spirit hath placed it far from us. They have spoken—let them die.

Let them die, if we are to remain, to appease the angry Spirit; and the food that now keeps life lingering in their shrivelled and useless carcasses may then nerve the limbs of our young hunters, or keep our children from perishing. Let them die, if we are to move hence, for their presence will but bring a curse upon our path—their worn-out frames will give way upon the march, and the raven that hovers over their corses, will guide our enemies to the spot, and scent them like wolves upon our trail. Let them die, my brothers, and because they are still our tribesmen, let us give them the death of warriors—and that before we leave this ground."

And with these words the young barbarian, pealing forth a ferocious whoop, buried his tomahawk in the head of the old man nearest to him. The infernal yell was echoed on every side—a dozen flint hatchets were instantly raised

by as many remorseless arms, and the massacre
was wrought before one of those thus horribly
sacrificed could interpose a plea of mercy. But
for mercy they would not have pleaded, had op-
portunity been afforded them.   For even in the
moment that intervened between the cruel sen-
tence and its execution, they managed to show
that stern resignation to the decrees of fate
which an Indian warrior ever exhibits when
death is near; and each of the seven old men
that perished thus barbarously, drew his wolf-
skin mantle around his shoulders and nodded
his head as if inviting the deathblow that fol-
lowed.

The parricidal deed was done; and it now
became a question, how to dispose of the re-
mains of those whose lamp of life, while twink-
ling in the socket, had been thus fearfully
quenched for ever. The act, though said to
have been of not unfrequent occurrence among

certain Indian tribes at similar exigencies, was
one utterly abhorrent to the nature of most of
our aborigines; who, from their earliest years,
are taught the deepest veneration for the aged.
In the present instance, likewise, it had been
so outrageous a perversion of their customary
views of duty among this simple people, that it
was thought but proper to dispense with their
wonted mode of sepulture, and dispose of the
victims of famine and fanaticism in some pecu-
liar manner. They wished in some way to
sanctify the deed, by offering up the bodies of
the slaughtered to the Master of Life, and that
without dishonouring the dead. It was there-
fore agreed to decapitate the bodies and burn
them; and as the nobler part could not, when
thus dissevered, be buried with the usual forms,
it was determined to sink the heads together in
the bottom of the lake.

The soul-less trunks were accordingly con-
sumed and the ashes scattered to the winds.
The heads were then deposited singly, in sepa-
rate canoes, which were pulled off in a kind of
procession from the shore. The young chief
who had suggested the bloody scene of the
sacrifice, rowed in advance, in order to desig-
nate the spot where they were to disburden
themselves of their gory freight. Resting then
upon his oars, he received each head in succes-
sion from his companions, and proceeded to tie
them together by their scalp-locks, in order to
sink the whole, with a huge stone, to the bot-
tom. But the vengeance of the Master of Life
overtook the wretch before his horrid office was
accomplished; for no sooner did he receive the
last head into his canoe than it began to sink—
his feet became entangled in the hideous chain
he had been knotting together, and before his

horror-stricken companions could come to his rescue, he was dragged shrieking to the bottom. The others waited not to see the water settle over him, but pulled with their whole strength for the shore.

The morning dawned calmly upon that un-hallowed water, which seemed at first to show no traces of the deed it had witnessed the night before. But gradually as the sun rose up higher, a few gory bubbles appeared to float over one smooth and turbid spot, which the breeze never crisped into a ripple. The parri-cides sat on the bank watching it all the day; but sluggish, as at first, that sullen blot upon the fresh blue surface still remained. Another day passed over their heads, and the thick stain was yet there. On the third day the floating slime took a greener hue, as if coloured by the festering mass beneath; but coarse fibres of darker dye marbled its surface: and on the fourth day these began to tremble along the water like weeds growing from the bottom, or the long tresses of a woman's scalp floating in a pool when no wind disturbs it. The fifth morning came, and the conscience-stricken watchers thought that the spreading-scalp—for such now all agreed it was—had raised itself from the water, and become rounded at the top as if there were a head beneath it. Some thought, too, that they could discover a pair of hideous eyes glaring beneath the dripping locks. They looked on the sixth, and there indeed was a monstrous head floating upon the surface, as if anchored to the spot, around which the water —notwithstanding a blast which swept the lake—was calm and motionless as ever.

Those bad Indians then wished to fly, but the doomed parricides had not now the courage to encounter the warlike bands through which they must make their way in flying from their native valley. They thought, too, that as nothing about the head, except the eyes, had motion, it could not harm them, resting quietly as it did upon the bosom of the waters. And though it was dreadful to have that hideous gaze fixed for ever upon their dwellings, yet they thought that if the Master of Life meant this as an expiation for their frenzied deed, they would strive to live on beneath those unearthly glances without shrinking or complaint.

But a strange alteration had taken place in the floating head on the morning of the seventh day. A pair of broad wings, ribbed, like those of a bat, and with claws appended to each tendon, had grown out during the night; and, buoyed up by these, it seemed to be now resting on the water. The water itself appeared to ripple more briskly near it, as if joyous that it was about to be relieved of its unnatural burden; but still for hours the head maintained its first position. At last the wind began to rise, and, driving through the trough of the sea, beneath their expanded membrane, raised the wings from the surface, and seemed for the first time to endow them with vitality. They flapped harshly once or twice upon the waves, and the head rose slowly and heavily from the lake.

An agony of fear seized upon the gazing parricides, but the supernatural creation made no movement to injure them. It only remained balancing itself over the lake, and casting a shadow from its wings that wrapped the valley in gloom. But dreadful was it beneath their withering shade to watch that terrific monster, hovering like a falcon for the stoop, and know not upon what victim it might descend. It was then that they who had sown the gory seed from which it sprung to life, with one impulse sought to escape its presence by flight. Herding together like a troop of deer when the panther is prowling by, they rushed in a body from the scene. But the flapping of the demon pinions was soon heard behind them, and the winged head was henceforth on their track wheresoever it led.

In vain did they cross one mountain barrier after another—plunge into the rocky gorge or thread the mazy swamp to escape their fiendish watcher. The Flying Head would rise on tireless wings over the loftiest summit, or dart in arrowy flight through the narrowest passages without furling its pinions: while their sullen threshing would be heard even in those vine-webbed thickets, where the little ground bird can scarcely make its way. The very caverns of the earth were no protection to the parricides from its presence; for scarcely would they think they had found a refuge in some sparry cell, when, poised midway between the ceiling and the floor, they would behold the Flying Head glaring upon them. Sleeping or waking, the monster was ever near; they paused to rest, but the rushing of its wings, as it swept around their resting-place in never-ending circles, prevented them from finding forgetfulness in repose; or, if in spite of those blighting pinions that ever fanned them, fatigue did at moments plunge them in uneasy slumbers, the glances of the Flying Head would pierce their very eyelids, and steep their dreams in horror.

What was the ultimate fate of that band of parricides, no one has ever known. Some say that the Master of Life kept them always young, in order that their capability of suffering might never wear out; and these insist that the Flying Head is still pursuing them over the great prairies of the Far West. Others aver that the glances of the Flying Head turned each of them gradually into stone, and these say, that their forms, though altered by the wearing of the rains in the lapse of long years, may still be recognised in those upright rocks which stand like human figures along the shores of some of the neighbouring lakes; though most Indians have another way of accounting for these figures. Certain it is, however, that the Flying Head always comes back to this part of the country about the times of the equinox; and some say even, that you may always hear the flapping of its wings whenever such a storm as that we have just weathered is brewing.

———

The old hunter had finished his story; but my companions were still anxious that he should protract the narrative, and give us the account of the grotesque forms to which he had alluded as being found among these hills. These, however, he told us more properly belonged to another legend, which he subsequently related, and which I may hereafter endeavour to recall.

The storm of the last night had not subsided on the morrow, and Major Peabody proclaimed authoritatively that it was folly to leave our comfortable quarters in such weather. The Major presented a singular appearance as I first viewed him engaged in taking an observation, when I awakened in the morning. Being in his stocking-feet he had avoided the disagreeableness of stepping upon the wet ground without the Shantie to study the elements, by raising his tall body erect upon the place where he had slept, and thrusting his head through the bark roof much after the fashion of a man in the pillory. Hearing his voice on the outside of the wigwam, I had stepped through the

doorway without observing his lean and Quix-
otic figure within: and when this lantern-
jawed countenance, reposing as it were upon
the roof, first met my eyes, I rubbed them in
doubt whether the Flying Head of which I had
heard the night before, was not yet bewilder-
ing my senses.

Our party generally was disposed to abide by
the counsels of Major Jake, and remain within
doors amusing themselves by putting their
various hunting accoutrements in order for the
morrow. One or two, however, went off to
catch some lake-trout for our dinner; and as
the Indians philosophically got rid of a rainy
day by sleeping like hounds before the fire, the
Major had but a small audience, when, after
calling in vain for another Iroquois legend to
amuse us, my friend and I prevailed upon him
to relate the principal adventures of his own
life, which he did in nearly the following words.

CHAPTER III.

THE MAJOR'S STORY.

" For earthly goods he cared not, more because
    He went to work to carve his proper share
From out the common stock, as coolly as
    You would a morsel from a pippin pare.
A shrewd, but wild and wayward chap he was,
    Cautious—but danger ready still to dare
(If by it he could rise or win), on field or flood ;
    A pedlar even of his heart's best blood!"

                         The Yankee Rhymer.

" You mustn't think because you're hearn me called Major by all the folks round the country, that I'm much stuck up by the title, for it's only a militia one, which, you know, is not of much account to a man who has once been a breveted captain in the regular service. This, however, is neither here nor there; for though I had worn Uncle Sam's livery for some years, and smelt gunpowder upon more than one occasion—ay, and killed my man too, in a duel, yet natur never meant me for an officer. I never took to the thing in the best of times, and I never now can account for my luck in getting an epaulet on my shoulder, and being thought the fire-eater, which some of my old comrades will describe to you when you ask them about Jake Peabody. But this again is neither here nor there; let me begin with the commencement of my story, which, when it tires you, you will please to interrupt just as you please.

" I was born in Albany, in Old York state, in a small house, which is, perhaps, still standing at the north end, down by Fox Creek. My father was a Connecticut horse-doctor, or, as he more politely styled himself in latter years, a veterinary surgeon. My mother was born of Yankee parents, in Rensselaer county; but she was the widow of an old Dutchman up in the colony, when my father took her to wife, and stepped into Mynheer's property along the creek.

" Being the youngest son, I came into the world after my father had got his head pretty well above water, and had, therefore, greater advantages of education than the rest of my family. The old gentleman, who took particular delight in being addressed as Doctor Peabody, hoped that the son who bore his name, might some day turn out a real M. D.; and, as the first step towards such a consummation, I was taken from the academy, when a boy of eleven, and placed in a druggist's shop.

" The person to whom I was apprenticed,

kept his office upon the water-side, near the skirts of the town, where, what with keel-boatmen from the Mohawk, Schenectady teamsters, Sacondaga raftsmen, and an occasional North river skipper for customers, he contrived to drive a pretty brisk trade in certain medicines, and initiate his pupil in a branch of practice, which had a wonderful tendency to give me an insight into what, in larger cities, is called 'life.' You will not wonder, therefore, that, in exchange for the vegetable and mineral nostrums, which it was my duty to vend to our customers, I readily imbibed a moral poison, hardly less pernicious; nor that I was sent a packing by my bos before I was fifteen, because he had discovered that I was too old to continue longer the playmate of his daughter Nantie, and he knew not how, otherwise, to break off an intercourse which had ripened into too great familiarity.

" I was in no want of friends, however. My father, indeed, was dead; and my mother having taken unto herself a third helpmate, my brothers troubled themselves but little about such a scapegrace as they considered me. But among raftsmen and skippers, I was favourably known; and one of the latter readily took me on board of a coasting schooner, until something better should offer.

" Our first voyage from Albany was to a port in Long Island Sound, whither the skipper was bound with a cargo of shingles. Here I met with a Connecticut medicine pedler, who was about starting to Georgia with a large supply of a patent carminative, of which he attempted to force some sales among our crew. This fellow conceived a fancy for me from the moment I exposed his quackery, and was very solicitous to employ so cute a lad, as he called me, in the manufacture of an article which I seemed to

understand so well. But I declined his over-
tures from having higher things in view. The
truth is, upon our first landing at the place, I
had seen a newspaper in the bar-room of an
inn, which set my ambition all on fire. It was
an advertisement, which ran as follows :

"'To young Gentlemen wishing to Travel.

"'A middle-aged gentleman, engaged in an
agreeable and lucrative business, which leads
him to take extensive tours over various parts
of the Union, is desirous of a young and intel-
ligent companion, whose duties would be merely
nominal, and who, in forming a most improving
connexion, would have an opportunity of visit-
ing the most interesting cities and towns of the
United States, without incurring a particle of
expense. Applicants for the situation will
address *Viator*, at this office; and none but

young gentlemen of the first respectability need apply.'

"You may think me presumptuous in preferring a claim to such a place; but, nevertheless, I immediately answered the advertisement by asking an interview with Viator at such time and place as he should choose to designate. I confess I thought that I was attempting a pretty high flight, and therefore kept my hopes and schemes to myself. Indeed, it required all the ingenuity of the pedler, who thought I must have some prospect in view, from so peremptorily declining his offer—it required all his skill, I say, to worm my real purpose out of me. I did, however, communicate it to him, and you may judge of my surprise, when, upon my telling him that I hourly expected an answer to my note, he produced it from his pocket, and quietly announcing himself as the 'middle-aged gentleman' with whom I had been treating anonymously, added, that there was now no difficulty in at once arranging matters. The first castle in the air I had ever built was thus demolished in a moment. But I suppressed the mortification of my feelings; and having now made up my mind to see the world in some way or other, I closed at once with the overtures of the pedler. The connexion, it is true, did not elevate me in the world, but it might open the means of rising.

"I passed two or three years in travelling with this man through the south-western states; he was frugal, kind, and considerate, and of the most scrupulous honesty in every respect, save where the disposal of his patent medicine was concerned; and I verily believe that he would have sold a bottle of this to his best friend, though the use of it might destroy the purchaser in an hour afterwards. With regard to me, he exhibited ever the care of a father, until his stock in trade becoming one day exhausted while at a thriving village in East Tennesee, I became exceedingly ill shortly afterwards, and had good reason to believe that my worthy master had induced the sickness by experiments upon me with some simples, from which he hoped to prepare a new compound that might enable him to supply his customers. I kept the suspicion to myself, however; and after seeing some fifty persons in the neighbourhood hurried off by what in that country is called the milk-sickness—whose worst symptoms, by-the-by, were always aggravated by the vegetable remedies which my associate exhibited — we decamped one night, and took our way along the mountain-ridge which enters Virginia not far north of this point. But here I and my master were doomed to part company, in a way that makes us unlikely to meet again in the United States.

"A disbanded regulator of the Georgia guard, with a Lynch-ing corn-cracker from that state, accompanied by a couple of enterprising counterfeiters lately thrown out of employ in Kentucky, had scented the contents of my master's saddle-bags, and dogged our steps to the wild mountain-passes about the Cumberland Gap. Here, in a woody ravine, to which we had withdrawn to take our noonday meal, apart from the dust of the highway and the heat of the sun, these worthies joined our society in a way which, to say the least of it, was exceedingly abrupt. The first intimation of their presence was a couple of shots, which killed the pedler's fine Kentucky horse, and wounded my Indian tackey. The latter was a tough and spirited little animal, for which I had exchanged a broken-down nag while passing through the

Creek nation. He was not wounded so badly, however, but that he bore me quickly out of danger, when I leaped upon his back as the robbers rushed from the bushes upon the unarmed pedler.

" I have often since believed that my patron might have escaped the dreadful fate which overtook him a few moments afterward, if he had kept a quiet tongue between his teeth ; but his Connecticut notions of justice impelled him to mutter something about the law of highway robbery, when he saw the plump saddle-bags which his legs had so often caressed in the possession of the freebooters. There was then but a brief parley, the words of which I could not make out, though I still hovered near, having secured my pony in a thicket : its purport, though, was soon apparent. They seized the pedler, and, reckless of his cries, dragged him up a rocky hill, thick-set with bushes, to the mouth of one of those limestone caverns with which this part of the country abounds. Here they paused for a moment, but not to listen to the passionate pleadings for liberty which were redoubled by the victim; who, however, seemed to anticipate nothing more than confinement in so dreary a place.

"'Strike a light, Jim,' cried one, who appeared to be the leader.

"'You don't want no light,' said the other; 'it's not far from the mouth, and Angus, who has been in a dozen times, can take your hand and guide you.'

"At the word, a carroty-headed fellow stepped forward, and, taking the hand of the leader, moved in advance as his pioneer, while the two assisted him in dragging the pedler within the cave. The mouth was thick-grown with tall weeds, and much obscured with fallen boughs and brush of one kind or another, which had from time to time accumulated over it. Supple and active, I did not hesitate to worm my way through this screen, and penetrate into the dark region beyond, which once gained, I knew I must be safe. The struggles and out-cry of the pedler prevented the robbers from observing any rustling I might make in moving through the thicket beside them, and I gained the cover of the cavern before their forms had wholly darkened the entrance. The pedler did not struggle much as they pushed and dragged him through the passage; indeed, he seemed rather to catch at their garments, lest they should suddenly retrace their steps and close up the entrance; and he besought them, in the most piteous terms, not to imprison him in the vault without a chance of escape.

"'I shall starve—I shall certainly starve in

this cavern! For God's sake, if you would murder me by inches, gentlemen, let me be tied to a tree, and die in the light of day.'

" He spoke; but his pleadings did not for an instant defer a fate more appalling than any he yet anticipated: a fate which Providence alone prevented me from sharing, as the nearness of the ruffians now was all that hindered me from penetrating farther into the cavern, when my instant doom would have been that which was intended only for my poor patron. But, fearful of my footfalls being heard, I remained still; placing my body in a cleft of the rock, while the whole party groped their way along the wall, so near to me that, while by a miracle they failed to touch me, it seemed as if the beatings of my heart must have been audible. They paused within two yards in advance of where I stood.

"'Are we near it, Angus?' cried the captain.

"'Hand me a stone, and I'll try; or do you chuck one before me from where you stand.'

"The stone was thrown. It seemed long in coming to the earth, but at last, after one or two rebounds, which sounded hollowly against the sides of a deep pit, it reached its destination, and the last faint echo seemed to rise from beneath the very spot where we were standing.

"'By G——!' cried the ruffian pioneer, 'I am on the brink of the precipice myself; one step more, and I should have pulled you all to h—l along with me! Stand exactly where you are, captain; and you and Humphrey take the Yankee nigger by his shoulders. Jim, do you move this way—step carefully though, G—— d——n you—and seize the other leg.'

"'Ah, I take the idea.'

"'Are you all ready?' said the captain, when the victim was secured in the manner indicated, and swung like a pendulum between the four; 'have you got a fair hold, Jim?'

"'Yes—but we'd better yet have a light— my place here in front is cursed pokerish.'

"The suggestion awakened the hope of a moment's respite in the pedler's bosom.

"'Yes, a light—a light in the name of Jesus the merciful, gentlemen!—let me look on my death—let me see your faces! Ye are changed into fiends, are ye—since we came into this horrible place—I cannot—I will not—I—' Here his struggles became so violent that I lost the rest that he said. A burst of merriment, that rung like the laughter of demons through the vault, told that this last effort for liberty was fruitless; and, overcome with exhaustion, he lay panting upon the floor of the cavern.

"'Now for a game of Alligator, Jim.'

"'As quick as you please, captain; he'll launch easily, now, if you'll give the word at once.'

"'Lift,' said the captain.

"'All up,' was the answer.

"'Now then, together, boys.'

"'One to make ready.'

"'Two to show.'

"'Three to make ready.'

"'And four to g—o !'

"A hideous yell of more than mortal agony drowned the last word. To give force to the heave, they had swung the pedler's body so far back the fourth time, that the hair of his head actually grazed my body. The cry of his parting soul seemed to spring at first from my own bosom—it swelled to its highest pitch in the moment that he was launched over the brink of the abyss—and it died away in a hissing moan a thousand feet below me. A dull reverberation from the falling body followed, and then all was still.

" 'Well, Yankee, you'll tell no tales,' said the ruffian called Humphrey, who had not before spoken, and who seemed more of a novice at such business than the others. The party then left the cavern in silence, as if the affair, once despatched, was not worth an afterthought. I stood for some time transfixed with horror. The whole scene had passed amid total darkness, the dropping vault of the cavern near the entrance not allowing the light of day to penetrate thus far into these now accursed chambers; and I felt like one who had intruded upon some doings of the damned, deep within the bowels of the earth. At last, moved by better feelings, reckless whether or not any of the gang might hear me, if still loitering about the place, I shouted to my ill-fated friend as the idea flashed across me that life might possibly yet linger in his mutilated form. I screamed to him at the top of my voice, and a dismal howl seemed to answer from the gulf; I shrieked again, but heard only as before the same fearful echo to my own voice. The place had been turned into a grave, and *that* gives no reply. A supersti tious terror seized upon me; I felt as if some- thing were dragging me backward to that horrid chasm, and groping anxiously till I met a ray of light from the entrance of the cavern, I rushed from it in an agony of fear, the bitterest I have ever known.

"The land pirates had disappeared, without molesting my tackey, who soon carried me to a safer region farther east. Abingdon, in Wash- ington county, Virginia, was the first place where I ventured to stop and seek employment. The valley used to be a beautiful green basin among the hills in those days; and here the principal hotel being in want of a barkeeper, I was glad to fill a station, among people who knew nothing about me, which, at the same time that it was comfortable in itself, gave me an opportunity of mixing, after a fashion, with all the young bucks and politicians. There were too, at that time, many of your real old-fashioned Virginny gentlemen in Abingdon; good fellows, who wouldn't disdain to hold a chat with a white man while mixing a julep, though he did stand behind a bar. Well, during all the two years I was there, I never let out where I came from nor where I was going to. Jacobs was the name I bore, and under this name I used to mingle with all sorts of people during court-week, and pick up something about books and manners, which has served my turn ever since. For you may depend, that a man can never play gentleman well, unless he has served some sort of apprenticeship to it; and that, I take it, is the reason why in our northern cities, where fortunes are made so quick, you so often see servants better bred than their masters. Well, after I had laid up a little money, and learnt how your quality folks conduct themselves toward each other, I left Abingdon, and made my way to Charleston, on the Kenhawa, where I fitted myself out with some new clothes, and took my passage in a salt-boat to Cincinnati. Here I provided myself with a pair of saddle-bags, and a stock of medicines to fill them, crossed over into Kentucky, and bought a good horse at Georgetown, and then returning to Ohio, took up my line of march for the interior.

" Now, it chanced that about this time the breaking out of the war had brought some levies of Western volunteers and drafted militia, on their way to the frontier, to the village of Urbanna, where I had put up, announcing myself as Dr. Peabody. Well, most of the officers

were real harem-scarem fellows; they seemed
to be marching in loose detachments, loitering
from day to day for the baggage to come up,
and drinking confusion every night to those in
authority, who had as yet, not even made any
medical provision for so large a body of men.
In fact, disease had already broken out among
them, from robbing the orchards as they came
along; and during a halt of three days, I made
myself so useful and agreeable, in prescribing
for the sick and frolicking with the well, that
by the time the general and his staff came up
with the fourth regiment of infantry, who joined
us at this point, every officer had signed a
paper, which I soon set afloat, recommending
me as an army surgeon. And, in fact, soon
after I received a demi-official appointment as
assistant-surgeon of the drafted forces. I was
already mounted, and my blue coat was soon

converted into a uniform, by clapping a collar of black velvet on it, and sticking a button on either side. I appropriated the sword of a dead drummer as my fee for easing him off handsomely, during an attack of cholera morbus, which compelled him to beat his last tattoo: and now Surgeon Peabody, who was already a favourite with the officers, could ruffle it with the best of them. My tavern experience had given me a knowledge of the kitchen, which made my services highly valued by some of the old cocks in catering for the mess; and I had a sort of knowledge of life, which took mightily with the younkers.

"The presence of so large a body of regulars, infused something like discipline into our ranks, and our men reached the Miami of the lakes in such good condition, that I began to have quite an opinion of my medical skill; when my talents as a surgeon were put to their first proof, in a way that took the conceit out of me a little.

" I was one day holding a pleasant talk with a militia colonel, who rode at the head of his division, when I was suddenly called to the rear, to look after a man that had been accidentally shot through the arm by a fellow volunteer, who, to exhibit at once his soldierly discipline and skill as a marksman, had discharged his rifle across the face of the platoon in which he was marching, at a squirrel that was skipping along a log by the roadside. The wounded man was sitting upon the log when I reached the spot, and all so covered with blood, that I could hardly find the place of his hurt. Not knowing exactly how to treat a gunshot wound, I still thought common sense dictated that the first thing to be done, was to plug up the hole which the bullet had made, and I therefore tried very hard to fill it with a pledget of tow ; but all my squeezing and pushing, only made the blood flow the faster; the tow was forced out as fast as I stuck it in, and at last I saw that nothing could be done until I had got this effusion of blood under. I had more than once assisted my old masters at ordinary bleedings, and had sometimes helped to tie the bandages afterwards: and these, I remembered, always stopped the flow of blood from the veins, by being tied below the venesection; and, God forgive me, but I never dreamt of there being such a thing as an artery, much less did I know any thing of the circulation of the blood when I clapped a tourniquet below the wound, upon that poor fellow's arm. He bled like an ox; and seeing that I could do nothing to stop it, I told his friends, who had left the ranks to gather round him, that he was mortally wounded, and beyond the reach of surgery. I helped to place him upon a smooth stump, that he might go off with some comfort, and felt mightily relieved at the kind manner in which he welcomed his fate; especially when I used to think afterward of the tomahawking upon the river Raisin, which he thus escaped. The last thing I heard him say, before I left him to his friends, and resumed my place in the line, was addressed to the man that shot him, in these terms: ' Well, Evert, don't be cast down now, because you've done for me; I'll allow it was a nation bad shot at the squirrel, and that's enough to make you feel ugly; but as for your hitting me, why that was all along of my bad luck; only tell the old man that I died game. Kiss Nan for me, and take good care of my mare, poor cretur, she'll break her legs between some of these cursed logs, afore the campaign's ove—r.' The last word was uttered with a sort of hiccough, and the backwoodsman fainted, never to revive again, as they told me afterwards.

"My next case was rather more fortunate, being taken off my hands before I could enter fairly upon its treatment. I had been left in the rear with some sick men, who, as soon as convalescent, joined a company of Ohio volunteers, who, under the command of Captain Brush, had arrived at the river Raisin with supplies for the army. Major Van Horn, you may remember, was sent with a detachment from Detroit to escort Brush's company to head-quarters, but was used up by Tecumseh, near Brownstown, before he could join us. A larger force was therefore sent to perform this duty; and when I learned from a scout that Colonel Miller, with three hundred regulars of the gallant 4th, the old Tippecanoe regiment, was marching towards us, I volunteered to push through the woods, and warn him that

Major Muir of the Britishers, was waiting for
him at Magagua, with a large force of Indians
and regulars. Making a circuit through the
woods, I reached Muir's position, just as Cap-
tain Snelling, who commanded the American
advance, had entered the ambuscade, and the
Indians broke their cover. The red-skins had
a cool chap to deal with in Snelling. The
painted devils came yelling upon him as if
they had their fingers already twisted in the
scalps of his men. But—Lord, it's pleasant
to see regulars fight—why, Snelling did not
even think it worth while to fall back on the
main body. His little corps there kept its
ground until Miller came up, and made the
British regulars, who had moved to the support
of the Indians, give way before his solid charge;
i'faith, it was Greek meeting Greek. There are
no troops better with the bayonet than the
British, but Miller is just the fellow to lead

men of blood as good as theirs. The battle though was not yet over. Tecumseh drew off his Indians to the woods on each side of our people, and fought from tree to tree, and bush to bush, as if he meant to make each inch of ground his last halting-place. The British regulars rallied with desperate rivalry of their Indian allies; and then came a sight I have never seen but that once, though they tell me the same thing happened at Bridgewater — bayonet crossed bayonet, and the opposing columns met and waved to and fro for a moment in one reeling line of bristling steel; while near them the painted Indians, who yelled like demons as they rushed from the forest to aid in turning the fortunes of the day, were fighting hand to hand with the grim backwoodsmen. It was strange, when the crisis of the instant was over, to see the order that came out of such confusion, when the British, though borne down by the furious charge of Baker, Sarabie, and Peters, kept closing up their ranks, and retreated to their boats as coolly as if upon field-parade. The stars and stripes never had a braver sword to guard them than that wielded by Ensign Whistler on that day; but old England's banner waved hardly less proudly even in defeat.

"Ah! it's a pretty sight to see real soldiers cut each other's throats in a business-like way, and I was peskily worried when they called me off as I sat upon the breastwork from which the reserve of the enemy had been driven, to look after the poor devils whose business had been only half done for them. The first wounded man they brought me had been bored through the thigh by a British bayonet. It was but a boy, and I did not wonder that he howled like a wild Indian, when I applied the probe to his hurt as he lay upon the rampart.

Not knowing what next to do, I told a couple of fellows to move him, when, just as one had raised his head, a ball took him right through the throat, and freed me at the same time from patient and assistant. The man that was helping him, threw a kind o' back somerset from the breastwork. He seemed to think at first that nothing but the shock of the fall disabled him so suddenly. He floundered about so curiously in trying to regain his feet, striking out the while, for all the world like an awkward swimmer, or a chicken that beats his wings when the cook wrings his head off, that I could not forbear from laughing; though I tell you it made me feel all over, when, with a wriggle of his neck, he suddenly came to a stand-still, with eyes broad open, and so set in death upon my own face, that they appeared to look me through and through. I have often heard soldiers laugh in battle when a gunshot wound makes a comrade cut these antics in dying, and you know we do become kind o' heathens about such matters; but, seeing that I was not then a soldier, I never could forgive myself for laughing at that poor fellow's expiring agonies.

"The regular surgeon, who accompanied Miller's detachment took the worst cases off my hands that day, and my next opportunities of practice were in the fever-hospital of Detroit, where I had not been many days, before the vacillating movements of Hull upon the opposite side of the river, began to dispirit the whole army, which, as is always the case, soon swelled the sick list, and I was superseded in my duty by an older and more capable surgeon. My patients were spread out upon the floor in their blankets when this officer came to relieve me of their charge, and examine me as to the course of treatment I had pursued. 'Well, to business, to business, doctor,' said he, turning up his nose, and filling it with a huge pinch of snuff, as he first scented the apartment upon entering it; "you get along with these poor fellows, eh—eh? Not lose many of them I hope, eh, doctor, eh?'

" 'Why, sir, when the river is at as low a stage as it is now, with no wind from the lower lakes to prevent the water from running out and exposing the decomposing matter upon the banks, they tell me that this country-fever is incurable. My Creole assistant, the other day told me that a man who had just died, introduced him to a New Orleans acquaintance in going off; and since then we have had ten other cases of black vomit.'

" 'Eh—indeed—hum—hah—we—eh—we must be mum about all that sort o' thing— bad, very bad—plenty of calomel in the medicine chest though, I suppose?'

" 'Yes, sir, some ; also some salts. In exhibiting my remedies, I administer both medicines in equal quantities, in order that one shall not become exhausted before the other. This I call the saline side of the room, and the row of patients opposite are all under the influence of calomel.'

" 'Ah—eh—indeed—strange mode of treatment, but military, eh? Doctor you draw your men up in regular lines for their last march. Good! ha! ha! ha! hum! But from which platoon do you count off the most convalescent?'

" 'The average of cures is about the same, sir, upon either side; is it not, Alphonse?' said I, turning to my Creole assistant, who at that moment approached us.

" 'Oui, monsieur—certainement—we buries about de same from both rows every day.'

" But confound those hospital days, it always makes me gloomy to talk them over. I had

been making interest for a commission long be-
fore I was relieved from my disagreeable duty
in this place; a friendly representation of one
or two little things which I had done in the
way of knocking down an Indian or so, while
mingling as an amateur in the affair of Magagua,
procured me an ensign's commission, which I
received just in time to include me among the
regulars as a prisoner of war, in Hull's capitu-
lation; but as the militia were allowed to re-
turn to their homes after the fall of Detroit, I
thought it better to pocket my unseasonable
honours and march off as plain Dr. Peabody.
The circumstance afterwards gave rise to a dis-
pute as to the actual date of commission, and
my consequent place in the line of my pro-
motion; but the only officer whose rank thus
jostled with mine was fool enough to force a
hostile meeting upon me two years afterward,
when, you know, a proper regard to the situa-

tion of my name upon the army-list, compelled
me to shoot him.

" Poor Raffles, we were at one time more
intimate than any two men in the mess. We
both of us played the flute, and were in the
habit of practising duets together; and though
our fight was all arranged six weeks before it
took place, yet we kept up our music as usual
till the last. The thing happened pretty much
in this way: You see, one night, out of sheer
kindness, I had volunteered to carry a challenge
for a poor devil, whom his brother officers had
put in Coventry, because he was seen taking a
scalp, like a wild Indian, upon the field of
battle. He came and told me of having been
grievously insulted, without ever letting off
that my friend Raffles was the man who had
put upon him; and knowing that no officer in
the regiment would stand by the forlorn cretur,
I, out of sheer kindness, offered to carry his

message. The paper was written right off hand; several other officers were standing by at the time, and, though it made me feel a little ridiculous when I saw my principal coolly put the name of my most intimate friend upon the back of the note, you know it was too late to withdraw from my pledge.

" Poor Harry, how he stared when I gave him the note.

" ' Why, Jake,' he cried, ' d—n it, what's the meaning of this ? you don't mean to stand in that fellow's shoes, do you?'

" ' In his shoes? why, God's weather! Harry, you will meet the man, won't you?'

" ' My dear Jake, can you expect me to put myself upon a level with a scoundrel who has actually scalped a British officer? What the devil possessed you to thrust yourself into such a business as this?'

" ' That is neither here nor there, Mr.

Raffles; the person of whom you speak stands in the relation of my friend at present, and I cannot hear you talk in that style about him.'

" ' Mr. Raffles! your friend? Well, sir, you know best how to play your own game, and for my part I shall use the privilege which the laws of honour allow in these matters. I will meet the representative of your friend, sir. I will—but stay—d—n it, Jake, let the thing lie over till to-morrow morning, and I'll try and make up my mind to meet your principal.'

" ' It is for your pleasure to determine that matter, Raffles. My friend, you know, is no shot, and I—'

" ' And you are the best in the regiment. I see the inference that may be drawn. I thank you for the hint. Mr. Peabody, I will send a friend to you in the morning. I wish you a good night, sir.'

" Now blister my blistering tongue; I never

meant my friend to give such a turn to this last suggestion; I merely intended to hint that he might meet my scalping friend, and tap him gently in the shoulder without exposing himself to any inconvenience, and so the affair might pass up to the satisfaction of all parties; but Raffles, when his honour was concerned, was just one of those fiery fellows that will go off upon a half-cock in the hands of the friends who try to guide him.

" Well, the morning came, but the affair was still in abeyance. My principal had been ordered off, with a detachment for supplies, in the course of the night. He was not expected to return for a month, and all the officers agreed that Raffles ought not to make public any decision in regard to his choice of an antagonist, until Scalpy, as he was generally called, should return among us. In the mean time, when the first sensation of this affair had blown over, our winter-quarters were as dull as ever, and for want of something else to amuse us, Raffles and I resumed our flute practising. Occasionally, too, when the weather would permit, we took our fowling-pieces and went out together after wild-ducks. I don't think, however, that we were exactly the same to each other as formerly; neither of us would, of course, show any concern as to what might happen, before the other officers; but we had mighty little to say to each other when alone. We became, somehow, cooler and cooler, until it was no longer ' Jake' and ' Harry,' but ' Mr. Raffles,' and ' Mr. Peabody.' Still, however, we kept up our fluting until the source of all this mischief came back to camp. And sorry enough were both of us, I guess, to see him. He had been on a long tramp, through woods alive with out-lying Indians, and the chances were ten to one that some of Tecumseh's people would have made dogsmeat of him. But your bad penny, somehow, always comes back to hand. The fellow did return safe and sound, and we had to make the best of it. He had been living all the while hand and glove with the vilest of his rangers, and returned more coarse and vulgar than ever. Raffles could not bring himself to acknowledge such a chap as his equal; and I, though I wished the varmint to the devil, was obliged to fight his battles for him. We met—poor Harry and I. His pistol snapped, and I threw away my first fire; but I did it so unskilfully, that he saw I meant to let him off, and became furious for another exchange of shots. The truth is, the man was mad. The doom of bad luck had gone out against him, and his eyes were sot' upon hurrying to his fate. I shot my friend through the heart, sir, and rose one on the army-list."

The major here gave a dry cough, while a slight trembling of his eyelids betrayed that he was not the wholly emotionless being that he would paint himself.

" It was soon after this that General Winchester had orders to break up his cantonment near the mouth of the Au Glaize, and push forward to the Rapids, which we reached through the deep snows of mid-winter, with about one thousand effective men. Here we received those expresses from the inhabitants of Frenchtown, urging us to march upon the enemy near that point. The appeal fired the souls of our officers, who burned for action. The gallant Colonel Allen, who took a conspicuous part in Winchester's military council, advocated an. immediate movement. A corps, composed of regulars and Kentucky volunteers was organized, and the command given to Colonel Lewis. We reached the river Raisin, which was covered by thick and strong ice. The British and Indians were posted among the straggling houses along the banks. They were apprized of our approach, and we displayed and marched forward under the fire of musketry and how-itzers. The battalions of Graves and Maddison, preceded by Ballard's light infantry, charged across the river, and dislodged the enemy from the houses and pickets. The Indians fought like fiends incarnate, and Reynolds twice rallied his Englishmen to the charge; but Allen, with the Kentucky brigade, dashed amid a shower of bullets upon his left, and the fortune of the day was soon ours.

" But never was a victory attended with such disastrous consequences. Infatuated with our success, we determined to maintain our position, though no provision had been made by our commander-in-chief, to strengthen us in a proper manner. We had not a single piece of artillery; and though General Winchester himself joined us with two hundred and fifty men, yet the most ordinary precautions to keep our troops together were neglected; nor did he even place a picket guard upon the only road by which our position could be conveniently approached. Our force consisted altogether of only seven hundred and fifty men, and many of those lay encamped in open field, when, on the morning of the fatal twenty-second, Proctor came down upon us with a combined force of fifteen hundred British and Indians, and six pieces of artillery. The body of men belonging to the encampment were instantly overpowered, and my company and another, which sallied out to their rescue were at once cut off; I, only, with a couple of privates, making good my retreat within the line of our picketing defences. The artillery, in the mean time, opened upon this slight breastwork of pickets, while the British forty-first charged under cover of the fire; no soldiers could come on more coolly and steadily, but the British bayonet was no match then for the Kentucky rifle. They made three successive assaults, but at each time were driven back with heavy loss. The terrible slaughter in his ranks now made Proctor pause. The general, and half of our little force, were already in his hands; and though he had the means of crushing the rest of us, it could only be done with immense loss to himself. He sent a flag proposing a surrender, but we rejected his terms.

"Our volunteers consisted chiefly of gentlemen; young lawyers, physicians, Kentucky planters, and other people of condition, each of whom, though serving as a private, had an individual character as well as his country's honour, to sustain; and all of us were well armed, and elated with the repulse we had already given the enemy. We had yet thirty-five officers and four hundred and fifty men, after fighting six hours against artillery and five hundred British troops, backed by a thousand savages.

" Proctor sent another flag, with better terms ; but his message hinted something about the fate we were likely to meet at the hands of his red allies in case he was compelled to carry the place by assault; while the Indians yelled, during the brief conference, like wolves ravening for their prey. This, however, instead of scaring us into compliance, only served to rally our men. It was, in fact, only a roundabout way of bullying, to say the best of it. We again rejected his terms, and resolved to make a die of it.

" But Proctor was too many for us ; it was in his power to use us up, and he was determined to do it, only after his own fashion. He now sent a third flag, with a communication from our general, that he, General Winchester, had surrendered us as prisoners of war, under an explicit engagement that we were to be protected in our persons and private property, and have our side-arms returned to us. And now came the first dissensions among our little force. Some were wearied out with the toil of the day, and ready at once to adopt the terms of capitulation; others were more full of fight than ever, and eager to go ahead; some argued that it was mutinous not to come into the terms which our commanding-officer had made for us; and others, again, insisted that, being a prisoner in the hands of the enemy, he had no right to make terms for us. But Winchester, though wanting in conduct as a general, was as benevolent as he was brave, and had still the love and confidence of most of us: his advice, rather than his order, prevailed, and we surrendered. Never did men do a weaker thing than surrender themselves, with arms in their hands, to such an enemy as Proctor, with the hope that a fellow, whom Tecumseh afterwards rowed up Salt river, as well for his want of faith as his inefficiency in using injuns, could protect them against a horde of infuriated savages.*   I

* When General Proctor began to prepare for retreating from Malden, Tecumseh, having learned his intention, demanded an interview, and, in the name of all the Indians, remonstrated in these terms :

" Summer before last, when I came forward with my red brethren, and took up the hatchet for my British father, you told us to bring our women and children to this place, and we did so ; you also promised to take care of them—they should want for nothing, while the men would go and fight the Americans.   You also told your red children that you would take good care of your own garrison here, which made our hearts glad.

" Father, listen !—Our fleet has gone out—we know they have fought—we have heard the great guns—but we know nothing of what has happened to our father with one arm.*   Our ships have gone one way, and we are

* Commodore Barclay, of the British flotilla on Lake Erie.

don't know whether or not the man quailed before the ferocious demands of his allies, but notwithstanding the humane remonstrance of his own officers, he did not leave a guard of British soldiers for his prisoners, as he had

much astonished to see our father tying up every thing and preparing to run away the other, without letting his red children know what his intentions are. You always told us to remain here, and take care of our lands; it made our hearts glad to hear that was your wish. Our great father, the king, is the head, and you represent him. You always told us you would never draw your foot off British ground. But now, father, we see you are drawing back, and we are sorry to see our father doing so without seeing the enemy. We must compare our father's conduct to a fat dog, that carries its tail upon its back, but, when affrighted, it drops it between his legs and runs off.

" Father!—You have got the arms and ammunition which our great father sent for his red children. If you have an idea of going away, give them to us, and you may go and welcome for us. Our lives are in the hands of the Great Spirit. We are determined to defend our lands; and, if it be His will, we wish to leave our bones upon them."—*Thatcher's Indian Biography.*

pledged himself. The Indians were set on drinking blood, and he marched off with his regulars, leaving them to revel in it. Contrary to express stipulations, the swords were taken from the sides of our officers, and then, unarmed, and stripped almost naked, our prisoners were left to be driven by the Indians in the rear of the English forces upon their retrograde march to Malden. Few, however, ever reached that British garrison. Many were slaughtered upon the spot. Some were carried off to be roasted at the stake by the bands of savages, that from time to time dropped off from the main body, and stole home to make merry with their captives at a feast of blood. But the most gallant and distinguished of our officers perished upon the spot. I saw Colonel Allen, with four kinsmen of the same name, the youngest a boy of seventeen, butchered within a hundred yards of the Raisin. Simpson, the member of congress, with Majors Madison and Ballard, and Captains Bledsoe, Hickman, Mason, Woolfolk, Kelly, M'Cracken, Williams, and Hamilton, with many a private who had the best blood of Kentucky in his veins, all perished in that field of slaughter. Young Hart, the kinsman of Harry Clay, who claimed the protection of an old college chum that he met in the British ranks, was dragged, wounded, from his horse, and tomahawked and scalped like the rest. It made my flesh crawl to hear the shrieks of those dying men as they howled curses upon the unheeding Proctor, mingled with bitter imprecations upon their own folly in trusting to the mercy of such a foe. But this was not the worst scene which that day presented.

"There were about sixty of our people, who

being wounded or ill, had sought shelter from the cold in the house of a Canadian on the banks of the Raisin. Some had crawled thither amid the confusion of the fight, others had been conveyed there by friends immediately after the surrender, and a few, like myself, had sought the place to look after a wounded comrade. The rear-guard of the British regulars had scarce taken up their line of march before this house was beset by the savages and fired in a dozen places. I was kneeling on the floor in an upper story beside a poor fellow, who, fevered with his wounds, was swallowing eagerly a handful of snow which I had just reached to him from the window-sill, when I heard the Indians whooping beneath the window, and smelt the smoke coming up the passage-way. Almost at the same moment there was a simultaneous cry among the wounded in the room below us, followed by a rush toward the door, and yells and groans of agony, as the savages, rushing into the entry, brained those who attempted to escape with their tomahawks. A heavy burst of smoke, which seemed to come up from the cellar, succeeded; and looking out, I saw the Indians springing by dozens from the window below me. But while these thus hastened to escape from being stifled, as many more were pouring into the house to snatch their scalps from the inmates before the fire could consume them. The fire had as yet only burst into flame in the cellar, and the wet clapboards on the outside of the house smoked like a pile of green timber with live coals beneath it. The Indians as yet had not come up to where we were, and when we heard the live flames roaring below, some prayed for the fate of their friends who had but now perished with the tomahawk; others, though half stifled with smoke, seemed only to dread the Indians, who yelled like wild devils as they glanced in and out from the building. But now came a grand crash, which seemed to tell that their fate, whatever it might be, was at hand. The floor in the room below gave way, and the sharp yells of sudden agony which mingled with the moans of the dying prisoners, told that some of the savages must have gone down with it. I could hear some of them, too, exhorting each other as they clung to the steep staircase above them, and tried to mount to the place of momentary safety where we were. But two succeeded; and the shaven crowns and begrimed faces of these emerged through the well of the staircase along with a burst of flame, which seemed, as it were, to hoist them into our room like demons lifted upon their native element. God's weather! had you seen those horrible faces glowering upon you from out the fire, you would have cowered in a corner as I did.

" The devils! instead of making at once for the window, and escaping from the house, as I thought they would, they began at once to pay about them with their scalping-knives. They never stopped to tomahawk men who were too feeble to resist, but peeled their heads as readily as you would strip the skin from a ripe peach. Accident, or the eddying smoke-wreaths which came thicker and thicker into the apartment, prevented their seeing me until one of them had engaged in a death-grapple with a stout sergeant, who, being only wounded in his knee-pan, could make good fight with the fellow who threw himself upon his body to take his scalp.

" The first sound of resistance put new life into my limbs, and I braced myself for a tussle with the other savage, in the same moment that a puff of wind, wrapping the combatants from view, revealed me to the Indian who was spring-ing to the assistance of his comrade. He turned upon me so abruptly that he stumbled over a dead body by my side, and I flung myself upon him, and plucked his scalping-knife from the floor, as it stood quivering where his hand had drove it in falling. He was a stout and heavy savage; and though not slow myself at wrestling, he turned me under him at the first grapple and planted his fingers at my throat with a grip like an armourer's vice. The knife was still in my hand, but it was bent nearly double; and if I had lifted my arm he would have wrenched it from me to a certainty. I pretended, therefore, to be quite spent while straightening the knife by pressing the blade beneath my wrist against the floor. The next moment I made another struggle—the Indian raised himself a little to get a better hold, and then, as he came down with his full weight upon my body, I slipped aside so adroitly, that the knife, which I had raised on the butt-end, entered his bosom clean up to the haft, and the warm blood, spouting over my face, made it as red as his own.

"All this, as you may conceive, passed in less time than I take in telling it. Yet even in that space of time the fire had gained upon us fearfully, and put an end to the fight of the sergeant and his Indian in the same moment that I despatched mine. The rafters on the opposite side of the room gave way; and the white and red man, with hands clutched in each other's hair, were plunged amid the roaring flames below.

"Now the sight of those flames was just what saved my life after all. I seized my Indian's blanket, to shield me from the fire until I could reach the window, and sprang with it wrapped around me among the crowd of devils who were howling for blood below. I fell into a deep snow-bank, which covered my boots and trousers as did the blanket my body. My hair was burnt off, and my face, red with blood, and begrimmed with smoke, made me look so much like a real Indian, that, having plenty to do on their own account, the others let one of their comrades, as they thought me, lie there like an old log. The roof fell in soon afterwards; the flames shot high into the air, and the smoke and embers rolled far and wide, as the sides of the house came crashing down in the midst of the flames. The savages gave an exulting yell, as if contented that they had done their worst, and then trooped like a pack of ravening wolves after the detachment of prisoners which followed in Proctor's rear. Few of them, as we know, ever reached Malden; and for a fact, I thought at the time when I crawled half-frozen from that snow-bank, that my chance was probably the luckiest in all the army that was captivated on the river Raisin.

"The wolves had succeeded their Indian

brothers, and were already busy upon the dead when I crept from my hiding-place. The night was raw and gusty, and the snappish growl of the creturs, as they quarrelled over the food, when there was enough for all of them, the varmints! sounded on the fitful blast like the wrangling of Christian men. There was no need of making a circuit to avoid them, for though by the light of the snow we could see each other as plain as day, they did not even stop to look at me as I crossed the clearings to get to the woods in the rear of Frenchtown. This I didn't do though without meeting with a sort o' interruption which was queer, to say the least of it. There was a little knoll near the banks of the Raisin which I rather chose to go round than to cross over the top, thinking that it was not best to bring my body clean against the sky as a mark for any loitering drunken Indian that might still by possibility be outlying near the scene of his hellish orgies. Well, as I wound round the hillock and got within a hundred yards of the forest, which was close upon it, what should I meet upon the other side but a great buck bear, who had just dragged a body around the opposite side of the knoll, and was under full sail for the woods in the very direction that I was steering for them. The brute might have been a few paces in advance of me when I stumbled upon him, and he seemed considerably taken aback, though he had no idea of dropping his prize. A half-starved, half-frozen man has not much active courage to spare, but if he has gone through scenes such as I witnessed that day, he feels pretty indifferent as to what next may turn up on his hands. It seemed to warm my natur, too, within me, to have something upon which I could pour the vengeful feelings that I felt just then ag'inst all creation; and though armed with nothing but my dead Indian's scalping-knife, I made a spring toward the bear and planted my foot upon the body he was dragging. The cretur let go the other end, and sat right up on his hinderparts, looking first at me and then at the dead body, but never offering to harm me. The moon at that moment broke through a cloud, and, for the first time, I saw that it was only an Indian that my opposite neighbour was carrying off for his supper, and I thought there was such a sort of gravity about his appeal in looking from me to the Indian, and from the Indian to me, as if the dumb brute know'd that I had only made a mistake and didn't mean to molest him wantonly, that I took off my foot, stepped backward a pace or two, and let him pass on. But bears have their hour of fate as well as men; for this one had not gone twenty steps farther when I heard the crack of a rifle, and he tumbled over in the snow, scratching his head with his fore-paws in a way that showed a bullet must have gone through it. In a moment afterward, leaving time only to reload, a white hunter stepped from the edge of the forest, and levelling his rifle upon me beckoned with his forefinger for me to come into him, addressing me at the same time in the half-French, half-Indian lingo at that time prevailing in this district—'Venez ici needji.'

" 'Throw up your shooting-iron, and don't call me *needji*, old gumbo, unless you mean friend and not Indian by it. I'm a half-starved white man, and should like a bit of your bear that you knocked over so handsomely.'

" 'Nesheshin—chemocomow! ah! c'est bon, Monsieur c'est un Americain,' he rejoined, advancing from the edge of the wood, and giving me his hand. I saw at once that it was an old gumbo hunter, and knowing what a guileless set they are I felt instantly at ease, for one of his class was the only man who could now help me out of those infernal woods, and guide me to the nearest United States' post.

"I helped him to drag the wounded bear within the forest so soon as he had despatched him with his tomahawk. A few moments sufficed to flay him, and then, after cutting some tender bits from the carcass, we retired deeper into the woods to sup upon bruin, who, half an hour before, might have made a supper of me. The wood we were in was only a narrow belt dividing the Frenchtown settlement from a large wet prairie, which we were obliged to circuit for some miles before taking up a direct route for the Rapids, whither I prevailed upon the Frenchman to guide me. In summer time the tall reeds of this prairie would have afforded ample shelter in traversing it, if indeed it be possible, but it was now only a frozen snowy waste, where the figure of a man might have been descried for miles, and I felt considerably relieved when we had safely navigated along the borders and got in the deep forest to the south. I needn't tell of all I suffered in struggling through the heavy snows until I reached Carrying River, to which Harrison, after hearing of the disaster of Frenchtown, had retreated, for the purpose of forming a junction with the troops in his rear. I arrived here in such a condition that I was placed at once upon the sick list.

" After that I was pretty much useless to myself and to all others till after the war; when, at the reduction of the army I was dropped like many a more deserving fellow who like myself lacked the education to do his country credit upon her peace establishment. Uncle Sam gave me some broad lands in the far west, however, but though one of his territorial governors promised to commission me in a corps of rangers, in case I settled upon them, I somehow could never go to them flat western prairies. I longed for the woods and mountains of Old York State. I swapped my bounty-lands for one thing and another that I could turn into ready money, until I was able to buy me a farm down among the hills of Montgomery county; from which I can easily take a run up among these mountains whenever it jumps with my humour; and that's all I've got to tell you about Old Major Jake Peabody. He's not so old though neither except from his experience in studying human natur."

Though sometimes losing the phraseology of the worthy Major in repeating the history he gave of his adventures, the conclusion being precisely in his own words, will give the reader some idea of the conceit that was blended with a character at once shrewd and simple, and often recklessly, if not gamesomely bold amid much habitual and inborn selfishness. There were many such men who raised themselves from the ranks in our quickly-created army of 1812-13, and being like the major, suddenly dropped from the list of its reduction, or gradually weeded out from the service by a more accomplished and high-minded race of officers, fell into penury and intemperance and finished their lives so deplorably that the gallantry of their early career has been too often forgotten in the debasement that sullied its close.

When the hour of dinner arrived, and pipes and cigars were laid aside for more substantial refreshment, the introduction of some parched corn among the condiments of our repast raised a discussion between "the barrister" and myself, as to the Asiatic, or American origin of this

great staple of our farmers; and upon asking
the opinion of Captain Gill, as to how the maze
was first obtained, the old chief nodded to
one of his dusky satellites, who straightway set
the question at rest for ever by giving an ex-
planation, of which the following is the pur-
port.

CHAPTER IV.

THE ORIGIN OF INDIAN CORN.

" THERE is a place on the banks of the softly-flowing Unadilla, not far from its confluence with the Susquehannah, which in former years was an extensive beaver-meadow. The short turf sloped down almost to the brink of the stream, whose banks in this place nourish not a single tree to shadow its waters. Here, where they flow over pebbles so smooth and shiny that the Indian maid who wandered along the margin, would pause to count over her strings of wampum, and think the beads had slipped

away, there came one day some girls to bathe;
and one, the most beautiful of all, lingered be-
hind her companions to gather these bright
pebbles from the bed of the river.

" A water-spirit who had assumed the form
of a musquosh, sat long watching her from the
shore.   He looked at her shining shoulders—
at her dripping locks, and the gently swelling
bosom over which they fell; and when the maid
lifted her rounded limbs from the water, and
stepped lightly upon the green sod, he too raised
himself from the mossy nook where he had been
hidden, and recovering his own shape, ran to
embrace her.

" The maiden shrieked and fled, but the
enamoured spirit pressed closely in pursuit, and
the meadow affording no shrub nor covert to
screen her from her eager pursuer, she turned
again towards the stream she had left, and made
for a spot where the wild flowers grew tall and

rankly by the moist margin. The spirit still followed her; and, frightened and fatigued, the girl would have sunk upon the ground as he approached, had she not been supported by a tuft of flags while hastily seizing and twining them around her person to hide her shame.

"In that moment her slender form grew thinner and more rounded; her delicate feet became indurated in the loose soil that opened to receive them; the blades of the flag broadened around her fingers, and enclosed her hand; while the pearly pebbles that she held resolved themselves into milky grains, which were kept together by the plaited husk.

"The baffled water-spirit sprang to seize her by the long hair that yet floated in the breeze, but the silken tassels of the rustling maze was all that met his grasp."

CHAPTER V.

THE HUES OF AUTUMN.

A GLORIOUS sunset succeeded the day of storms, and all our arrangements being completed for a grand hunt on the morrow, I sallied out to observe the effect of the golden light upon the rainbow foliage of autumn still dripping with the shower. Accompanied by Major Jake, and guided by one of the Indians, we made our way to an elevation some distance from the lake, commanding an extensive view of the unbroken forest that rose in billowy masses on every side.

The hillock where we paused was surmounted by the slight remains of one of those singular mounds which, though not unfrequently found in the state of New York, are beheld in so much greater variety and perfection upon the prairies of the Far West; where their enormous size, not less than their profusion of numbers, astounds and bewilders the speculations of the antiquary. In ascending to the top of this one, I chanced to trip over some bones projecting from the side of the mound, where some wild animal had removed the turf while making his burrow, and I paused to ask the Indian guide if he knew any thing about them.

"Those old bones!" cried Major Jake, turning round, "why, that ignorant varmint can tell you nothing about them, squire—they were the framework of men who kicked their shins against these knobs a million of years before his people came here to scare game and scalp white folks."

The Iroquois evidently understood the words of the rough hunter, though he did not vouchsafe a reply to the slur upon his race. He did not seem, however, to take offence at the rude and officious answer to a question addressed to himself, but waiting patiently until the other had finished speaking, he drew his blanket around him, and turning with his face westward as he planted his last steps upon the summit, stood erect upon the mound. The light of the setting sun was thrown full upon his attenuated features, and lit them up with almost as ruddy a glow as that which bathed the autumnal foliage around him. He was mute for some moments, and then spoke to this effect:

"Yes! they were here before my people,

but they could not stay when we came, no more than the red man can now bide before the presence of the Long Knife. The Master of Life willed it, and our fathers swept them from the land. The Master of Life now wishes to call back his red people to the blessed gardens whence they first started, and he sends the pale-faces to drive them from the countries which they have learned to love so well as to be unwilling to leave them.

"It is good. Men were meant to grow from the earth like the oak which springs in the pine barren, or the evergreen that shoots from the ground when the tree with a falling leaf has been cut down.

"But listen, brother!—Mark you the hue that dyes every leaf upon that sumach? It is born of the red water with which its roots were nourished a thousand years ago. It is

the blood of a murdered race which flushes
every autumn over the land when yearly the
moon comes round that saw it perish from this
ground."

CHAPTER VI.

A SACONDAGA DEER-HUNT.

Up, comrades, up! the morn's awake
   Upon the mountain side,
The wild-drake's wing hath swept the lake,
And the deer has left the tangled brake,
    To drink from the rippling tide.

Up, comrades, up! the mead-lark's note,
And the plover's cry o'er the prairie float,
The squirrel he springs from his covert now
To prank it away on the chestnut bough,
Where the oriole's pendant nest high up,
    Is rocked on the swaying trees,
While the humbird sips from the harebell's cup
    As it bends to the morning breeze.

Up, comrades, up! our shallops grate
   Upon the pebbly strand,
And our stalwart hounds impatient wait
    To spring from the huntsman's hand.

THE September dawn broke brilliantly upon

Sacondaga Lake. The morning did not slowly awake with a yellow light that gradually warmed into the flush of day; but, ruddy and abrupt, the bold streaks shot from behind the mountains high into the heavens, spreading themselves on their path like the fires of the aurora borealis, and dyeing the lake, in which they were reflected, with hues as vivid as those of the pointed forests that walled its waters. We had left our camp, however, long before the stars grew dim.

The hunt was divided into three parties, each with different duties assigned to them by one who took the direction.

The first, who were the drivers, had the hounds in charge; they were to take three different routes, and slip their leashes, after a certain time had elapsed, wherever they might find themselves. They had light guns, and from knowing every creek and swamp in the country, could follow the dogs to advantage, even when on a fresh track. The second party, who were all armed with long rifles, were to go on the stations; these were old foresters, who knew every run-way for miles about, and each of whom might be relied upon as stanch at his post should the chase last for hours. The third party took the skiffs and canoes; a number of the latter being easily shifted to the adjacent waters, so that every lake within several miles of our rendezvous had two or more boats upon it. Lastly, upon a hill overlooking the cluster of lakes, was placed a keen-eyed lad, furnished with a horn, whose duty it was to blow a signal, the moment he saw the deer take the water.

My friend and myself were attached to the boat party; a skiff with light sculls fell to my lot alone, but my companion, more fortunate,

was assigned to a bark canoe with one of the
Indians. These arrangements having been
made the night before, were put in action in a
very few moments. The strand seemed alive
with figures, for a minute only, as we emerged
from the thicket wherein our wigwam was
secreted, and then, while some plunged into
the forest, and others glided in their gray
shallops around the dusky headlands, the scene
of our last night's revels became as silent as if
nothing but the chirp of the squirrel or the
scream of the jay had ever awakened its echoes.
So still indeed was it at that early hour in the
morning, when the birds had hardly begun to
rouse themselves, that I was almost startled by
the click of my own oars in the rowlocks as
they broke the glassy surface of the lake, while
I pulled with an easy stroke for a little islet,
which I had ample leisure to gain before the

dogs would be let slip. Here the drooping boughs of a tall hemlock, which seemed to flourish not less luxuriantly because the towering stem above them was scathed and blasted, screened my boat from view as I ran her under the rocky bank. Having deposited my gun in the bow, with the breech still so near me that I could reach it from midships in so small a craft, I arranged the wooder-yoke, or halter, with the pole at my feet and the noose hanging over the stern; so that I was prepared for action in any way that it might offer itself. This yoke is nothing more nor less than a forked sapling with a noose of rope or grape-vine at the end, to throw over a wounded deer's horns when your shot does not stop his swimming. If unskilfully managed, the animal is likely to upset your boat in the effort to take him thus; but there are men upon these lakes so adroit in the use of this rude weapon, that they prefer it to fire-arms when a hunting-knife is at hand to give the game the *coup de grace.**

There is nothing in the world like being a few hours on a hunting-station, with every sense upon the alert to familiarize one with the innumerable sounds and noises that steal up in such " creeping murmurs " from the stillest forest. A man may walk the woods for years and be conscious only of the call of birds or the cry of some of the larger animals, making themselves heard above the rustling of his own footsteps. But watching thus for young quarry, in a country abounding in game, and when it may steal upon you at any moment, interest approaches almost to anxiety; and intense eagerness for sport makes the hearing as nice as when fear itself lends its unhappy instinct to the senses.

Myriads of unseen insects appear to be

* See vol. i., chap. xix.

grating their wings beneath the bark of every tree around you, and the "piled leaves," too damp to rustle in the breeze, give out a sound as if a hundred rills were creeping beneath their plaited matting. It is, in fact, no exaggeration to say that the first bay of a hound at such a moment breaks almost like thunder upon the ear. So, at least, did it come now upon mine, as a long, deep-mouthed yell, was pealed from a valley opposite, and echoed back from hill to hill around me. The sharp crack of a rifle followed, and then cry after cry, as some fresh dog opened, the stirring chorus came swelling on the breeze. Each second I expected to hear the signal-horn, or see the chase emerging from the forest wherever the indented shore indicated the mouth of a brook along its margin.

Not a bush, however, moved near the water,

the mountains were alive around, but the lake was as untroubled as ever, save when a flock of ducks feeding near me flapped their wings once or twice at the first outcry, and then resumed their unmolested employment. The sudden burst had died away in the distance, the chase had probably been turned by the single piece that was discharged; and now, leading over the farther hills, its sounds became fainter and fainter, until, at last, they died away entirely.

An hour had elapsed, and, damp, chilly, and somewhat dispirited, I still maintained my motionless position. A slight breeze had arisen upon the lake, and the little waves rippling against my boat made a monotonous flapping sound that almost lulled me asleep. I was, indeed, I believe, fairly verging upon a most inglorious nap upon my post, when a sharp

eager yell started me from my doze, and made
me seize my oars in a moment. It came from
a broad deep bay locked in by two headlands
on my right. The farther side of the bay was a
marsh, and there, bounding through the tall
sedge, I beheld a noble buck, with a single
hound about a gunshot behind him. Strangely
enough, he seemed to have no disposition to
take the water, but leaping with prodigious
strides over the long grass, he kept the margin
for a few moments, and then struck into a
tamarack swamp that fringed the opening. It
was but an instant that he was lost, however;
a simultaneous cry from half-a-dozen hounds
told that he was turned in that direction. He
appeared again upon a rocky ledge where some
lofty pines, with no underwood, were the only
cover to screen him. But now his route carried
him unavoidably out of the line of my station.
I knew that there were those beyond who would

care for him, but in the vexation of my heart at losing my own shot, I could hardly help cursing the poor animal as I saw him hurry to destruction. The height of the cliffs seemed alone to prevent him from taking the water; and I could almost fancy that he looked hurriedly around, while bounding from crag to crag, for a spot where he might best make his plunge. The dogs were now silent—they had not yet issued from the covert—but the moment they emerged from the wood and caught sight of the game, they opened with a yell which made the deer spring from the high bank as if he were leaping from the very jaws of his pursuers. Now came my first moment of action; I might even yet, I thought, be not too late: I seized my oars, and the tough ash quivered in my hands as I sent the skiff flying over the water.

The buck was swimming from me, but he had a broad bay to cross before he could gain the opposite side of the lake. In this bay, and between me and his direct track, was a wooded islet, and by taking an oblique direction I tried, as well as possible, to keep it between myself and the hard-pressed animal, in order that, not seeing me, he might still keep on the same course. I must have been nearly abreast of the islet. The route of the deer was only a few hundred yards in advance, and directly at right angles to that which I was steering—I might yet cut him off the opposite shore—the dogs would prevent him returning from that he had left, and I would certainly overtake him should he attempt to make for the bottom of the bay, which was still distant. The moisture started thick upon my brow from exertion, and the knees of my frail shallop cracked as I impelled her through the water.

But there were other players in the game beside myself—cooler, more experienced, equally alert, and better situated for winning. The canoe, in which was my friend, " The Barrister," with the Indian, was concealed on the opposite side of the islet, and having watched the whole progress of the chase, waited only for the buck to come in a line with it before launching in a pursuit sure to be successful. The moment for striking arrived just as I passed the islet, and then, swift as a falcon on the stoop, the arrowy bark shot from its covert and darted across the water. The effect was more like a vision than any scene I can recall. My friend was nearly concealed from view as he lay on his breast, with his piece levelled directly over the prow of the canoe waiting for the Indian to give the word to fire; but the person of the latter was fully exposed and with the most striking effect, as he stood erect in the stern, stripped to the waist, and with every muscle in his swarthy frame brought into action as he plied his flashing paddle. His long hair streamed on the wind, and, with the piercing eyes and features strained with eager and intense excitement, gave an almost unearthly aspect to his countenance. The dogged and listless look which characterized him a few hours before, seemed to have been thrown off with the tattered garb that disguised without covering his person; and the keen-eyed, clean-limbed hunter now revealed to view, bore no more resemblance to the sullen and shabby vagrant of yesterday, than does a thorough-bred and mettlesome racer, spurning the green turf with glowing hoof, to the rickety and broken-down hackney that steals through the dirty suburbs of a city. The ludicrous cries, however, that broke from him at every moment, afforded a most whimsical contrast to his picturesque appearance. "Yarh! whiteman!" —"San Marie! no fire!"—"Howh! diable

Poagun !"*—" Dame de Lorette ! Corlaer,† be
ready—Sacre—Weenuc !" and a dozen other
epithets and exclamations, Catholic and heathen,
Indian, English, and Canadian, burst in a tor-
rent from his lips. Suddenly, however, disco-
vering he had gained sufficiently upon the buck,
he stopped paddling, and, in good calm Eng-
lish, gave his directions to his companion as
coolly as if now certain of the prize.

The other then covered the deer's head with
his rifle as he swam directly from him, but still
he waited for the proper moment. It came
just as the buck touched the ground with his
fore feet; a projecting rock received him, and
he reared his antlers high above the water,
while his hinder parts were yet submerged in

---

* Poagun, or Tmewawgun, "Pipe," was a name he
gave my friend, "The Barrister."

† New-Yorker.

making good his landing. " Fire !" cried the
hunter, and at that instant the ball struck him
in the spine, a few inches behind the ears. The
animal bent forward beneath the blow, and
then endeavouring to raise his head, he toppled
over backwards, and slipped off the rock into
the lake, an unresisting carcass.

My skiff shot alongside the canoe at that
instant; but though within hearing of all that
passed, I was, of course, too late for a shot.
The buck, which proved a noble fellow, was
soon lifted into the boat, while together we
pulled leisurely for the rendezvous on the oppo-
site side of the lake. There the different mem-
bers of the hunt came gradually dropping in,
one after another. A yearling, with its horns
yet in the velvet, and a doe in tolerable condi-
tion, were the only other fruits of the hunt.
But all were loud in praising the buck as the

finest and fattest that had been taken near the
lake during the season. For several hours the
woods rung with merriment, as, kindling our
fire upon a broad rock, we feasted upon the
spoils of the chase; and our revel was only
brought to an end by the close of the day,
when, embarking leisurely to steer for our
camp, the echoing halloo of the last loiterer
faded over the hills as his boat rounded the
nearest headland and finally left the shore to
solitude and silence.

> The hunt is up—
> The merry woodland shout
> That rung these echoing glades about
> An hour agone
> Hath swept beyond the eastern hills;
> Where pale and lone,
> The moon her mystic circle fills.

And now from thicket dark,
  When by the mist-wreathed river
The firefly's spark
  Will fitful quiver,
And bubbles round the lilies cup,
From lurking trout come coursing up,—
The doe hath led her fawn to drink,
  While scared by step so near,
Uprising from the sedgy brink,
The lonely bittern's cry will sink
  Upon the hunter's ear ;
Who, startled from his early sleep,
  Lists for some sounds approaching nigher—
Half-dreaming lists—then turns to heap
  Another fagot on his fire,
And then again in dreams once more,
Pursues his quarry by the shore.

The next day's hunt I took no share in,
owing to an indisposition incurred while lying
at my station, in a wet boat inactive for hours.
I therefore amused myself in writing out a
narrative which forcibly struck my fancy as told
by one of the party during our row homewards
the evening before, and which, upon my visiting

the scene of its chief incident some year after-
ward,* assumed in my portfolio the shape of the
following story.

* Vide " A Winter in the Far West," vol. i.

CHAPTER VII.

THE TWIN-DOOMED.

" Twin-born they live, twin-born they die ; in grief and
    joy twin-hearted;
Like buds upon one parent bough, twin-doom'd, in death
    not parted."

THE superstition imbodied in the above
distich is very common in those parts of New
York and New Jersey, which were originally
settled by a Dutch population. It had its in-
fluence with Dominie Dewitt from the moment
that his good woman presented him with the
twin-brothers, whose fortunes are the subject of

our story. He regarded them from the first as children of fate—as boons that were but lent to their parents to be reclaimed so soon, that it was a waste of feeling, if not an impious intermeddling with Providence, to allow parental affection to devolve in its full strength upon them.

They were waifs, he thought, upon the waters of life, which it hardly concerned his heart to claim.

The death of the mother, which soon followed the birth of the twins, confirmed this superstitious feeling, and their forms were henceforth ever associated with images of gloom in the breast of their only surviving parent. Old Dewitt, however, though a selfish and contracted man, was not wanting in the ideas of duty which became his station as a Christian pastor. He imparted all the slender advantages of education which were shared by his other children to the two youngest; and though they had not an equal interest in his affections with the rest, he still left them unvisited by any harshness whatsoever. The indifference of their father was, in fact, all of which the twins had to complain.

The consequence was natural; the boys being left so much to themselves, became all-in-all to each other. Their pursuits were in every respect the same. At school, or in any quarrel or scene of boyish faction, the two Dewitt's were always named as one individual; and as they shot up toward manhood, they were equally inseparable. If Ernest went out to drive a deer, Rupert always must accompany him to shoot partridges by the way; and if Rupert borrowed his brother's rifle for the larger game, Ernest in turn would shoulder the smooth-bore of the other, to bring home some birds at the same time. Together, though, they always went.

The " Forest of Deane," which has kept its name and dimensions almost until the moment when I write, was the scene of their early sports. The wild deer at that time still frequented the Highlands of the Hudson; and the rocky passes which led down from this romantic forest to the river, were often scoured by these active youths in pursuit of a hunted buck which would here take the water. Many a time then have the cliffs of Dundenberg echoed their woodland shout, when the blood of their quarry dyed the waves which wash its base. Their names as dead shots and keen hunters were well known in the country below, and there are those yet living in the opposite village of Peekskill, who have feasted upon bear's meat, which the twin-huntsmen carried thither from the forest of Deane.

Our story, however, has but little to do with the early career of the Rockland hunters, and I have merely glanced at the years of their life which were passed in that romantic region of a state whose scenic beauties are, perhaps, unmatched in variety by any district of the same size, in order to show how the dispositions of the twins were fused and moulded together in early life. It was on the banks of the Ohio (Oh-ey-o, or Beautiful River, as it is called in the mellifluous dialect of the Senecas), that the two foresters of Deane first began to play a part in the world's drama. As the larger game became scarce on the Hudson, they had emigrated to this, then, remote region; and here they became as famous for their boldness and address in tracing the Indian marauder to his lair, as they were previously noted for their skill in striking a less dangerous quarry.

The courage and enterprise of the two brothers made them great favourites in the community of hunters, of which they were now members. A frontier settler always depends more upon his rifle than on his farm for subsistence, during the infancy of his " improvements ;" and this habit of taking so often to the woods, brings him continually into collision with the Indians. It has ever, indeed, been the main source of all our border difficulties. The two Dewitts had their full share of these wild adventures. They were both distinguished for their feats of daring; but upon one occasion, Rupert, in particular, gave such signal proofs of conduct and bravery, that upon the fall of the chief man in the settlement, in a skirmish wherein young Dewitt amply revenged his death, Rupert was unanimously elected captain of the station, and all the cabins within the stockade were placed under his especial guardianship. Ernest witnessed the prefer-

ment of his brother with emotions of pride as
full as if it had been conferred upon himself;
and so much did the twins seem actuated by
one soul, that in all measures that were taken
by the band of pioneers, they insensibly fol-
lowed the lead of either brother. The super-
stition which had given a fated character to
their lives at home, followed, in a certain de-
gree, even here, and their characters were sup-
posed to be so thoroughly identified, their for-
tunes so completely bound up in each other,
that, feeling no harm could overtake the one
which was not shared by the other, their fol-
lowers had equal confidence in both, and volun-
teered, with the same alacrity, upon any border
expedition, when either of the brothers chanced
to lead.

It was about this time that General Wayne,
who had been sent by government to crush the
allied forces of the North-western Indians,

established his camp upon the Ohio, with the intention of passing the winter in disciplining his raw levies, and in preparing for the winter campaign, which was afterward so brilliantly decided near the Miami of the Lakes. The mail route from Pittsburg to Beaver now passes the field where these troops were marshalled, and the traveller may still see the rude fireplaces of the soldiery, blackening the rich pastures through which he rides. He may see, too——but I must not anticipate the character of my story, whose truth is indicated by more than one silent memento.

The western militia, large bodies of which had been drafted into Wayne's army, were never remarkable for military subordination, of which, not to mention the Black Hawk war of 1832, the more notable campaigns with the British, afforded many an instance. They are a gallant set of men, but they have an invincible propensity, each man to " fight on his own hook;" and not merely that, but when not employed upon immediate active service, it is almost impossible to keep them together. They become disgusted with the monotony of military duties; revolt at their exacting precision, and though full of fight, when fight is to be had, are eager to disperse upon the least intermission of active service, and come and go as individual caprice may lead them. General Wayne's camp, indeed, was for a while a complete caravanserai, where not merely one or two, but whole troops of volunteers could be seen arriving and departing at any hour. This, to the spirit of an old soldier, who had been bred in the armies of Washington, was unendurable. But as these flitting gentry constituted the sharpshooters, upon whom he chiefly depended, the veteran officer bore with them as long as possible, in the hope that by humouring the volunteers, he might best attach them to the service for which this species of force was all-important.

At length, however, matters reached such a pass, that the army was in danger of complete disorganization, and a new system must necessarily be adopted. " Mad Anthony," as Wayne's men called him (who when he really took a thing in hand, never did it by halves), established martial law in its most rigid form, and proclaimed that every man on his muster-roll, of whatsoever rank, who should pass beyond the lines without a special permit from himself. should be tried as a deserter, and suffer accordingly. The threatened severity seemed only to multiply the desertions; but so keen were the backwoods militiamen in making their escape, from what they now considered an outrageous tyranny, that, with all the vigilance of the regular officers, it was impossible to seize any, to make a military example of them.

Fresh volunteers, however, occasionally supplied the place of those who thus absented themselves without leave; and one morning in particular, a great sensation was created throughout the camp by the arrival of a new body of levies, which, though numerically small, struck every one as the finest company that had yet been mustered beneath the standard of Wayne. The troop consisted of mounted riflemen, thoroughly armed and equipped after the border fashion, and clad in the belted hunting-frock, which is the most graceful of modern costumes. Both horses and men seemed picked for special service, and their make and movement exhibited that union of strength and agility, which, alike in man and beast, constitutes the perfection of that am-

phibious force—the *dragoon;* whose original
character, perhaps, is only represented in
modern armies, by the mounted rangers of our
Western prairies.

The commandant of this corps seemed wor-
thy to be the leader of so gallant a band. His
martial figure, the horse he rode, and all his
personal equipments, were in every respect
complete, and suited to each other. The eagle
feather in his wolf-skin cap, told of a keen eye
and a long shot; the quilled pouch, torn with
the wampum belt, which sustained his hatchet
and pistols, from the body of some swarthy
foeman—spoke of the daring spirit and iron
arm; while the panther-skin which formed the
housings of his sable roan betrayed that the
rider had vanquished a foe, more terrible than
the red savage himself. His horse, a cross of
the heavy Conestoga, with a mettlesome Vir-
ginia racer, bore himself as if proud of so gal-

lant a master; and as the fringed leggin pressed his flank, while the young officer faced the general in passing in salute before him, he executed his passages with all the graceful precision of a charger trained in the *manège*.

A murmur of admiration ran along the ranks as this gallant cavalier paced slowly in front of the soldiery, and reined up his champing steed before the line of his tall followers, as they were at length marshalled upon the parade. But the sensation which his air and figure excited was almost equally shared by another individual, who had hitherto ridden beside him in the van, but who now drew up his rough Indian pony apart from the rest, as if claiming no share in the lot of the new comers.

It was a sunburnt youth, whose handsome features afforded so exact a counterpart of those of the leader of the band, that were it not for the difference of their equipments, either of the two might at first be taken for the other; and even upon a narrower inspection, the dark locks and more thoughtful countenance of Ernest, would alone have been distinguished from the brown curls and animated features of his sanguine and high-spirited brother. The former, as we have mentioned, had drawn off from the corps the moment it halted and formed for inspection. He now stood leaning upon his rifle, his plain leather hunting-shirt, contrasting not less with the gay-coloured frocks of his companions, than did the shaggy coat of his stunted pony, with the sleek hides of their clean-limbed coursers. His look, too, was widely different from the blithe and buoyant one which lighted their features; and his eye and lip betrayed a mingled expression of sorrow and scorn, as he glanced from the lithe and noble figure of his brother to the buckram regulars, whose platoons were marshalled near.

The new levies were duly mustered, and after the rules and articles of war had been read aloud to them, several camp regulations were promulgated; and among the rest the recent order of the commander-in-chief, whereby a breach of discipline, in going beyond the chain of sentinels, incurred the penalty of desertion.

"No, by heaven!" shouted Ernest, when this was read, "Rupert, Rupert, my brother, you shall never bear such slavery! Away—away, from this roofless prison, and if your life is what they want, let them have it in the woods—in your own way. But bind not yourself to these written laws, that bear chains and death in every letter. Away, Rupert, away from this accursed thraldom!" And leaping into his saddle before half these words were uttered, he seized the bridle rein of his brother and nearly urged him from the spot while pouring out his passionate appeal.

" By the soul of Washington !" roared old Wayne, " what mad youngster is this ? Nay, seize him not," added he, goodhumouredly, seeing that Rupert did not yield to his brother's violence, and that the other checked himself and withdrew abashed from the parade, as a coarse laugh, excited by his Quixotism, stung his ear. " By the soul of Washington," cried the general, repeating his favourite oath, " but ye're a fine brace of fellows ; and Uncle Sam has so much need of both of you, that he has no idea of letting more than one go." And calling Rupert to his side, he spoke with a kindness to the young officer, that was probably meant to secure a new recruit in his brother; who had, however, disappeared from the scene.

The parade was now dismissed, and so soon as Rupert had taken possession of his quarters, and seen that his men and horses were all properly taken care of, he parted from his comrades

to take a farewell of Ernest, who awaited him
in a clump of trees upon the bank of the river,
a short distance from the camp. Ernest seemed
to have fully recovered his equanimity; but
though, youth-like, ashamed of the fit of heroics
which had placed his brother in a somewhat
ridiculous position a few hours before, he had
not altered the views which he had entertained
from the first, about Rupert's taking service
under General Wayne.

" You will not start homeward to-night?"
cried Rupert, at length changing a subject it
was useless to discuss.

" Yes, to-night I must be off, and that soon,
too, Rupert. Little Needji must pace his
thirty miles before midnight. I don't know
that I have done wisely in coming so far with
you; but, in truth, I wanted to see how our
hunters would look among the continentals
Mad Anthony has brought with him."

" Wait till we come to the fighting, Ernest, and the old general will soon find out who's who. His regulars may do in civilized war, but a man must live in the woods to know how to fight in them."

" Ay, ay, that's it; a hound may do for a deer that isn't worth a powder-horn stopper upon a panther track. But you must remember," continued his brother, fixing his eyes sadly upon Rupert, " that you will have to fight just in the way that the general tells you— whichmeans, I take it, that real manhood must go for nothing. Why, there's not a drummer in the ranks that will not know his duty better than you; ay, and for aught I see, be able to do it, too, as well."

A flush of pride—perhaps of pain—crossed the countenance of the young officer as his brother thus spoke; and, laying his hand upon his arm, added, with the indignant tone of a caged hunter, "Why, Rupert, you must not dare even, soldier that you now are, to take the bush, and keep your hand in by killing a buck occasionally."

"Believe it not, Ernest. My men will never stand that, for all the Mad Anthony's or mad devils in the universe."

"You must, you must, my brother," answered Ernest, shaking his head, "and now you begin to see why I would not volúnteer upon this service. I am quieter than you, and therefore saw further into matters than you did, when you chose to come hither rather than give up the command of your company. But where's the use of looking back upon a cold trail? You are now one of Uncle Sam's men, and Heaven knows when he will let go his grip upon you."

Conversing thus, the brothers had walked some distance. The moon was shining brightly above them, and a silver coil of light trailing along the rippling Ohio, seemed to lure them onward with the river's course. At length, however, the more considerate Ernest deemed it prudent that they should part, and catching the pony, which had followed them like a dog, he mounted and prepared to move off. But Rupert would not yet leave his brother and retrace his steps to camp. It might be long before they should meet again—they who had never before thus parted—who had been always inseparable, alike in counsel and in action, and who were now about for the first time to be severed, when stout hearts and strong hands might best be mutually serviceable.

"I don't think I will leave you just yet, Ernest. I may as well walk with you as far as the branch; and we are hardly without shot of the soldier who is standing sentry yonder.

What a mark the fellow's cap would be from that clump of pawpaws !"

" Yes," said Ernest, lifting his rifle from his lap as the musket gleamed in the moonlight. " I am almost tempted to pick that shining smooth-bore out of his fingers, just to show how ridiculous it is to carry such shooting-irons as that into the woods. But come; the time has gone by for such jokes; if you will go farther with me, let us push on." They reached the " branch," or brook, and crossed it; and still they continued increasing the distance between themselves and the camp.

" Well, I suppose we must now really bid good-bye," exclaimed Rupert at last, seizing the hand of his brother. " But here, Ernest, I wish you would carry home my Indian belt, and these other fixings; they will remind you of old times if I'm kept away long, and the sutler will give me something to wear more in camp fashion." As he spoke thus, he tied the wampum sash around the waist of his brother, and while throwing the Indian pouch over his shoulder, their arms met in the fold of brotherhood, and the twins parted with that silent embrace. Rupert, rapidly retracing his steps toward the camp, soon reached the brook, and a half-hour's walk might yet have enabled him to regain his quarters in safety; but the finger of Fate was upon him, and he, who had already been led away from duty by the strong lure of affection, was still further induced to violate it by an instinct not less impulsive in the bosom of a borderer.

Pausing to drink at the rivulet, Rupert, in stooping over the bank, thought that he discovered a fresh moccasin-print, and bending down the branches which embowered the spot, so as to bring the rays of the moon full upon it, a more thorough examination fully satisfied him that an Indian had lately passed that way. A regular soldier, upon thus discovering traces of a spy in the neighbourhood of the camp, would at once have reported it to the officer of the day, and allowed his superior to take measures accordingly. But such an idea never occurred to the backwood ranger. He had discovered an Indian trail, and there were but two things, in his opinion, to be done : first to find out its direction, and then to follow it to the death. A sleuth-hound upon the scent of blood could not be impelled by a more irresistible instinct than that which urged the fiery Rupert on that fatal chase.

It boots not to tell the various chances of his hunt; how here he missed the trail upon rocky ground, where the moccassin had left no print; how there he was obliged to feel for it in some tangled copse, where no betraying moonbeam fell; and how, at last, when the stars grew dim, and the gray dawn had warmed into ruddy day, he for the first time rested his wearied limbs upon the banks of a stream, where the trail disappeared entirely.

Let us now follow the fortunes of the doomed Ernest, who, like the hero of classic story, bore about his person the fatal gifts that were to work his destruction. Not a half-hour elapsed from the time that he had parted from his brother, before he found himself the prisoner of a sergeant's guard, which had been despatched to " take or slay the deserter, Rupert Dewitt."

Apprehending no ill, Ernest allowed himself to be seized; the equipments he had just received from Rupert, not less than the similitude of likeness to his twin-brother, in the opinion of the party that captured him, fully established his identity; and the horror which he felt at discovering how Rupert had forfeited his life, was almost counterbalanced by a thrill of joy, as it suggested itself to the high-souled Ernest that he might so far keep up the counterfeit as to become a sacrifice in place of the brother on whom he doted. The comrades of Rupert, who might have detected the imposition, chanced to be off on fatigue parties in different directions; and this, together with the summary mode of proceeding that was adopted upon his reaching camp, favoured his design.

A drum-head court-martial was instantly called to decide upon the fate of a prisoner, to whose guilt there seemed to be, alas! too many witnesses. The road that he had taken, the distance from camp, the time of night he had chosen to wander so far from the lines,— nay, the fact of his leaving his blood-horse at the stable, as if fearing detection through him, and stealing off upon an Indian pony,—all seemed to make out a flagrant case of desertion. But why dwell upon these painful details of an affair which was so amply canvassed in all its bearings, throughout the western country, long afterwards? Let the reader be content with the bare historical fact, that the ill-starred militiaman was condemned to be shot to death as a deserter, under the circumstances as I have stated them. It seemed a terrible proceeding when these attending circumstances were afterwards reviewed; but though at the time General Wayne was much censured for signing that young man's death-warrant, yet both military men and civilians, who knew the condition of his army, have agreed that it was this one example alone which prevented that army from falling to pieces.

The heart of Ernest was so thoroughly made up to meet the fate which was intended for his brother, that his pulses did not change in a single throb when he was told that he had but an hour to prepare himself for death. "The sooner that it be over the better for Rupert," exclaimed he, mentally. And then, man as he was, his eyes filled with tears when he thought of the anguish which that darling brother would suffer at learning the fate which had overtaken him.

"Oh, God!" he cried aloud, clasping his hands above his head as he paced the narrow guard-room in which he was now immured, "God of Heaven! that they would but place us together with our rifles in the forest, and send this whole army to hunt us down." And the features of the wild bushfighter lighted up with a grim smile as he thought of keeping a battalion at bay in the green wood, and crippling it with his single arm. The proud thought seemed to bear with it a new train of views. "If Rupert knew," said he, pausing in his walk — "if he but dreamed how matters were going, he would soon collect a score of rifles to strike with, and take me from beneath their very bayonets. But this is madness——"

"Ay! that it is, my fine fellow," answered the sentinel, who guarded his door, and who now, hearing the last words uttered while the steps of those who were to have the final charge of the prisoner were heard upon the stair, thought it incumbent upon him to remind the youth where he was. Ernest compressed his lip, and drawing himself to his full height, as he wheeled and faced his escort, motioned to them to lead on. He was at once conducted to the esplanade in front of the camp, upon the river's bluff.

The morning was gusty and drizzling, as if nature shuddered in tears at the sacrifice of one who from his infancy had worshipped her so faithfully. The young hunter scarcely cast a glance at the military array as he stepped forward to take the fatal position from which he was never to move more. Pride alone seemed to prompt the haughty mien and averted but unblenching eye, that were, in fact, governed by a nobler impulse—the fear of a personal recognition by some of the soldiery before his substitution as a victim to martial law was completed; but of the many in his brother's band who had so often echoed his own shout upon the joyous hunt, or caught up his charging cheer in the Indian onslaught, there was now not one to look upon the dying youth. Considerations of feeling, or the fear, perhaps, of exciting a mutinous spirit among those hotheaded levies, had induced the general to keep the comrades of the twin-brothers at a distance from the fatal scene. As already stated, they had originally been detained upon some fatigue duty, which took them to a distance from the camp, and measures had been since adopted to prolong their absence until the catastrophe was over. Once, and once only, did Ernest trust himself to run his eye along the formal files of stranger faces; and then—while the scenes of his early days by the bright river of the north flashed athwart his memory—he felt a momentary sinking of the heart to think there was no home-loved friend who could witness the manner of his death; and yet, when he remembered that one such witness might, by identifying him, prevent his sacrifice and endanger the life of Rupert, he was content that it should be thus.

A platoon of regulars was now drawn up in front of him, and waited but the word of their officer—when suddenly a murmur ran along the column, which was displayed upon the ground in order to give solemnity to the scene. It was mistaken for a symptom of mutiny, and precipitated the fatal moment.

" FIRE !" cried the officer; and, even as he spoke, a haggard figure, in a torn hunting-shirt — with ghastly look, and tangled hair that floated on the breeze—leaped before the line of deadly muzzles! He uttered one piercing shriek—whether of joy or agony it were impossible to tell—and then fell staggering with one arm across the bosom of Ernest, who breathed out his life while springing forward to meet the embrace of his brother!

They were buried in one grave; and the voyager upon the Ohio, whose boat may near the north-western shore, where the traces of Wayne's encampment are yet visible, still sees the shadowy buckeye, beneath which repose THE TWIN-DOOMED FORESTERS OF DEANE !

Upon the return of the party, the close of evening found us seated around the fire discussing the day's sport, while the older hunters enlightened those less versed in woodcraft with the detail of various feats and adventures, of which, in bygone days, the forests around us had been the scene and themselves the heroes. Moose, panther, and bear hunting were their favourite themes; and I took an opportunity, when the latter was mentioned, to ask the old Indian, who was the most intelligent of the party, if any grizzly bears had ever been found in this region, as some naturalists have asserted. His reply indicated that there was a tradition of that ferocious animal being known to his ancestors, by whom its race was said to have been extirpated. The information was, however, so mixed up with what was evidently fable, that it was impossible to tell how much of his account was true; and not the least extravagant portion of it was imbodied in a story, the strange tissue of which I can by no means recall to my own satisfaction.

CHAPTER VIII.

OTNE-YAR-HEH, OR THE STONE GIANTS.

A LEGEND OF TSEKA LAKE.*

" Alas! when he told of the flinty heel,
    That trampled his tribesmen down in wrath ;
To the hearts of flint would he make appeal,
    That saw them swept from the white man's path !"

THEY who have hunted over the wild lands
that lie between the sources of Moose river on

---

* A large and beautiful sheet of water, lying a few
miles to the south-west of Lake Pleasant and Saçondaga
Lake in Hamilton county, New York. Its name is
sometimes written Pseka, and more often *Piseka*.

the west, and the Talking Water,* where it falls
into the northern branch of the great Mohegan
on the east, tell of certain strange forms, re-
sembling men, that appear to be carved out of
the solid rock, as they stand like sentinels along
the shores of some of the lakes which are so
numerous in this region. The stunted hem-
locks which are occasionally rifted among their
fissures, and the wild vines that here and there
are tangled among their groups, prevents a
close examination of their shape ; and some
white people insist that these upright rocks
bear little or no resemblance to the human
figure. But it is probable that they who under-
take to speak thus positively upon the subject,
have never seen the particular cliffs with which
the Indian hunter is familiar ; and which,

* Commonly called " Jessup's River," a famous trout-
ing brook that forms one of the tributaries of the Hud-
son.

N 2

though with the lapse of every year assuming more and more the aspect of the common rocks around them, still preserve so much of their original appearance as to be easily identified. Few, however, would suspect that these mute forms were once animated, and gifted with powers of destruction proportionate to their huge size; and yet, if tradition can be believed, such was formerly the case. The wars with Otne-yar-heh lasted for many generations before they were utterly subdued and reduced to their present harmless condition; and the century of continual conflicts with Ononthio (the French) was not half so destructive to the warriors of the Aganuschion,* as a single battle with these monsters.

It was on the shores of the Tseka Lake that

* Thus the confederated Five Nations called themselves. — *Clinton's Discourse before the New York Historical Society.*

they were first discovered, though some say that they came originally from the great salt water, and had cut their way through the Mahikanders and other river tribes up to this point. But they who talk thus confound these giants with a band of strangers that were destroyed upon this lake the year before, and whose bodies afterwards became, as it were, the shells in which these monsters were hatched.

These wanderers had encamped upon the sand-beach of Tseka, about a gunshot from the cove where the inlet of Oxbow Lake flows from it into the swamp that lies between them : being discovered, they were set upon by a war-party of the Aganuschion on its way to strike a blow at the Abenaquis. The warriors of the confederacy mistaking them for Hurons or some other hostile band of the north, attacked them with such fury, that every one of their number was either killed or wounded before the head-long assailants could be brought to a parley. It was then discovered, when too late, that they had never been among the foes of the Five Nations, and were, in fact, strangers, of whom no one could give an account. The assailing party were overcome with confusion; but the victims of their rashness were so completely cut up, that sympathy was of no avail, and they were wholly at a loss what to do with the wounded survivors. They had not a single "medicine-man" in their own party to assist them on the spot, and, if they undertook to carry the strangers back to their own towns, they must have perished on the way; while the delay would be fatal to the enterprise upon which these fierce warriors had left their homes.

Some proposed to tomahawk those of the strangers who were most badly wounded to put

them out of their pain, and to carry forward
the others upon the expedition. This, however,
was strenuously opposed by the hotheaded
young men upon whom the task of carrying the
disabled would have fallen: and, after several
other propositions had been made with the
same effect, it was determined to leave the
victims to their fate upon the spot where their
calamity had overtaken them.

The vengeance of the Master of Life was as
summary as it was enduring. That war-party
marched on its way, and reached the Cadaraqui,
but not one of their number ever after returned
to the lodges of the Aganuschion; while for
many a long year their tribesmen suffered for
the judgment they had brought upon their
people, and the butchered strangers were made
the instruments of the punishment.

The bleeding band, left with their raw wounds
upon the open beach, would crawl to the wa-

ter's edge to quench the thirst that consumed them; and then, as they suffered new anguish in reviving for a moment, they would roll and twist upon the sand, until, adhering to the gore that covered them, the flinty particles covered the whole surface of their bodies; and, as their limbs stiffened in death, congealed almost like solid rock around them. But their cruel thirst remained to the last. And they drank and drank until each one expired where he lay; while their bodies and limbs became swollen into frightful bulk before they gasped out their last breath.

The winter, which soon set in, preserved these crusted remains from decay; and when the snows, which are very deep and lasting in this mountain region, had subsided, each stark and grim corpse had gained still more in size; while the waves of the lake, in washing its shells and pebbles over them, appeared, in the lapse of a few months, to have turned the giant sleepers into solid masses of stone. This was not the case, however, as the grizzly bears knew full well when the last troop of these monsters, driven from the low country by the hunters of the Iroquois, scented them for prey upon that shore.

At first, however, their prize availed them nothing; for the bodies were so protected by their shell of stone that it seemed impossible to get at them. But the grizzly bear is the keenest hunter of his kind, and when half famished as now, his cunning is equal to his strength. These animals then commenced at the soles of the feet, where the hard casing was thinnest, and being of a supple nature, they eat their way forward until the body and limbs of each were completely enclosed within those gigantic moulds.

The bears at first wished to withdraw from

their strange dwellings, thinking after all they might be nothing but some new kind of traps which their enemies had been setting for them: but in struggling to turn round, they found that the flinty casing upon their limbs yielded so to each motion, that, provided they only stood erect, they could walk as formerly. And then it was that, for the first time, he who looked upon that shore would have seen those unearthly monsters raising themselves one by one from the ground, until, tall as a thrifty pine, with frames proportioned to their height, and cased from head to heel in shining flint, the terrible band of the Otne-yar-heh was marshalled by their leader.

"My brothers," said the chief in a voice that sounded like the wind rushing through a mighty cavern, "we are not tortoises, though we have shells; nor need we wait here until our enemies set the swamp on fire and smoke us out like musk-rats! Let us move to the lodges of the Aganuschion, and see how they will receive us."

The woods cracked as if a tornado had been let loose among them as the hard-heeled giants strode from mountain to mountain crushing the stoutest saplings like rushes beneath their feet. Their trail was as broad as that of a gang of moose, but the trampled and twisted trees lay so thick upon it, that man with mortal limbs could never have followed upon their path. Straight as the flight of a pigeon was the road they took. The swollen torrent or dizzy precipice was no obstacle to their footsteps; they stepped from the tall crag or stalked through the raging stream with equal ease. The trees which their leader trampled beneath him, afforded a firm passage for his followers over the deep morass, and they waded the lakes in storm and tempest, while the waves that lashed their sides as they advanced, broke into foam against their rocky ribs as if it were the very mountain cliffs that opposed them.

What could the warriors of the Five Nations do against such an enemy? They were not then, indeed, though they hunted and fought together, a united people; and the wars with the Stone Giants, devastating as they were, were at least the cause of one happy event, in giving rise to the league that was formed against them, and producing in the Aganuschion a race of men that surpasses all others.* But hundreds of brave men were destroyed before this grand end was accomplished, and the Mohawks and Oneidas, who met the first descent of the Otne-yar-heh were vanquished again and again in battle. Their weapons seemed to pro-

---

* *Onwe-honwe*, or "the men that surpass all others," was a title arrogated by the Five Nations.—*Colden's History.*

duce no effect upon their terrible opponents. They tried first to cut off the chief of the band, but their arrows would rattle like hail against his marble hide; and when a score of hatchets at a time were aimed at his head, though they made the fire shower from its flinty hood as if a flame-stone from the moon* were bursting near, yet it seemed to produce no effect upon the giant.

At length it was determined that all the chief men of the Five Nations should meet at Onondaga, in order to take measures for acting in concert against the common enemy; and then that famous league was formed, whose power, for centuries afterward, was acknowledged alike by the white and red man, wherever its name was known.

Tradition has preserved no exact record of the mode of warfare it was then determined to

* An aereolite is thus called by some tribes.

employ against the Stone Giants; but it is gene-
rally believed that the Master of Life himself
looked so benignantly upon the councils of this
band of brothers, that he interposed his arm to
shelter so heroic a people from destruction. It
is said that he sent his lightnings among the
Otne-yar-heh, which drove them back to the
glens from which they first emerged, and draw-
ing there a circle of thunderbolts around the
unhallowed region, so that no game ever tra-
versed it, the Stone Giants perished in the fast-
nesses where they had sought a refuge. Their
only traces are now the uncouth forms of rock
that are scattered here and there among these
hills; nor since that time has a grizzly bear
been seen within a hundred miles of these lakes,
and the last of the race is supposed to have
animated the forms, and perished with the band
of the OTNE-YAR-HEH.

"God's weather!" cried the Major, when the

story was ended, " but I have never seen those
sculptured rocks of which the old fellow tells
us, and I know every stone of the size of a flint
in the country."

Captain Gill replied to the discredit that was
thus thrown upon his narrative only with a look
of scorn at the party who thus sought to dis-
parage it; but a young Iroquois hunter took up
the matter more feelingly, by observing that the
white man never saw with the same eyes as the
Indian, and that the traces of " The Spirit,"
alike in trees, and stones, and running streams,
were never discovered by him, who only studied
how he could best turn these objects to pur-
poses the very reverse of those for which
Owaneyo intended them.

" Well, well," said the Major, goodnaturedly
" you are more than half right, young un; for
what with mining among the mountains, dam-

ming the rivers, and turning the timber into shingles, they will soon play the mischief with all the trout and deer in the country. But we've had enough of Injun matters now, I want a story with a gal in it. By your leave, sir," added he, turning to my friend the barrister, " we've not had a word from you yet, though being a lawyer you ought to be as slick with your tongue as you are with your rifle. Here's the last night we are to be together—the very last, perhaps, you will ever spend in the woods with old Jake Peabody; so do turn us out something nice in the way of a story, something that has plenty of women in it, for tho'f we never see the creturs in these parts we like to hear about 'em sometimes."

Thus eloquently besought, my friend could not but comply, and promising that he would take the Major at his word, and make the story entirely about women, he related the particulars of a remarkable law-case, which are imbodied in the following version of " The Barrister's Story."

CHAPTER IX.

ROSALIE CLARE.

" Men have died, and worms have eaten them,
But not for love."

So saith the poet! meaning by his speech
not men in a numeric sense—not mankind at
large, but only the males of the *genus homo*.
Shakspeare, perhaps, was right in regard to
men, but had he spoken of women, he would
have told a different story. Love, indeed, is
" the worm i' the bud," which hath devoured

the life-germ in many a female bosom, leaving only a frail and hollow shell for death to crush between his iron fingers. Truly hath Byron said, that " woman's love is a fearful and dangerous thing;" for it is both mystical in its birth and perilous in its being. It maketh realities out of a shadow. It linketh things unsubstantial with things real, until they become part of woman's very being, making a tangible substance of that which is in its nature " an essence incorporeal"—rooting its fibres in the heart, and interweaving them with the very filament and texture of the brain.

The personal memoirs of former times, not less than the periodicals of our own day, are rife with records proving this. But one of the most extraordinary instances of misplaced affection, clinging to its object until reason was extinct, is one which, though often repeated in society, has never yet, to our knowledge, found its way into print.

I allude to the singular story of Miss ***** (the Rosalie Clare of our tale), the niece of that eccentric old tory, Mrs. C****, of Nova Scotia; who, after emigrating to New Brunswick during the revolution, made herself so conspicuous in our courts of law, when she returned hither to recover some forfeited estates, about the year 179—. The family is, I believe, now extinct; and I have therefore less hesitation in speaking here of events, which must already be familiar to many of my readers.

The estates, to recover which Mrs. C. embarked in such expensive litigation, were claimed only in behalf of her son, to whom they had been devised by the will of his maternal grandfather. With regard to the identity of this son, there were strange surmises abroad, from the moment he landed with his supposed mother in New York. It seems that Mrs. C., when she retired to Nova Scotia, at the breaking out of the revolution, had carried her two orphan children with her from their native city. These were a little girl, and a boy still in petticoats, and one of them never reached their destination. The child was lost overboard at sea; and when the vessel landed, the provincial papers announced the melancholy loss which Mrs. C. had met with in the untimely fate of her only daughter. Such a misfortune, one would think, were enough to gratify the vindictiveness of the old lady's enemies, at least for a season; yet there were many who had the malice to whisper doubts as to which of the two children had actually perished. " It was easy amid the confusion of the times," said they, " for one leading so unsettled a life as Mrs. C., to find, in her various journeyings, some male infant of

similar age, which she might readily substitute
for the lost heir.   She had then only to keep
the daughter out of the way, and his fortune was
made."   This gossip, however, was soon swal-
lowed up by more exciting themes; and when,
years afterward, Mrs. C. appeared in New
York with a handsome youth of eighteen, whom
she called her son, there were a few who hinted
that the boy was hers only by adoption, and
that Mrs. C. had done what history proves has
often been attempted in the assertion of higher
claims than hers—namely, to pass off the son
of another as her own.

Young Ludlow C., so was the youth called,
was not the less popular, however, on account
of such surmises, if they did exist.   He was a
young man of exceeding beauty and accom-
plished manners, with a voice gentle and soft as
a woman's, and an eye brilliant with all the fire
of opening manhood.   His, indeed, was just the

union of qualities that most readily captivate
the female fancy. He had that high flow of
spirits which is often mistaken for talent in
youth, and which is generally so attractive to
those who are thrown much in the society of
the fortunate possessor. This constitutional
blessing gave him an agreeableness, which those
who know more of the subject than we affect
to know, aver as all-important in pleasing the
sex. But agreeableness, however it may enter-
tain, is not the quality to interest a woman, and
young C. had another arrow in his sheaf, which,
perhaps, flew the farther from being seldom
shot. There was at times a shade of sadness
about him—a melancholy so deep and absorb-
ing, that it made the subject of this altered
mood differ for a season not less from himself
than he did at other times from all around him.
This, as the cause of the depression was wholly
unknown, threw a veil of mystery over his cha-

racter, and completed the list of lover-like qualities which are the source of so much bedevilment to girls of nineteen; and nineteen was just the age of Rosalie Clare, when for the first time she became acquainted with her all-conquering cousin.

Some female writer has said that none of her sex reach the age of sixteen without having had at least one affair of the heart. If there were ever an exception to the rule it was in the case of Rosalie Clare. Love, like wonder, is half the time the child of ignorance. It is an exhalation that springs from young hearts, and settles upon the nearest object, however unsuited by character or "imperfect sympathies," as Coleridge expresses it, to inspire or to reciprocate true affection. Perhaps there is no greater protection against these idle fancies, than the placing those who may become the subject of them early in the world of reality.

Rosalie, as the only female of her father's family, had been thrown into society so early that she could hardly remember the time when she had not been surrounded by admirers. A petted and half-spoiled child of six or seven, she had often taken her mother's place, and sat in mock dignity at the head of her father's table; while, as a girl of twelve, she had habitually done the honours of his house during the time that New York was occupied by the British troops. Living thus in the very vortex of gay society, and surrounded by the handsome cavaliers, who are only known in the day-dreams of girls of her age, imagination had never a chance to act. She became habituated to the compliments and attentions of the other sex before the feelings of womanhood began to assert themselves in her bosom; and the flatteries which had always been received as a matter of course by the forward child of

twelve, made no impression on the blooming
girl of seventeen. Some dispositions would
have been entirely ruined by such an educa-
tion, whose tendency would seem to make the
whole character artificial. It was not thus,
however, with Rosalie Clare, whose candid and
happy temperament resembled one of those
easily - raised plants that seem to flourish
equally well in the conservatory or the par-
terre, adapting themselves alike to the free
exposure of the atmosphere, or the measured
heat of the forcing-house; and exhibiting all
their characteristic properties in either situa-
tion. Such natures must be either very superior
to, or below, the general standard. They are
either so elevated as to be independent of cir-
cumstances, or so common that no training can
much alter or improve them; and so far as
mind is concerned, it must be confessed that
Rosalie did not soar above the latter class.

Yet, while the illnatured observer might have confounded her with those of her sex whom Pope tells us "have no character at all," her fond and most unchanging affectionateness of disposition would, not less than her rare beauty, have entitled her to sit for the original of any of Byron's heroines but Gulnare.

It was this affectionateness, this disposition to cling to, and rely upon, whatever seemed loveable and reliable, that made Rosalie become attached to her cousin almost from the moment she knew him. The nearness of their relationship, united to the frank, winning manners of Ludlow, was an immediate passport to her confidence. The idea of regarding him as a lover she did not dream of, but they were friends from the moment they met. There would, indeed, be occasionally some little interchange of lively sensibilities between them, but it could

hardly be otherwise with two young persons of
different sexes, who were thrown so continually
together.   If Rosalie ever thought of the ten-
dency of such an intercourse when she was
rallied about it by others, she always had an
answer which fully satisfied herself.   Ludlow
was scarcely a year older than herself, and was,
therefore, " a boy," with whom it was no harm
to be upon the easiest terms of familiar acquaint-
ance.   Besides, was he not her cousin?—a first
cousin!—and where's the harm of a good-
humoured flirtation with a cousin?—if flirtation
it might indeed be called.   Yet it was strange
that Rosalie Clare did not like cousin Ludlow
to flirt with any one else but her!

"What! cousin, you are not going to dance
again with that horrid Laura T. to-night?" said
she pettishly, laying her hand upon our hero's
arm, as he passed her in a crowded ball-room.

"And why not, Rosalie? I am engaged to walk a minuet with Miss T., and you know it is *impossible* now to withdraw."

"Why, you have hardly spoken to me yet to-night, Ludlow!"

The youth answered only by taking a single flower from the *bouquet* which the beaux of that day wore in their buttonholes, and gracefully placing it in the high head-dress of the pretty pleader. The next moment he took the hand of his partner, the band struck up the inspiriting *gavotte*, and he stepped off in the featly minuet with an air that would have done honour to a courtier of Versailles; while, half-pleased and half-provoked, his deserted cousin looked on with the admiring crowd.

This was but one of a thousand little passages between the cousins that marked the progress of a flirtation which soon assumed the appear ance of a serious entanglement. And now one would have thought that some coolness had arisen between them, they met, comparatively, so seldom. The air of Ludlow, too, when they did meet, was absent and dejected, as he walked by the side of the radiant girl, who rattled away with all the thoughtless vivacity of a triumphant belle who has the preferred admirer of her train for a listener. Rosalie, however, had also her hours of listlessness, if not of dejection; and while her cousin lost his wonted flow of spirits when with her, she, on the contrary, seemed happy only in his society.

Nor did Rosalie want for other lovers; as that little ballad which goes by her name, and which may not inaptly be introduced here, to show how her beauty fired the gallants of the day, is a genuine record of the otherwise forgotten belle.

SONG.—ROSALIE CLARE.

Who owns she's not peerless? who calls her not fair?
Who questions the beauty of Rosalie Clare?
Let him saddle his courser and spur to the field,
And, though harnessed in proof, he must perish or yield;
For no gallant can splinter—no charger can dare
The lance that is couched for young Rosalie Clare.

When goblets are flowing, and wit at the board
Sparkles high, while the blood of the red grape is poured,
And fond wishes for fair ones around offered up
From each lip that is wet with the dew of the cup—
What name on the brimmer floats oftener there,
Or is whispered more warmly, than Rosalie Clare?

They may talk of the land of the olive and vine—
Of the maids of the Ebro, the Arno, or Rhine;—
Of the Houris that gladden the east with their smiles,
Where the sea's studded over with green summer isles;
But what flower of far-away clime can compare
With the blossom of ours—bright Rosalie Clare?

Who owns not she's peerless? who calls her not fair?
Let him meet but the glances of Rosalie Clare!
Let him list to her voice—let him gaze on her form—
And if, hearing and seeing, his soul do not warm,
Let him go breathe it out in some less happy air
Than that which is blessed by sweet Rosalie Clare!

It was to her, too, during some desponding moment, that a forgotten provincial poet addressed that lively impromptu, that we have more than once seen copied in the albums of our fair acquaintance by some admirer who would rally their pettishness in the language of another.

TO A BELLE WHO TALKED OF GIVING UP THE WORLD.

You give up the world? Why, as well might the sun,
　When tired of drinking the dew from the flowers,
While his rays, like young hopes, stealing off one by one,
　Die away with the Muezzin's last note from the towers,
Declare that he never would gladden again,
　With one rosy smile, the young morn in its birth;
But leave weeping Day, with her sorrowful train
　Of hours, to grope o'er a pall-covered earth.

The light of that soul, once so brilliant and steady,
　So far can the incense of flattery smother,
That at thought of the world of hearts conquered already,
　Like Macedon's madman, you weep for another!

Oh! if, sated with this, you would seek worlds untried,
 And fresh as was ours, when first we began it,
Let me know but the spot where you next will abide,
 And, that instant, for one, I am off for that planet.

But all this idolatry of the gay world was un-
heeded by her who cared for one only worship-
per, and a careless little song of her cousin's,
which we have seen as copied out in the faded
characters of Rosalie's own fair hand, was dearer
to her than all the more elaborate compliments
of others; for she, fond girl, imagined that none
other than herself had inspired Ludlow's muse
when he ventured upon so confident a strain as
that which prompts the conceits of the follow-
ing

CHANSONETTE.

I know thou dost love me—ay! frown as thou wilt,
 And curl that beautiful lip,
Which I never can gaze on without the guilt
 Of burning its dew to sip:
I know that my heart is reflected in thine,
And like flowers that over a brook incline,
 They toward each other dip.

Though thou lookest so cold in these halls of light,
  'Mid the careless, proud, and gay,
I will steal like a thief in thy heart at night,
  And pilfer its thoughts away.
I will come in thy dreams at the midnight hour,
And thy soul in secret shall own the power
  It dares to mock by day.

Such an affair seldom proceeds far in any circle without there being many who discover its existence, and watch its progress with as lively an interest as if their own welfare were identified with that of the parties chiefly concerned. The two cousins, as time wore on, were not exempted from this disinterested surveillance, and manifold were the speculations about the termination of their loves. There was that in the conduct of Ludlow which puzzled the most acute of these gossips. In the first place, they were certain that he must be conscious of possessing the affections of the guileless Rosalie, whose heart was reflected too faithfully in her speaking countenance to admit of the concealment of its feelings. Ludlow, in the course of six months, must certainly have found out what, in the first six weeks of their acquaintance, was apparent to every one except the lovely and unconscious betrayer of her own gentle emotions. Why, then, did he not claim the hand when the heart was beyond all question his own? True, he was very young, and his precarious fortunes, with the fact of his never having been brought up to any profession, might make his youth an objection when thinking seriously of matrimony. But yet, when other circumstances seemed to remove every real obstacle, why should such fancied impediments be allowed to prevail? They might become engaged at least; and supposing even that they waited until the family lawsuit was decided, they had still some years of youth to spare, and his cousin's means were sufficiently ample if

the cause were decided against Ludlow and his
mother.   But then, again, did Ludlow love
Rosalie?   Did he seriously return her attach-
ment; or, if requiting it, did he give up the
whole tide of his heart, in all its warmth and
fulness, to this one only object?   It seemed
impossible to tell how far his feelings actually
did go.   If he thus loved her, there was some-
thing unaccountably irresolute, not to say in-
consistent, in his conduct.   The capricious
youth certainly preferred the society of his
cousin to that of all other women.   Though not
apparently enjoying it, he always courted it, or
rather, almost without any act of volition on his
part, he seemed to find himself constantly near
her.   He had been seen to watch Rosalie with
more than a lover's solicitude, when some of
the gay and dissipated young men of his ac-
quaintance hovered round her in society.   He
listened when they engaged her in conversation,

and her slightest tone of kindness filled him with strange agitation. Still, on the other hand, he allowed the most trivial engagement to take him from her company; and it was observable, that, though often, of his own accord, addressing Rosalie in terms of affection, he never returned any of those little endearments—attentions, perhaps, we should rather call them—which a guileless girl cannot help showing toward the man of her choice, when deeming herself secure of his affection.

It was remarked, too, that none of the reports which were occasionally circulated about Rosalie and her other admirers—for she was still a belle —seemed to awaken any jealousy in her eccentric cousin. He scrutinized every one who approached her in the guise of a lover—yet his watchfulness was more like the discreet care of an affectionate and considerate brother, than the anxiety of an earnest and passionate admirer.

But if he were not such an admirer, what be-
came of Ludlow's honour as a gentleman, what
of his principles as a man, when he allowed a
dreaming and fond-hearted girl to yield up her
whole soul to him, in the delusive belief that he
was all hers in return? True, he had never
told Rosalie that he loved her. True, he had
not even passed those trifling compliments—the
light currency of fancy—so often mistaken for
the sterling coinage of the heart: yet Rosalie
treasured up a thousand little proofs of tender-
ness—expressions which told, from day to day,
how often he thought of her when absent—
looks which spoke how much he felt for her
when near. How often had she caught herself
smiling in her heart, at what she believed to be
the jealous mood of her lover as he watched her,
while talking with others, with that expression
of sadness in his eyes, which often betokens the
overflow of a heart filled up with feeling! He

watched her when he spoke not; and when he did speak, his voice took ever a softer tone that surely was reserved for her alone!

There had, then, been no moment when Rosalie had said to herself, " Now, surely, he loves me," for she believed in Ludlow's affection before she ever *dreamed* the question. Her trust grew from her own heart—it was not founded upon his actions. She loved too sincerely to reason about her own feelings—too devotedly to scan those of her lover. It seemed as if they had been always meant for each other, and must of necessity be united; and so little could the doting girl conceive the void in her heart, which bereaved affection might create, that she looked upon the love of her cousin as something belonging to her from the first, and of right exclusively her own.

But the day was now at hand when all that

was enigmatical about the character of young Ludlow C., was to be fully solved in the eyes of the world.

Mrs. C.'s long-protracted civil suit was at length brought into court. The trial involved a large amount of property, and the celebrity of counsel on both sides, had drawn together an unusual assemblage of spectators. It was said that HAMILTON would speak; and the name of that great man, already becoming as distinguished at the bar as he had been in the cabinet, had attracted a great many ladies to the court-room in the old City-hall. Among the most beautiful of these—yet peerless in her own loveliness—might be seen the happy and blooming features of Rosalie Clare.

The court was opened, and the trial proceeded, exhibiting but little in its progress to gratify the expectations of the larger part of the audience, who became wearied with the dry and technical details which were minutely entered into by the old-fashioned lawyers, most of whom had studied their profession under the English regime. An incident soon occurred, however, which effectually dispelled the insipidity of this scene, and which can never be forgotten by those who were so situated as fairly to witness the whole circumstance. An exclamation of General Hamilton was the first thing that called general attention to what was going forward. Hamilton had as yet taken but little part in the conduct of the cause—leaving the drudgery, perhaps, to some less distinguished member of the profession—while he reserved himself for the cross-examinations and the summing up. At a particular point of the testimony for the C.'s, however, he interrupted the witness upon the stand, by exclaiming, "That is only hearsay evidence : may it please your honour (rising and bowing to the judge), this evidence is inadmissible; let the young gentleman alluded to by the witness be himself produced in court." The remark created instant confusion upon the opposite side of the table, at which the counsel were sitting. Old Mrs. C. bustled forward and whispered to her lawyer, who instantly rose and stated to the court, that " The son of the plaintiff—the young gentleman alluded to—had left town the evening before, and as the point in question was quite unimportant, he was willing to wave it in behalf of his client, rather than have the cause delayed until the averment of the person on the stand could be substantiated by what he, the counsel, admitted was the only proper evidence."

Mrs. C., in the mean time, seemed much agitated, and forthwith despatched a note to Ludlow, who, notwithstanding the statement which

had just been made in his name, she believed
to be at the moment reading quietly at home.
But her message was never doomed to reach
that unconscious victim of parental tyranny and
all-grasping avarice; for, even while the case in
point was still under the advisement of the
court, the name of young C. was pronounced
by one of the marshals, who, with officious
politeness, ushered him to a seat near his
mother, within the bar. The announcement of
the name caught the quick ear of Hamilton in a
moment.

"Let that young gentleman take his place on
the stand," cried he, with great presence of
mind, before his antagonist could recover from
the infectious embarrassment into which the
confusion of his client, at this untoward ap-
pearance, had thrown him.

"Swear him, Mr. Clerk." The oath was
administered. It probably was the first time

that Ludlow had gone through this solemnity, which might account for his seeming perturbed. His eye roamed uneasily around the court, as if in quest of something to rest upon.

"Young gentleman, you will please to look me steadily in the face," said the experienced barrister. "Now, sir, the question I am about to ask you, affects only a simple act of recollection; and you can therefore use what deliberation you please in your reply, provided it be explicit. The witness who has just left that stand, stated that yourself and another person —the name is immaterial—were present when your mother delivered the paper which I hold in my hand to the gentleman who sits opposite to you. Now, without stopping here to identify this third individual, I ask you, whether it be true that yourself and another man—" The features of the youth became much agitated, and the examiner, pausing an instant, resumed, as he fixed his eye keenly upon him, "I say, another person and yourself—" Ludlow was again reassured, but only to be more completely overwhelmed the next moment; as the deliberate lawyer, interrupting himself again to remind the witness of the solemnity of his oath, at last brought the question out in a shape that admitted of no prevarication—" Answer me, in a monosyllable, Ay! or No! Were you, or were you not, present upon the occasion alluded to—with *another* MAN ?"

The last words were pronounced with a significant whisper, that was heard in every part of the crowded court-room. The witness hesitated for a moment, and turned deadly pale. His lips were slightly convulsed, as if unable to syllable the words his tongue would fain record. His mother leaned forward with clasped hands and an appealing, agonized expression, that was wholly indescribable. The youth caught her eager and anxious eye, uttered an indistinct cry, and fainted upon the spot.

"Stand back!—stand back!" cried the agitated mother; "my child!—my child!—let me take care of my own child!" And she struggled through the crowd to get near the insensible object of her anxiety.

"One moment, madam," exclaimed the lawyer, feelingly, but with firmness, as he stretched across the table and held her back with an air that was not the less decided from being perfectly respectful.—"Dr. Hosack already has his hand upon the pulse of the youth, and the swoon will be over the moment his lungs have play." And even as he spoke, the physician had thrown open the frilled bosom of poor Rosalie's lover, while a cry of astonishment filled the court, as the fair

and feminine proportions of a beautiful Wo-
MAN were disclosed !

It has never been known exactly what be-
came of the accomplished female who so long
figured in the society of New York under the
name of Ludlow C. Few thought it strange,
however, knowing the eccentric and unprin-
cipled character of old Mrs. C., that she should
thus have trained her only daughter to play an
unconsciously dishonest part in her legal in-
trigues. As for the mere fact of a girl thus
acting in male character upon the theatre of
life, the example of the celebrated Chevalier
D'Eon had found too many imitators, both
among ladies of the best families in Europe,
and among the enthusiastically patriotic of her

sex in our own country, to make this feature of the case at all remarkable.*

And what became of poor Rosalie Clare? —she, whose kind and gentle heart had withstood so many assaults from the other sex, only to be yielded up at last to the delicate arts of a spoiler of her own. The false lover, who doted upon her like a sister, is said to have had all the painful emotions which her career might well have excited, swallowed up in contrition for the ruin she had so unintentionally wrought upon the happiness of the confiding Rosalie; but the

* One of these amazons, who had for fifty years drawn the pay of a revolutionary pensioner, died at an advanced age lately in New England. The new work of the Duchess d'Abrantes—"The Lives and Portraits of Celebrated Women"—records many remarkable instances of women thus unsexing themselves; and Mr. Henry Bulwer, in his work on France, avers, that among the slaughtered conscripts of Napoleon's fields, the bodies of females were found after almost every battle.

heart of that unfortunate had been too completely thrown away ever to be recalled, or again to beat aright. Her brain was either blasted by the sudden blow, or else it became so perverted that she could never fully comprehend the circumstances by which she was overwhelmed, so as to reconcile them to each other, and think rationally upon the subject. In a word, her mind, which had never been a strong one, was broken completely. The presence of her cousin, who, for some weeks, was not withdrawn by her mother from the scene of her disgrace, seemed only to increase the malady. She shrank from her nursing and feminine endearments as if they were the caresses of a monster; yet she was observed to listen to her masculine step upon the stair, and hail her approach with eagerness; while her colour would come and go when she heard her voice in another room, as if its tones awakened her softer sensibilities. But when

"Ludlow," as she still called her cousin, was forbidden by the physicians to see her more, and Rosalie was told that she had embarked with her mother for another land, the spirit of the faded and pining girl sank completely, and her mind lost its last gleams of intelligence.

Happy would it have been for her then, if death had intervened to close the scene! But no! the resources of an excellent constitution did not yet give way, and Rosalie Clare, for many a long year, still lived on. But how? Reader, were you ever at the Bloomingdale asylum? Did you ever look down into the enclosure, where the unhappy inmates may be seen at a certain hour, amusing themselves as each one listeth? Did you ever look in vain among that motley crew for that piteous, yet picturesque air of distraction, with which poets and painters have so often gifted the maniac? You have gazed there in vain, if you hoped to

find the romantic madness of a Hamlet, or an
Ophelia! And yet, among those common-
looking creatures—for all human creatures do
look *common* when the spirit of the mind that
once ennobled their forms hath departed, and
left them animated only by the instincts of
sense—among those common-looking creatures,
are many who have once been the loveliest of
the land. Ay! among those who are at this
moment gathered in that very yard, is one
who— But mark her as she sits crouched in
yon sunny corner! Those livid and sunken
eyes have once matched heaven's own blue in
colour, as they beamed with heavenly purity
and feeling! The fresh-blooming rose, in full-
ness, and softness, and colour, was once ri-
valled by that sallow and shrivelled cheek!
Freely did the eloquent blood—though disease
hath now

" Starved the roses on that cheek,
    And pinched the lily tincture of her skin,"

freely did it once course through the blue veins
of those shrunken temples ! Those leaden lips
—fevered—withered as they are—they—

But why dwell upon this appalling picture ?
The original was but now before us, in all the
light of youth and loveliness. Alas ! that the
copy, so strangely disfigured, should still be
true to all that remains of poor Rosalie Clare !
Reader, if thou knowest what woman's love is,
thou wilt not wonder that one who had thus
wooed a cloud, could not be released from its
embrace, without being scathed by its light-
ning.

" Well," said Major Jake, when the Barrister
had ended the narration (which he gave in lan-
guage, relishing still more of " the intensive
school," than that which I have ventured to

adopt), " that is indeed a real gal story. It's nothing but gal—as the fellow said down in Hoskimar, when his wife brought him a twentieth daughter! And now, let's take a cup all round, swear eternal friendship, and bid good bye, in case we separate to take an early start to home in the morning."

And thus end my early reminiscences of the Sacondaga country. I have frequently been there since, upon a trouting excursion, but the gay idlers of Saratoga springs have broken in upon those mountain fastnesses. The speculators have got hold of the sixpenny acres; old Captain Gill has been many years dead, and none of the new people remember " Major Jake," who is likewise no more: nor should I, perhaps, have attempted to recall their memory, if my recent visit to the Sources of the Hudson, which rises among the same group of mountains as the Sacondaga, had not awakened a vivid recollection of scenes which, enjoyed in early youth, possess far more interest for me in association, than I can hope they will inspire in the reader.

WILD SCENES

AMONG

THE APPALACHIANS.

CHAPTER I.

A NIGHT ON THE ENCHANTED MOUNTAINS.

It haunts me yet! that early dream
  Of first fond love;—
Like the ice that floats on a summer stream
  From some frozen fount above:
Through my river of years 'twill drifting gleam,
  Where'er their waves may rove!

It flashes athwart each sunny hour
With a strangely bright but chilling power,
  Ever and ever to mock their tide
    With its delusive glow;
  A fragment of hopes that were petrified
    Long, long ago!

            The Yankee Rhymer.

THERE are few parts of the United States which, for beauty of scenery, amenity of climate, and, I might add, the primitive character of the inhabitants, possess more peculiar attraction than the mountainous region of eastern Tennessee.

It is a wild and romantic district, composed of rocks and broken hills, where the primeval forests overhang valleys watered by limpid streams, whose meadowy banks are grazed by innumerable herds of cattle. The various mountain ridges, which at one point traverse the country almost in parallel lines, while at another they sweep off in vast curves, and describe a majestic amphitheatre, are all, more or less, connected, with the Appalachian chain, and share the peculiarities which elsewhere characterize those mountains. In some places the transition from valley to highland is so gradual, that you are hardly aware of the undulations of surface when passing over it. In others, the frowning heights rise in precipitous walls from the plains, while again their wooded and dome-like summits will heave upward from the broad meadows, like enormous tumuli heaped upon their bosom.

The hills also are frequently seamed with deep and dark ravines, whose sheer sides and dimly-descried bottom will make the eye swim as it tries to fathom them, while they are often pierced with cavernous galleries, which lead miles under ground, and branch off into grottos so spacious, that an army might be marshalled within their yawning chambers.*

Here, too, those remarkable conical cavities which are generally known by the name of

* The great limestone cavern of Kentucky, which has been explored twelve miles in one direction, is said, in the current phrase of the country, to extend under a *whole county.*

"sink-holes" in the western country, are thickly scattered over the surface; and so perfect in shape are many of them, that it is difficult to persuade the ruder residents that they are not the work of art, nor fashioned out as drinking-bowls for the extinct monsters whose fossil remains are so abundant in this region. Indeed the singular formation of the earth's surface, with the entire seclusion in which they live amid their pastoral valleys, must account for and excuse many a less reasonable belief and superstition prevailing among those hospitable mountaineers. "The Enchanted Mountains," as one of the ranges I have been attempting to describe is called, are especially distinguished by the number of incredible traditions and wild superstitions connected with them. Those uncouth paintings along their cliffs, and the footprints of men and horses stamped in the solid rock upon the highest summits, as mentioned by Mr. Flint in his Geography of the Western Country, constitute but a small part of the material which they offer to an uneducated and imaginative people for the creation of strange fantasies. The singular echoes which tremble through these lonely glens, and the shifting forms which, as the morning mist rises from the upland, may be seen stealing over the tops of the crags, and hiding themselves within the crevices, are alike accounted for by supernatural causes.

Having always been imbued with a certain love of the marvellous, and being one of the pious few, who, in this enlightened age of reality, nurse up a lingering superstition or two, I found myself, while loitering through this romantic district, and associating upon the most easy terms with its rural population, irresistibly imbibing a portion of the feeling and

spirit which prevailed around me. The cavern-
ous ravines and sounding aisles of the tall
forests had "airy tongues" for me, as well as
for those who are more familiar with their
whisperings. But as for the freakish beings
who were supposed to give them utterance as
they pranked it away in the dim retreats
around, I somehow or other could never obtain
a fair sight of one of them. The forms that
sometimes rose between my eyes and the mist-
breathing cascade, or flitted across the shadowy
glade at some sudden turn of my forest-path,
always managed to disappear behind some
jutting rock, or make good their escape into
some convenient thicket, before I could make
out their lineaments, or even swear to their
existence at all. My repeated disappointments
in this way had begun to put me quite out
of conceit with my quickness and accuracy of

vision, when a new opportunity was given me of testing them, in the manner I am about to relate.

I happened one day to dine at a little inn situated at the mouth of a wooded gorge, where it lay tucked away so closely beneath the ponderous limbs of a huge tulip-tree, that the blue smoke from the kitchen fire alone betrayed its locality. Mine host proved to be one of those talkative worthies who, being supplied with but little information whereon to exercise his tongue, make amends for the defects of education and circumstance by dwelling with exaggeration upon every trivial incident around him. Such people in polished society become the scandal-mongers of the circle in which they move, while in more simple communities they are only the chroniclers of every thing marvellous that has occurred in the neighbourhood " within the memory of the oldest inhabitant." I had hardly placed myself at the dinner-table, before my garrulous entertainer began to display his retentive faculties by giving me the exact year and day upon which every chicken with two heads, or calf with five legs, had been born throughout the whole country round. Then followed the most minute particulars of a murder or two which had been perpetrated within the last twenty years; and after this I was drilled into the exact situation and bearings of a haunted house which I should probably see the next day, by pursuing the road I was then travelling; finally, I was inducted into all the arcana of a remarkable cavern in the vicinity, where an " ouphe, gnome, moon-elf, or water-sprite," had taken up its residence, to the great annoyance of every one except my landlord's buxom daughter, who was said to be upon the most enviable terms with the freakish spirit of the grotto.

The animated and almost eloquent description which mine host gave of this cavern, made me readily overlook the puerile credulity with which he wound up his account of its peculiarities. It interested me so much, indeed, that I determined to stable my horse for the night, and proceed at once to explore the place. A fresh and blooming girl, with the laughing eye and free step of a mountaineer, volunteered to be my guide on the occasion, hinting, at the same time, while she gave a mischievous look at her father, that I should find it difficult to procure a cicerone other than herself in the neighbourhood. She then directed me how to find the principal entrance to the cave, where she promised to join me soon after.

A rough scramble in the hills soon brought me to the place of meeting, and entering the first chamber of the cavern, which was large, and well lighted from without, I stretched myself upon a rocky ledge which leaned over a brook that meandered through the place, and, lulled by the dash of a distant waterfall, surrendered myself to a thousand musing fancies.

Fatigue from an early and long morning ride, or possibly too liberal a devotion to the good things which had been placed before me at table, caused me soon to be overtaken by sleep. My slumbers, however, were broken and uneasy; and after repeatedly opening my eyes to look with some impatience at my watch, as I tossed upon my stony couch, I abandoned the idea of a nap entirely, momentarily expecting that my guide would make her appearance, and contented myself with gazing listlessly upon the streamlet which rippled over its pebbled bed beneath me. I must have remained for some time in this vacant mood, when my idle musings were interrupted by a new source of interest presenting itself.

A slight rustling near at hand disturbed me, and, turning round as I opened my eyes, a female figure, in a drapery of snowy whiteness, appeared to flit before them, and retire behind a tall cascade immediately in front of me. The uncertain light of the place, with the spray of the waterfall, which partially impeded my view of the farther part of the cavern, made me at first doubt the evidence of my senses ; but gradually a distinct form was perceptible amid the mist, apparently moving slowly from me, and beckoning the while to follow. The height of the figure struck me immediately as being about the same as that of the buxom daughter of my landlord ; and, though the proportions seemed more slender, I had no doubt, upon recalling her arch expression of countenance while her father was relating to me the wild superstitions of the cavern, that a ready solution of one of its mysteries, at least, was at hand. Some woman's whim, I had no doubt, prompted the girl to get up a little diversion at my expense, and sent her thither to put the freak in execution. I had been told that there were a dozen outlets to the cavern, and presumed that I was now to be involved in its labyrinths for the purpose of seeing in what part of the mountain I might subsequently make my exit. He is no true lover of a pair of bright eyes who will mar the jest of a pretty woman. The lady beckoned, and I followed.

I had some difficulty in scaling the precipice, over which tumbled the waterfall; but after slipping once or twice upon the wet ledges of rock, which supplied a treacherous foothold, I at last gained the summit, and stood within a few yards of my whimsical conductor. She had paused upon the farthest side of the chamber into which the cavern here expanded. It was a vast and noble apartment. The lofty ceiling swelled almost into a perfect dome, save where a ragged aperture at the top admitted the noon-day sun, whose rays, as they fell through the vines and wild flowers that embowered the orifice, were glinted back from a thousand sparry points and pillars around. The walls, indeed, were completely fretted with stalactites. In some places small, and apparently freshly formed, they hung in fringed rows from the ceiling; in others they drooped so heavily as to knit the glistening roof to the marble floor beneath it, or rose in slender pyramids from the floor itself until they appeared to sustain the vault above.

The motion of the air created by the cascade gave a delightful coolness to this apartment, while the murmur of the falling water was echoed back from the vibrating columns with tones as rich and melodious as those which sweep from an Æolian harp. Never, methought, had I seen a spot so alluring. And yet, when I surveyed each charm of the grotto, I knew not whether I could be contented in any one part of it. Nothing, indeed, could be more inviting to tranquil enjoyment than the place where I then stood; but the clustering columns, with their interlacing screen-work of woven spar, allured my eye into a hundred romantic aisles which I longed to explore; while the pendent wild flowers which luxuriated in the sunlight around the opening above, prompted me to scale the dangerous height, and try what pinnacle of the mountain I might gain by emerging from the cavern through the lofty aperture.

These reflections were abruptly terminated by an impatient gesture from my guide, and for the first time I caught a glimpse of her countenance as she glided by a deep pool in which it was reflected.

That glance had a singular, almost a preternatural effect upon me; the features were different from those I had expected to behold. They were not those of the new acquaintance whom I thought I was following, but the expression they wore was one so familiar to me in bygone years, that I started as if I had seen an apparition.

It was the look of one who had been long since dead—of one around whose name, when life was new, the whole tissue of my hopes and fears was woven—for whom all my aspirations after worldly honours had been breathed—in whom all my dreams of earthly happiness had been wound up. She had mingled in purer hours with all the fond and home-loving fancies of boyhood; she had been the queen of each romantic vision of my youth; and, amid the worldly cares and selfish struggles of maturer life, the thought of her had lived separate and apart in my bosom, with no companion in its hallowed chamber save the religion learned at a mother's knee—save that hope of better things which, once implanted by a mother's love, survives amid the storms and conflicts of the world —a beacon to warn us more often, alas! how far we have wandered from her teachings than to guide us to the haven whither they were meant to lead.

I had loved her, and I had lost her: how, it matters not. Perchance disease had reft her from me by some sudden blow at the moment when possession made her dearest. Perchance I saw her fade in the arms of another, while I was banned and barred from ministering to a spirit that stole away to the grave with all I prized on earth. It boots not how I lost her; but he who has centred every thought and feeling in one only object, whose morning hopes have for years gone forth to the same goal, whose evening reflections have for years come back to the same bourne, whose waking visions and whose midnight dreams have for years been haunted by the same image, whose schemes of toil and advancement have all tended to the same end—*he* knows what it is to have the pivot upon which every wheel of his heart hath turned wrenched from its centre—to have the sun, round which revolved every joy that lighted his bosom, plucked from its system.

Well, it was her face; as I live, it was the soul-breathing features of Linda that now beamed before me, fresh as when in dawning womanhood they first caught my youthful fancy—resistless as when in their noontide blaze of beauty I poured out my whole adoring soul before them. There was that same appealing look of the large lustrous eyes, the same sunny and soul-melting smile which, playing over a countenance thoughtful even to sadness, touched it with a beauty so radiant, that the charm seemed borrowed from heaven itself.

I could not but think it strange that such an image should be presented to my view in such a place; and yet, if I now rightly recollect my emotions, surprise was the least active among them. I cared not why or whence the apparition came; I thought not whether it were reality or mocking semblance, the fantasy of my own brain, or the shadowy creation of some supernatural power around me. I knew only that it was there; I knew only that the eyes in whose perilous light my soul had bathed herself to madness, beamed anew before me; that the lips whose lightest smile had often wrapt me in elysium; that the brow whose holy light—— But why should I thus attempt to paint what pencil never yet hath reached?—why essay a portrait whose colours I have nowhere found, save in the heart where they are laid so deeply

that death alone can dim them ?   Enough that
the only human being to whom my spirit ever
bowed in inferiority—enough that the idol to
which it had knelt in adoration, now stood pal-
pably before it.   An hour agone, and I would
have crossed the threshold of the grave itself to
stand one moment in that presence—to gaze, if
but for an instant, upon those features.   What
recked I now, then, how or whence they were
conjured up ?   Had the Fiend himself stood
nigh, I would have pressed nearer, and gazed
and followed as I did.   The figure beckoned,
and I went on.

The vaulted pathway was at first smooth, and
easily followed ; but, after passing through seve-
ral of the cavernous chambers into which it ever
and anon expanded, the route became more and
more difficult ; loose masses of rock encumber-
ing the floor, or drooping in pendent crags
from the roof, rendered the defiles between them

both toilsome and hazardous. The light which fell through the opening behind us soon disappeared entirely, and it gave me a singular sinking of the spirits, as we passed into deeper and deeper gloom, to hear the musical sounds, which I have already noted in the grotto from which we first passed, dying away in the distance, and leaving the place at last in total silence. Long, indeed, after they had ceased to reach my ear with any distinctness, they would seem at times to swell along the winding vault, and break anew upon me at some turn in our devious route. So strangely, too, do the innumerable subtle echoes metamorphose each noise in these caverns, that I continually found myself mistaking the muttered reverberations for the sounds of a human voice. At one moment it seemed in gay tones to be calling me back to the sparry grotto and bright sunshine behind me, while the very next it appeared with sudden and harsh intonation to warn me against proceeding further. Anon it would die away with a mournful cadence, a melancholy wailing, like the requiem of one who was beyond the reach of all earthly counsel or assistance.

Again and again did I pause in my career to listen to this wild chanting, while my feelings would for the moment take their hue and complexion from the sources which thus bewildered my senses. I thought of my early dreams of fame and honour, of the singing hopes that lured me on my path, when one fatal image stepped between my soul and all its high endeavour. I thought of that buoyancy of spirit, once so irrepressible in its elasticity, that it seemed proof alike against time and sorrow, now sapped, wasted, and destroyed by the frenzied pursuit of one object. I thought of the home which had so much to embellish and endear it, and which yet, with all its heart-cheering joys, had been neglected and left, like the sunlit grotto, to follow a shifting phantom through a heartless world. I thought of the reproachful voices around me, and the ceaseless upbraider in my own bosom, which told of time and talents wasted, of opportunities thrown away, of mental energies squandered, of heart, brain, and soul consumed in a devotion deeper and more absorbing than Heaven itself exacts from its votaries. I thought, and I looked at the object for which I had lavished them all. I thought that my life must have been some hideous dream, some damned vision in which my fated soul was bound by imaginary ties to a being doomed to be its bane upon earth, and shut it out at last from heaven; and I laughed in scornful glee as I twisted my bodily frame in the hope that at length I might wake from that long-enduring sleep. I caught a smile from the lips; I saw a beckon from the hand of the phantom, and I wished still to dream, and to follow for ever. I plunged into the abyss of darkness to which it pointed; and, reckless of every thing I might leave behind, followed wheresoever it might marshal me.

A damp and chilling atmosphere now pervaded the place, and the clammy moisture stood thick upon my brow as I groped my way through a labyrinth of winding galleries, which intersected each other so often both obliquely and transversely, that the whole mountain seemed honeycombed. At one moment the steep and broken pathway led up acclivities almost impossible to scale; at another the black edge of a precipice indicated our hazardous route along the brink of some unfathomed gulf; while again a savage torrent, roaring

through the sinuous vault, left scarcely room
enough for a foothold between the base of the
wall and its furious tide.

And still my guide kept on, and still I fol-
lowed. Returning, indeed, had the thought
occurred to me, was now impossible; for the
pale light which seemed to hang around her
person, emanating, as it were, from her white
raiment, was all that guided me through these
shadowy realms. But not for a moment did I
now think of retracing my steps, or pausing in
that wild pursuit. Onward, and still onward
it led, while my spirit, once set upon its pur-
pose, seemed to gather sterner determination
from every difficulty it encountered, and to
kindle again with that indomitable buoyancy
which was once the chief attribute of my
nature.

At length the chase seemed ended, as we ap-

proached one of those abrupt and startling turns
common in these caverns, where the passage,
suddenly veering to the right or left, leads you,
as if by design, to the sheer edge of some gulf
that is impassable. My strange companion
seemed pausing for a moment upon the brink
of the abyss. It was a moment to me of de-
lirious joy, mingled with more than mortal
agony; the object of my wild pursuit seemed
at length within my grasp. A single bound,
and my outstretched arms would have encircled
her person; a single bound — nay, the least
movement towards her — might only have pre-
cipitated the destruction upon whose brink she
hovered. Her form seemed to flutter upon the
very edge of that horrid precipice, as, gazing
like one fascinated over it, she stretched her
hand backward toward me. It was like in-
viting me to perdition. And yet, forgive me,

Heaven! to perish with her was my proudest hope, as I sprang to grasp it. But, oh God! what held I in that withering clasp? The ice of death seemed curdling in my veins as I touched those clammy and pulseless fingers. A strange and unhallowed light shot upward from the black abyss; and the features, from which I *could* not take my eyes away, were changed to those of a DEMON in that hideous glare. And now the hand that I had so longed to clasp closed with remorseless pressure round my own, and drew me toward the yawning gulf,— it tightened in its grasp, and I hovered still nearer to my horrid doom,—it clenched yet more closely, and the frenzied shriek I gave— AWOKE ME.

A soft palm was gently pressed against my own; a pair of laughing blue eyes were bent archly upon me; and the fair locks which floated over her blooming cheeks revealed the joyous and romping damsel who had promised to act as my guide through the cavern. She had been prevented by some household cares from keeping her appointment until the approach of evening made it too late, and had taken it for granted that I had then returned to my lodgings at the inn. My absence from the breakfast-table in the morning, however, had awakened some concern in the family, and induced her to seek me where we then met. The pressure of her hand in trying to awaken me will partially account for the latter part of my hideous dream; the general tenour of it is easily traceable to the impression made upon my mind by the prevalent superstition connected with the cavern; but no metaphysical ingenuity of which I am master can explain how one whose daily thoughts flow in so careless, if not gay, a current as mine, could, even in a dream, have conjured up such a train of wild and bitter fancies ; much less how the fearful tissue should have been so interwoven with the memory of an idle caprice of boyhood as to give new shape and reality to a phantom long—long since faded. And I could not but think, that had a vision so strange and vivid swept athwart my brain at an earlier period of life, I should have regarded it as something more than an unmeaning fantasy. That mystical romance, which is the religion of life's spring-time, would have interpreted my dream as a dark foreboding of the future, prophetic of hopes misplaced, of opportunities misapplied, of a joyless and barren youth, and a manhood whose best endeavour would be only a restless effort to lose in action the memory of dreary past.

If half be true, however, that is told concerning them, still more extravagant sallies of the imagination overtake persons of quite as easy and indolent a disposition as my own, when venturing to pass a night upon the Enchanted Mountains.

CHAPTER II.

THE LAST ARROW.

" And who be ye who rashly dare
   To chase in woods the forest child ?
To hunt the panther to his lair—
   The Indian in his native wild ?"

THE American reader, if at all curious about
the early history of his country, has probably
heard of that famous expedition, undertaken by
the vicegerent of Louis XIV., the governor-
general of New France, against the confederated
Six Nations of New York; an expedition which,
though it carried with it all the pomp and cir-

cumstances of European warfare into their wild wood haunts, was attended with no adequate results, and had but a momentary effect in quelling the spirit of the tameless Iroquois.

It was on the 4th of July, 1796, that the commander-in-chief, the veteran Count de Frontenac, marshalled the forces at La Chine, with which he intended to crush for ever the powers of the Aganuschion confederacy. His regulars were divided into four battalions of two hundred men each, commanded respectively by three veteran leaders, and the young Chevalier De Grais. He formed also four battalions of Canadian volunteers, efficiently officered, and organized as regular troops. The Indian allies were divided into three bands, each of which was placed under the command of a nobleman of rank, who had gained distinction in the European warfare of France. One was composed of the Sault and St. Louis bands and of

friendly Abenaquis; another consisted of the
Hurons of Lorette and the mountaineers of the
north; the third band was smaller, and com-
posed indiscriminately of warriors of different
tribes, whom a spirit of adventure led to embark
upon the expedition. They were chiefly Otta-
was, Saukies, and Algonquins, and these the
Baron de Bekancourt charged himself to con-
duct. This formidable armament was amply
provisioned, and provided with all the muni-
tions of war. Besides pikes, arquebusses, and
other small arms then in use, they were fur-
nished with grenades, a mortar to throw them,
and a couple of field-pieces, which, with the
tents and other camp equipage, were trans-
ported in large batteaux built for the purpose.
Nor was the energy of their movements unwor-
thy of this brilliant preparation. Ascending
the St. Lawrence, and coasting the shores of
Lake Ontario, they entered the Oswego river,

cut a military road around the falls, and carrying their transports over the portage, launched them anew, and finally debouched with their whole flotilla upon the waters of Onondago Lake.

It must have been a gallant sight to behold the warlike pageant floating beneath the primitive forest which then crowned the hills around that lovely water. To see the veterans who had served under Turenne, Vauban, and the great Condé, marshalled with pike and cuirass beside the half-naked Huron and Abenaquis; while the young cavaliers, in the less warlike garb of the court of the magnificent Louis, moved with plume and mantle amid the dusky files of wampum-decked Ottawas and Algonquins. Banners were there which had flown at Steenkirk and Landen; or rustled above the troopers that Luxemburgh's trumpets had guided to glory, when Prince Waldeck's battalions were borne down beneath his furious charge. Nor was the enemy that this gallant host were seeking unworthy of those whose swords had been tried in some of the most celebrated fields of Europe. " The Romans of America," as the Six Nations have been called by more than one writer, had proved themselves soldiers, not only by carrying their arms among the native tribes a thousand miles away, and striking their enemies alike upon the lakes of Maine, the mountains and morasses of Carolina, and the prairies of the Missouri; but they had already bearded one European army beneath the walls of Quebec, and shut up another for weeks within the defences of Montreal, with the same courage that, half a century later, vanquished the battalions of Dieskau upon the banks of Lake George.

Our business, however, is not with the main movements of this army, which we have already mentioned were wholly unimportant in their results. The aged Chevalier de Frontenac was said to have other objects in view besides the political motives for the expedition, which he set forth to his master, the Grand Monarque.

Many years previously, when the Six Nations had invested the capital of New France and threatened the extermination of that thriving colony, a beautiful half-blood girl, whose education had been commenced under the immediate auspices of the governor-general, and in whom, indeed, M. de Frontenac was said to have a paternal interest, was carried off, with other prisoners, by the retiring foe. Every effort had been made in vain during the occasional cessation of hostilities between the French and the Iroquois, to recover this child; and though, in the years that intervened, some wandering Jesuit from time to time averred that he had seen the Christian captive living as the contented wife of a young Mohawk warrior, yet the old nobleman seems never to have despaired of reclaiming his "nut-brown daughter." Indeed, the chevalier must have been impelled by some such hope when, at the age of seventy, and so feeble, that he was half the time carried in a litter, he ventured to encounter the perils of an American wilderness, and place himself at the head of the heterogeneous bands which now invaded the country of the Six Nations under his conduct.

Among the half-breed spies, border scouts, and mongrel adventurers that followed in the train of the invading army, was a renegade Fleming, of the name of Hanyost. This man, in early youth, had been made a sergeant-major, when he deserted to the French ranks in Flanders. He had subsequently taken up a military grant in Canada, sold it after emigrating, and then, making his way down to the Dutch settlements on the Hudson, had become domiciliated, as it were, among their allies, the Mohawks, and adopted the life of a hunter. Hanyost, hearing that his old friends, the French, were making such a formidable descent, did not now hesitate to desert his more recent acquaintances; but offered his services as a guide to Count de Frontenac the moment he entered the hostile country. It was not, however, mere cupidity, or the habitual love of treachery, which actuated the base Fleming in this instance. Hanyost, in a difficulty with an Indian trapper, which had been referred for arbitrament to the young Mohawk chief, Kiodago (a settler of disputes), whose cool courage and firmness fully entitled him to so distinguished a name, conceived himself aggrieved by the award which had been given against him. The scorn with which the arbitrator met his charge of unfairness, stung him to the soul, and fearing the arm of the powerful savage, he had nursed the revenge in secret, whose accomplishment seemed now at hand.

Kiodago, ignorant of the hostile force which had entered his country, was off with his band at a fishing-station, or summer-camp, among the wild hills about Konnedieyu ;* and, when Hanyost informed the commander of the French forces, that, by surprising this party, his long-lost daughter, the wife of Kiodago, might be once more given to his arms, a small, but efficient force, was instantly detached from the main body of the army to strike the blow. A dozen musketeers, with twenty-five pikemen, led severally by the Baron de Bekàncourt and the Chevalier de Grais, the former having the chief command of the expedition,

---

* Since corrupted into "Canada creek,"—Beautiful water; probably so called from its amber colour—now Trenton Falls.

were sent upon this duty, with Hanyost to guide them to the village of Kiodago. Many hours were consumed upon the march, as the soldiers were not yet habituated to the wilderness; but just before dawn on the second day, the party found themselves in the neighbourhood of the Indian village.

The place was wrapped in repose, and the two cavaliers trusted that the surprise would be so complete, that their commandant's daughter must certainly be taken. The baron, after a careful examination of the hilly passes, determined to head the onslaught, while his companion in arms, with Hanyost, to mark out his prey, should pounce upon the chieftain's wife. This being arranged, their followers were warned not to injure the female captives while cutting their defenders to pieces; and then a moment being allowed for each man to take a last look at the condition of his arms, they were led to the attack.

The inhabitants of the fated village, secure in their isolated situation, aloof from the war parties of that wild district, had neglected all precaution against surprise, and were buried in sleep, when the whizzing of a grenade, that terrible but now superseded engine of destruction, roused them from their slumbers. The missile to which a direction had been given, that carried it in a direct line through the main row of wigwams which formed the little street, went crashing among their frail frames of basketwork, and kindled the dry mats stretched over them into instant flames. And then, as the startled warriors leaped all naked and unarmed from their blazing lodges, the French pikemen, waiting only for a volley from the musketeers, followed it up with a charge still more fatal.

The wretched savages were slaughtered like sheep in the shambles. Some, overwhelmed with dismay, sank unresisting upon the ground, and, covering up their heads after the Indian fashion when resigned to death, awaited the fatal stroke without a murmur; others, seized with a less benumbing panic, sought safety in flight, and rushed upon the pikes that lined the forest's paths around them. Many there were, however, who, schooled to scenes as dreadful, acquitted themselves like warriors. Snatching their weapons from the greedy flames, they sprang with irresistible fury upon the bristling files of pikemen. Their heavy war-clubs beat down and splintered the fragile spears of the Europeans, whose corslets, ruddy with the reflected fires mid which they fought, glinted back still brighter sparks from the hatchets of flint which crushed against them. The fierce veterans pealed the charging cry of many a well-fought field in other climes; but wild and high the Indian whoop rose shrill above the din of conflict, until the hovering raven in mid air, caught up and answered that discordant shriek.

De Grais, in the mean time, surveyed the scene of action with eager intentness, expecting each moment to see the paler features of the Christian captive among the dusky females who ever and anon sprang shrieking from the blazing lodges, and were instantly hurled backward into the flames by fathers and brothers, who even thus would save them from the hands that vainly essayed to grasp their distracted forms. The Mohawks began now to wage a more successful resistance; and just when the fight was raging hottest, and the high-spirited Frenchman, beginning to despair of his prey, was about launching into the midst of it, he saw a tall warrior who had hitherto been forward in the conflict, disengage himself from the melée, and wheeling suddenly upon a soldier, who had likewise separated from his party, brain him with a tomahawk, before he could make a movement in his defence.

The quick eye of the young chevalier, too, caught a glance of another figure, in pursuit of whom as she emerged, with an infant in her arms, from a lodge on the farther side of the village, the luckless Frenchman had met his doom. It was the Christian captive, the wife of Kiodago, beneath whose hand he had fallen. That chieftain now stood over the body of his victim, brandishing a war-club which he had snatched from a dying Indian near. Quick as thought, De Grais levelled a pistol at his head, when the track of the flying girl brought her directly in his line of sight, and he withheld his fire. Kiodago, in the mean time, had been cut off from the rest of his people by the soldiers, who closed in upon the space which his terrible arm had a moment before kept open.   A cry of agony escaped the high-souled savage, as he saw how thus the last hope was lost.   He made a gesture, as if about to rush again into the fray, and sacrifice his life with his tribesmen ; and then perceiving how futile must be the act, he turned on his heel, and bounded after his re-treating wife with arms outstretched, to shield her from the dropping shots of the enemy.

The uprising sun had now lighted up the scene ; but all this passed so instantaneously, that it was impossible for De Grais to keep his eye on the fugitives, amid the shifting forms that glanced continually before him ; and when, accompanied by Hanyost and seven others, he had got fairly in pursuit, Kiodago, who still kept behind his wife, was far in advance of the chevalier and his party.

Her forest training had made the Christian,

captive as fleet of foot as an Indian maiden. She heard, too, the cheering voice of her loved warrior behind her, and pressing her infant in her arms, she urged her flight over crag and fell, and soon reached the head of a rocky pass, which it would take some moments for any but an American forester to scale. But the indefatigable Frenchmen are urging their way up the steep; the cry of pursuit grows nearer as they catch a sight of her husband through the thickets, and the agonized wife finds her onward progress prevented by a ledge of rock that impends above her. But now again Kiodago is by her side; he has lifted his wife to the cliff above, and placed her infant in her arms; and already, with renewed activity, the Indian mother is speeding on to a cavern among the hills, well known as a fastness of safety.

Kiodago looked a moment after her retreating figure, and then coolly swung himself to the ledge which commanded the pass. He might now easily have escaped his pursuers; but as he stepped back from the edge of the cliff, and looked down the narrow ravine, the vengeful spirit of the red man was too strong within him to allow such an opportunity of striking a blow to escape. His tomahawk and war-club had both been lost in the strife, but he still carried at his back a more efficient weapon in the hands of so keen a hunter. There were but three arrows in his quiver, and the Mohawk was determined to have the life of an enemy for each of them. His bow was strung quickly, but with as much coolness as if there were no exigency to require haste. Yet he had scarcely time to throw himself upon his breast, a few yards from the brink of the declivity, before one of his pursuers, more active than the rest, exposed himself to the unerring archer. He came leaping from rock to rock, and had nearly reached the head of the glen, when, pierced through and through by one of Kiodago's arrows, he toppled from the crags, and rolled, clutching the leaves in his death-agony, among the tangled furze below. A second met a similar fate, and a third victim would probably have been added, if a shot from the fusil of Hanyost, who sprang forward and caught sight of the Indian just as the first man fell, had not disabled the thumb-joint of the bold archer, even as he fixed his last arrow in the string. Resistance seemed now at an end, and Kiodago again betook himself to flight. Yet anxious to divert the pursuit from his wife, the young chieftain pealed a yell of defiance, as he retreated in a different direction from that which she had taken. The whoop was answered by a simultaneous shout and rush on the part of the whites; but the Indian had not advanced far before he perceived that the pursuing party, now reduced to six, had divided, and that three only followed him. He had recognised the scout, Hanyost, among his enemies, and it was now apparent that the wily traitor, instead of being misled by his *ruse*, had guided the other three upon the direct trail to the cavern which the Christian captive had taken. Quick as thought, the Mohawk acted upon the impression. Making a few steps within a thicket, still to mislead his present pursuers, he bounded across a mountain torrent, and then, leaving his foot-marks dashed in the yielding bank, he turned shortly on a rock beyond, recrossed the stream, and concealed himself behind a fallen tree, while his pursuers passed within a few paces of his covert.

A broken hillock now only divided the chief from the point to which he had directed his wife by another route, and to which the remaining party, consisting of De Grais, Hanyost, and a French musketeer, were hotly urging their way. The hunted warrior ground his teeth with rage when he heard the voice of the treacherous Fleming in the glen below him; and, springing from crag to crag, he circled the rocky knoll, and planted his foot by the roots of a blasted oak that shot its limbs above the cavern, just as his wife had reached the spot, and, pressing her babe to her bosom, sank exhausted among the flowers that waved in the moist breath of the cave. It chanced that, at that very instant, De Grais and his followers had paused beneath the opposite side of the knoll, from whose broken surface the foot of the flying Indian had disengaged stone, which, crackling among the branches, found its way through a slight ravine into the glen below. The two Frenchmen stood in doubt for a moment. The musketeer, pointing in the direction whence the stone had rolled, turned to receive the order of his officer. The chevalier, who had made one step in advance of a broad rock between them, leaned upon it, pistol in hand, half turning towards his follower; while the scout, who stood farthest out from the steep bank, bending forward to discover the mouth of the cave, must have caught a glimpse of the sinking female, just as the shadowy form of her husband was displayed above her. God help thee now, bold archer! thy quiver is empty; thy game of life is nearly up; the sleuth-hound is upon thee; and thy scalp-lock, whose plumes now flutter in the breeze, will soon be twined

in the fingers of the vengeful renegade! Thy
wife—— But hold! the noble savage has still
one arrow left!

Disabled, as he thought himself, the Mo-
hawk had not dropped his bow in his flight.
His last arrow was still griped in his bleeding
fingers; and though his stiffened thumb for-
bore the use of it to the best advantage, the
hand of Kiodago had not yet lost its power.*
The crisis which it takes so long to describe,
had been realized by him in an instant. He
saw how the Frenchmen, inexperienced in
woodcraft, were at fault; he saw, too, that the
keen eye of Hanyost had caught sight of the
object of their pursuit, and that further flight
was hopeless; while the scene of his burning
village in the distance, inflamed him with hate

---

* The European mode of holding the arrow is not
common among our aborigines, who use the thumb for a
purchase.

and fury towards the instrument of his misfortunes. Bracing one knee upon the flinty rock, while the muscles of the other swelled as if the whole energies of his body were collected in that single effort, Kiodago aims at the treacherous scout, and the twanging bowstring dismisses his last arrow upon its errand. The hand of THE SPIRIT could alone have guided that shaft. It misses its mark! But WANEYO smiles upon the brave warrior, and the arrow, while it rattles harmless against the cuirass of the French officer, glances toward the victim for whom it was intended, and quivers in the heart of Hanyost! The dying wretch grasped the sword-chain of the chevalier, whose corslet clanged among the rocks as the two went rolling down the glen together; and De Grais was not unwilling to abandon the pursuit, when the musketeer, coming to his assistance, had disengaged him, bruised and bloody, from the embrace of the stiffening corpse!

The rest is soon told. The bewildered Europeans rejoined their comrades, who were soon after on their march from the scene they had desolated; while Kiodago descended from his eyrie to collect the fugitive survivors of his band, and, after burying the slain, to wreak a terrible vengeance upon their murderers; the most of whom were cut off by him before they joined the main body of the French army. The Count de Frontenac, returning to Canada, died soon afterwards, and the existence of his half-blood daughter was forgotten. And— though among the score of old families in the state of New York who have Indian blood in their veins, many trace their descent from the offspring of the noble Kiodago and his Christian wife, yet the hand of genius, as displayed in the admirable picture of Chapman, has alone res cued from oblivion the thrilling scene of the Mohawk's LAST ARROW!

THE END.

WHITING, BEAUFORT HOUSE, STRAND.